PEARSON
Math
Makes Sense

5

WNCP Edition

Author Team

Ray Appel

Daryl Chichak

Sharon Jeroski

Peggy Morrow

Ricki Wortzman

Trevor Brown

Lalie Harcourt

Lorraine Kinsman

Cynthia Pratt Nicolson

With Contributions from

Ralph Connelly   Michael Davis   Jason Johnston

Don Jones   Bryn Keyes

PEARSON

Publisher
Mike Czukar

Research and Communications Manager
Barbara Vogt

Publishing Team
Claire Burnett
Enid Haley
Lesley Haynes
Ioana Gagea
Lynne Gulliver
Stephanie Cox
Jane Schell
Karen Alley
Judy Wilson

Photo Research
Karen Hunter

Design
Word & Image Design Studio Inc.

Composition
Integra Software Services Pvt. Ltd.

PEARSON

ISBN-13   978-0-321-49639-3
ISBN-10   0-321-49639-6

Printed and bound in the United States.

1 2 3 4 5 -- 12 11 10 09 08

The publisher wishes to thank the staff and
students of St. Stephen School and Wilkinson Public
School for their assistance with photography.

Consultants, Advisers, and Reviewers

Series Consultants

Trevor Brown
Maggie Martin Connell
Craig Featherstone
John A. Van de Walle
Mignonne Wood

Assessment Consultant
Sharon Jeroski

Aboriginal Content Consultants
Susan Hopkins
Tlicho Community Services Agency
Behchoko, NT

Angie Hall
Aboriginal Learning Services Consultant
Edmonton Catholic Schools, AB

Advisers and Reviewers

Pearson Education thanks its advisers and reviewers, who helped shape the vision for *Pearson Mathematics Makes Sense* through discussions and reviews of prototype materials and manuscript.

Alberta

Joanne Adomeit
Calgary Board of Education

Lona M. Ani
Edmonton Public Schools

Lana Babkirk
Calgary Board of Education

Bob Berglind
Calgary Board of Education

Allison Bobenic
Calgary Board of Education

Jacquie Bouck
Lloydminster Public School
Division 99

Auriana Burns
Edmonton Public School Board

Daryl Chichak
Edmonton Catholic School District

Lissa D'Amour
Medicine Hat School District 76

K. Demers
Calgary Board of Education

Theresa Dragatis
Calgary Board of Education

Brenda Foster
Calgary R.C.S.S.D. 1

Florence Glanfield
University of Alberta

Connie Haylett
Calgary Board of Education

Laurie Hornford
Calgary Board of Education

Kevin M.G. Howell
Calgary Board of Education

Jodi Mackie
Edmonton Public School Board

Deborah L. Owens
Calgary Public School Board

Kate Steinfeld
Calgary Board of Education

Jeffrey Tang
Calgary R.C.S.S.D. 1

Janet Way
Edmonton Catholic School District

Bobbi Whitlow
Edmonton Catholic School District

Heidi Zadderey
Golden Hills School Division

British Columbia

Lorraine Baron
Central Okanagan School District 23

Donna Beaumont
Burnaby School District 41

Bob Belcher
School District 62 (Sooke)

Steve Cairns
Burnaby School District 41

Marc Garneau
Surrey School District 36

Selina Millar
Surrey School District 36

Lenora Milliken
School District 70 (Alberni)

Chris Van Bergeyk
Central Okanagan School District 23

Christine VanderRee
Comox Valley School District 71

Denise Vuignier
Burnaby School District 41

Mignonne Wood
Formerly Burnaby School District 41

Manitoba

Rosanne Ashley
Winnipeg School Division

Neil Dempsey
Winnipeg School Division

Ralph Mason
University of Manitoba

Christine Ottawa
Mathematics Consultant,
Winnipeg

Gretha Pallen
Formerly Manitoba Education

Gay Sul
Frontier School Division

Northwest Territories

Melissa Davis
Yellowknife Catholic Schools

Saskatchewan

Susan Beaudin
File Hills Qu'Appelle Tribal Council

Robyn Blatz
Prairie South School Division 210

Edward Doolittle
First Nations University,
University of Regina

Lori Jane Hantelmann
Regina School Division 4

Angie Harding
Regina R.C.S.S.D. 81

Valerie Lees
S.E. Cornerstone School District

Kristi Nelson
Prairie Spirit School Division

Devona Putland
S.E. Cornerstone School District

Trish Reeve
Prairie Spirit School Division

Cheryl Shields
Spirit School Division

Victor Stevenson
Regina School District 4

Table of Contents

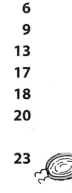

v

Fractions and Decimals ....

Geometry ....

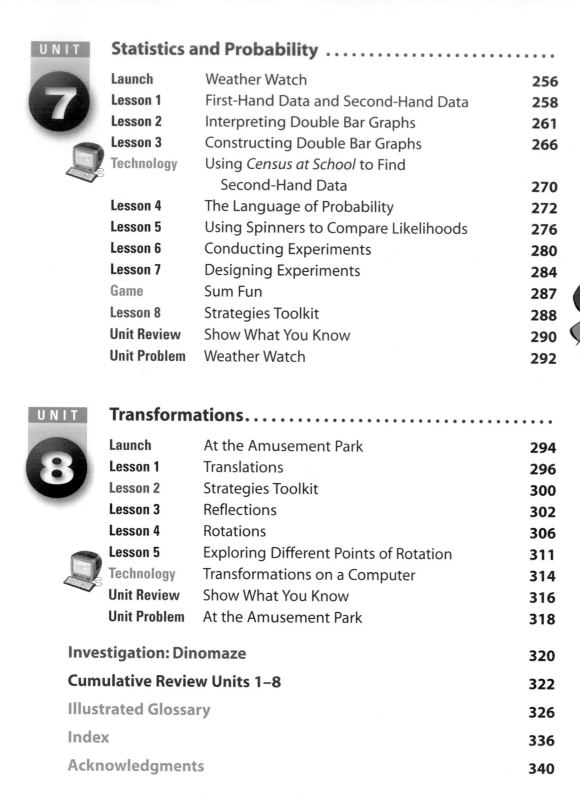

Welcome to
Pearson Math Makes Sense 5

Math helps you understand what you see and do every day.

You will use this book to learn about the math around you. Here's how.

In each Unit:

- A scene from the world around you reminds you of some of the math you already know.

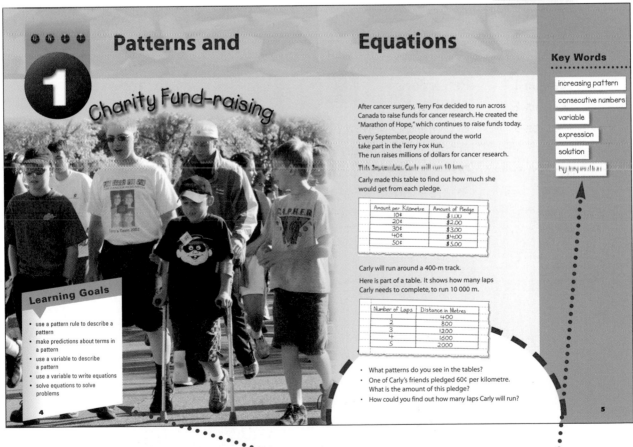

Patterns and Equations

1 Charity Fund-raising

Key Words
- increasing pattern
- consecutive numbers
- variable
- expression
- solution
- by inspection

After cancer surgery, Terry Fox decided to run across Canada to raise funds for cancer research. He created the "Marathon of Hope," which continues to raise funds today.

Every September, people around the world take part in the Terry Fox Run. The run raises millions of dollars for cancer research. This September, Carly will run 10 km.

Carly made this table to find out how much she would get from each pledge.

Amount per Kilometre	Amount of Pledge
10¢	$1.00
20¢	$2.00
30¢	$3.00
40¢	$4.00
50¢	$5.00

Carly will run around a 400-m track.

Here is part of a table. It shows how many laps Carly needs to complete, to run 10 000 m.

Number of Laps	Distance in Metres
1	400
2	800
3	1200
4	1600
5	2000

Learning Goals
- use a pattern rule to describe a pattern
- make predictions about terms in a pattern
- use a variable to describe a pattern
- use a variable to write equations
- solve equations to solve problems

- What patterns do you see in the tables?
- One of Carly's friends pledged 60¢ per kilometre. What is the amount of this pledge?
- How could you find out how many laps Carly will run?

4

5

Find out what you will learn in the **Learning Goals** and important **Key Words**.

In each Lesson:

You **Explore** an idea or problem, usually with a partner. You often use materials.

Then you **Show and Share** your results with other students.

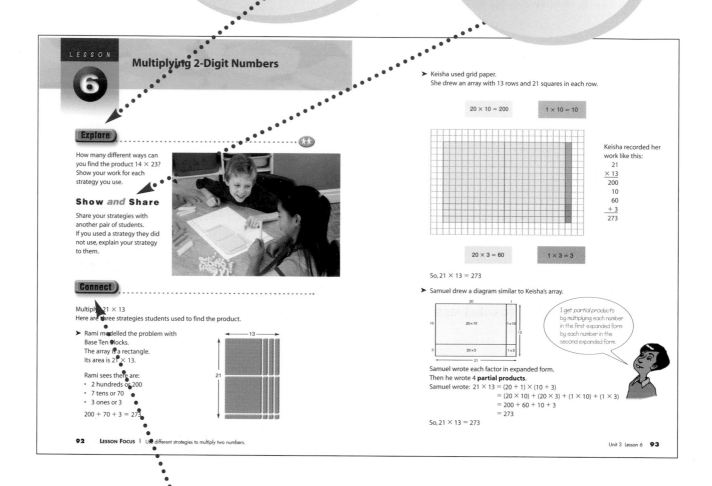

Connect summarizes the math. It often shows a solution, or multiple solutions, to a question.

Practice questions help you to use and remember the math.

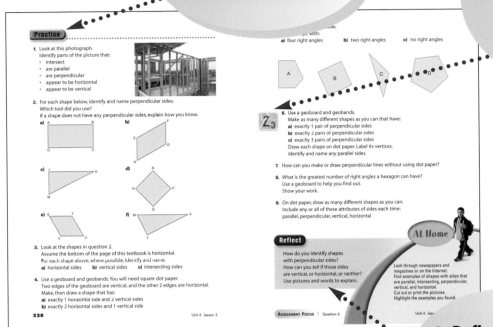

reminds you to use pictures, words, or numbers in your answers.

In **Reflect**, think about the big ideas of the lesson and about your learning style.

- Learn about strategies to help you solve problems in each **Strategies Toolkit** lesson.

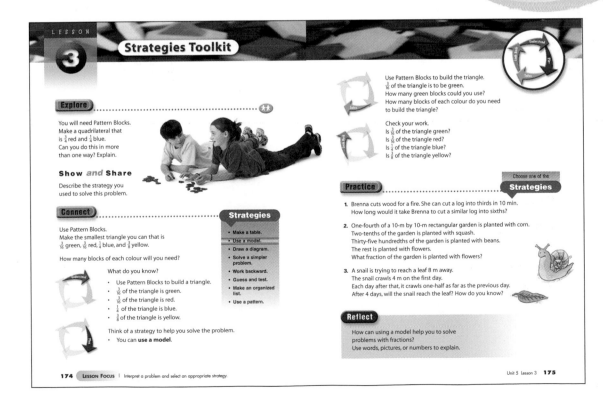

- Check up on your learning in **Show What You Know** and **Cumulative Review**.

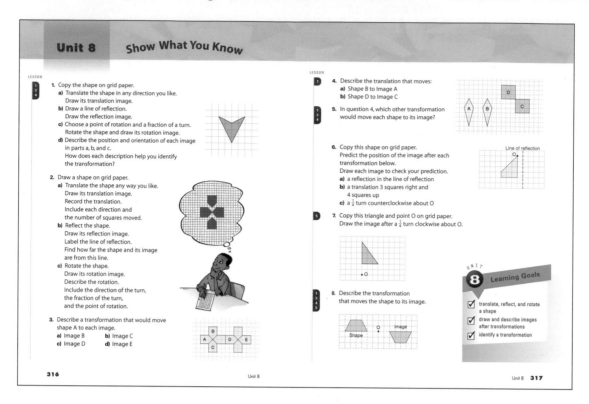

- The **Unit Problem** returns to the opening scene.

  It presents a problem to solve or a project to do using the math of the unit.

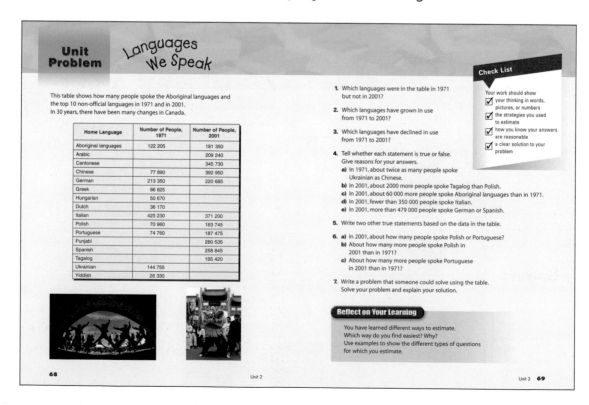

Explore some interesting math when you do the **Investigations**.

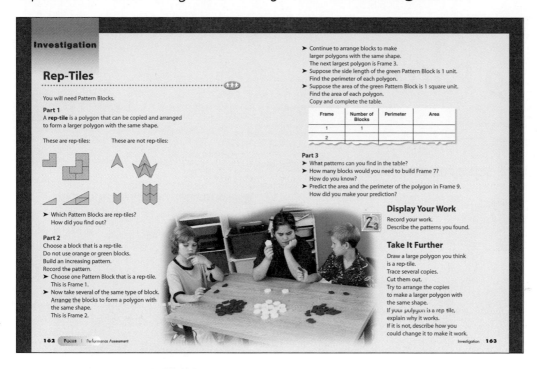

Investigation

Rep-Tiles

You will need Pattern Blocks.

Part 1
A **rep-tile** is a polygon that can be copied and arranged to form a larger polygon with the same shape.

These are rep-tiles: These are not rep-tiles:

➤ Which Pattern Blocks are rep-tiles? How did you find out?

Part 2
Choose a block that is a rep-tile.
Do not use orange or green blocks.
Build an increasing pattern.
Record the pattern.
➤ Choose one Pattern Block that is a rep-tile. This is Frame 1.
➤ Now take several of the same type of block. Arrange the blocks to form a polygon with the same shape. This is Frame 2.

➤ Continue to arrange blocks to make larger polygons with the same shape. The next largest polygon is Frame 3.
➤ Suppose the side length of the green Pattern Block is 1 unit. Find the perimeter of each polygon.
➤ Suppose the area of the green Pattern Block is 1 square unit. Find the area of each polygon. Copy and complete the table.

Frame	Number of Blocks	Perimeter	Area
1	1		
2			

Part 3
➤ What patterns can you find in the table?
➤ How many blocks would you need to build Frame 7? How do you know?
➤ Predict the area and the perimeter of the polygon in Frame 9. How did you make your prediction?

Display Your Work
Record your work.
Describe the patterns you found.

Take It Further
Draw a large polygon you think is a rep-tile.
Trace several copies.
Cut them out.
Try to arrange the copies to make a larger polygon with the same shape.
If your polygon is a rep-tile, explain why it works.
If it is not, describe how you could change it to make it work.

162 Focus | Performance Assessment   Investigation 163

Using *Census at School* to Find Second-Hand Data

How do you and your classmates compare to other students across Canada?
You can find out on a Web site called *Census at School*.
It provides data about students from age 8 to 18.

You can use questions from *Census at School* to collect first-hand data about your own classmates.
Then, you can check the Web site for second-hand data about students from other parts of the country.
You can even find out how students in other parts of the world answered the same questions.

Your teacher can register your class so you can complete a questionnaire online. The data from your class are then included with those already on the database.

Here are some of the questions you can answer:

• Do you have allergies?
• Which pets do you have?
• What is your favourite physical activity?
• How do you usually travel to school?

270 LESSON FOCUS | Find examples of second-hand data in electronic media.

Use **Technology.** Follow the instructions for using a calculator or computer to do math.

Look for  and  .

Sum Fun

You will need 2 number cubes each labelled 1 to 6.

➤ Take turns to roll the number cubes.

➤ Find the sum of the 2 numbers rolled. If the sum is even, you score a point. If the sum is odd, your partner scores a point.

➤ Record the results in a table.

➤ The first player to score 20 points wins.

➤ Who do you think will have more points after 36 turns? Explain.

➤ List the outcomes of the game.

➤ Which is more likely: an even sum or an odd sum? Or, are these sums equally likely? How do you know?

Unit 7 287

You will see **Games** pages.

Illustrated Glossary

a.m.: A time between midnight and just before noon.

Area: The amount of surface a shape or region covers. We measure area in square units, such as square centimetres or square metres.

Axis (plural: axes): A number line along the edge of a graph. We label each axis of a graph to tell what data it displays. The horizontal axis goes across the page. The vertical axis goes up the page.

Bar graph: Displays data by using bars of equal width on a grid. The bars may be vertical or horizontal.

Base: The face that names an object. For example, in this triangular prism, the bases are triangles.

Benchmark: Used for estimating by writing a number to its closest benchmark; for example,

1. For whole numbers: 47 532 is closer to the benchmark 47 500 than to the benchmark 47 600.

2. For fractions: $\frac{1}{3}$ is closer to $\frac{1}{2}$ than to 0 or to 1.

3. For decimals: 0.017 is closer to 0.020 than to 0.010.

Capacity: A measure of how much a container holds. We measure capacity in litres (L) or millilitres (mL).

Carroll diagram: A diagram used to sort numbers or attributes.

Centimetre: A unit used to measure length.
We write one centimetre as 1 cm.
1 cm = 0.01 m
1 cm = 10 mm
100 cm = 1 m

Certain event: An event that always happens.

Clockwise: The hands on a clock turn in a clockwise direction.

326

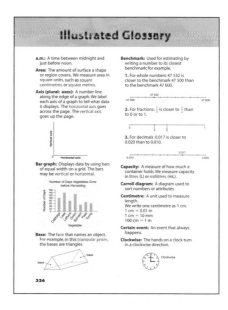

The **Glossary** is an illustrated dictionary of important math words.

Investigation

Building Patterns

You will need Pattern Blocks.
Be sure you have squares and triangles.

Part 1
Look at this pattern.

Frame 1

Frame 2

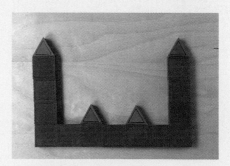

Frame 3

How many squares are in each frame?
How many triangles are in each frame?

Each block has a side length of 1 unit.
What is the perimeter of each frame?

Record the frame number, number of squares, number of triangles, and perimeter in a table.

Part 2

➤ Build Frame 4.
  How many squares and triangles did you use?
  What is the perimeter?
  Record the data in your table.
➤ How many squares and triangles will you need to build Frame 5?
  How did you find out?
  Build Frame 5 to check your prediction.
➤ Predict the number of squares and triangles needed to build Frame 10.
  How did you make your prediction?
➤ Write each pattern rule:
  • the numbers of squares in the frames
  • the numbers of triangles in the frames
  • the perimeters of the frames

Display Your Work

Record your work.
Describe the patterns you discovered.

Take It Further

Choose three different Pattern Blocks.
Build your own pattern.
Sketch the first 4 frames.
What number patterns can you find?

Patterns and

Charity Fund-raising

Learning Goals

- use a pattern rule to describe a pattern
- make predictions about terms in a pattern
- use a variable to describe a pattern
- use a variable to write equations
- solve equations to solve problems

Equations

increasing pattern

consecutive numbers

variable

expression

solution

by inspection

After cancer surgery, Terry Fox decided to run across Canada to raise funds for cancer research. He created the "Marathon of Hope," which continues to raise funds today.

Every September, people around the world take part in the Terry Fox Run.
The run raises millions of dollars for cancer research.

This September, Carly will run 10 km.

Carly made this table to find out how much she would get from each pledge.

Amount per Kilometre	Amount of Pledge
10¢	$1.00
20¢	$2.00
30¢	$3.00
40¢	$4.00
50¢	$5.00

Carly will run around a 400-m track.

Here is part of a table. It shows how many laps Carly needs to complete, to run 10 000 m.

Number of Laps	Distance in Metres
1	400
2	800
3	1200
4	1600
5	2000

- What patterns do you see in the tables?
- One of Carly's friends pledged 60¢ per kilometre. What is the amount of this pledge?
- How could you find out how many laps Carly will run?

Number Patterns and Pattern Rules

How would you describe this pattern?
What type of pattern is it?

What is a pattern rule for this pattern?

➤ For each number pattern below:
Identify a pattern rule.
Write the next 5 terms.
What did you do to one term to
get the next term?
- 3, 4, 6, 9, 13, . . .
- 3, 4, 6, 7, 9, . . .
- 1, 4, 3, 6, 5, 8, . . .
- 1, 2, 5, 10, 17, 26, . . .

➤ Choose one pattern above.
Use counters to show the pattern
and to check that the next 2 terms were correct.

1, 4, 3, 6, 5, 8, ...

➤ Make up a similar pattern.
Trade patterns with another pair of classmates.
Write a rule for your classmates' pattern.

Show and Share

Share your patterns with other classmates.
How do you know each pattern rule is correct?
For any pattern, did you find more than one rule? Explain.

Connect ●●

➤ Here is a number pattern.

5   6   8   11   15 ...
  +1 +2 +3 +4

> Each time, I add 1 more than I added before. This is an increasing pattern.

A pattern rule is:

Start at 5. Add 1.

Increase the number you add by 1 each time.

To get the next 5 terms, continue to increase the number you add by 1 each time.

5, 6, 8, 11, 15, 20, 26, 33, 41, 50,...

We can use counters to show the pattern.

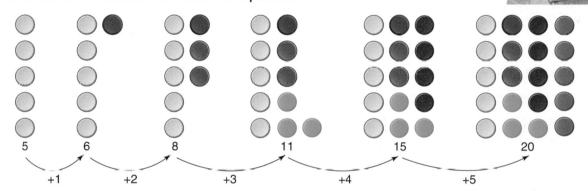

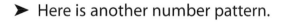
  5   6   8   11   15   20
    +1   +2   +3   +4   +5

➤ Here is another number pattern.

10   6   11   7   12 ...
  −4   +5   −4   +5

> I use mental math to subtract and add.

A pattern rule is:

Start at 10. Alternately subtract 4, then add 5.

To get the next 5 terms, continue to subtract 4, then add 5.

10, 6, 11, 7, 12, 8, 13, 9, 14, 10,...

When we alternately subtract, then add, there are two patterns in one.

10, 6, 11, 7, 12, 8, 13, 9, 14, 10,...   Add 1

                                          Add 1

1. Write the first 5 terms of each pattern.
   a) Start at 3. Add 2 each time.
   b) Start at 1. Add 2. Increase the number you add by 1 each time.

2. For each pattern in question 1:
   a) Use counters to show the first 5 terms.
   b) Predict the next 2 terms.
   c) Use counters to check your predictions.

3. Write the next 4 terms in each pattern.
   Write each pattern rule.
   What did you do to each term to get the next term?
   a) 1, 2, 4, 5, 7, 8, . . .   b) 2, 4, 3, 5, 4, 6, 5, . . .
   c) 98, 85, 87, 74, 76, . . .   d) 1, 10, 7, 70, 67, 670, . . .

4. Find each missing term. Describe the pattern.
   a) 3, 23, 13, 33, ☐, 43, 33, . . .
   b) 99, 98, 198, 197, ☐, 296, 396, . . .
   c) 2, 22, 12, 132, 122, 1342, ☐, . . .

5. What is the 7th term of this pattern?
   Start at 200. Subtract 8 each time.
   How could you find the 7th term without
   writing the first 6 terms?

6. What is the 10th term of this pattern?
   Start at 13. Alternately subtract 4, then add 5.

7. The first 2 terms of a pattern are 6, 12, . . .
   How many different patterns can you write with these 2 terms?
   For each pattern, list the first 6 terms and write the pattern rule.
   Show your work.

Reflect

How do you find the pattern rule for a number pattern?
Use an example to explain.

Using Patterns to Solve Problems

What are the missing numbers?
How do you know?

Explore

Sam charges $6 for each hour he baby-sits.

➤ How much does Sam earn when he works
2 hours? 3 hours? 4 hours? 5 hours?
Show your results in a table.

Time Worked (hours)	Money Earned ($)
1	6

➤ What patterns do you see in the table?
How is each term different from the term before?
Use the patterns to predict how
much Sam will earn working 21 hours.

➤ Will Sam earn exactly $40? $45? $50?
How do you know?

➤ Sam saves all the money he earns.
He needs $250 to buy a mountain bike.
How many hours does Sam need
to work?

➤ Make up your own problem you can
solve using this table.
Trade problems with another pair of classmates.
Solve your classmates' problem.

Show and Share

Share your answers with your classmates.
Did you solve the problems the same way? Explain.

LESSON FOCUS | Pose and solve problems by applying a patterning strategy.

9

One puzzle book costs $17.

➤ How much does it cost to buy 2 books? 3 books? 4 books?

Make a table.
When you add 1 to the
number of books,
you add $17 to the cost.

Number of Books	Cost ($)
1	17
2	34
3	51
4	68

These numbers
are multiples of 17.

Two books cost $34.
Three books cost $51.
Four books cost $68.

➤ Use a pattern to predict the
cost of 20 books.

 One pattern rule for the cost is:

Start at 17. Add 17 each time.

Another pattern rule for the cost is:

The number of books multiplied by 17

 To predict the cost of 20 books, multiply: $20 \times 17 = 340$
Twenty books cost $340.

➤ Suppose you have $200.
Can you buy puzzle books and have no money left over?

Extend the pattern to see if 200 is a term.
Use a calculator.

 Continue to add 17:
17, 34, 51, 68, 85, 102, 119, 136, 153, 170, 187, 204, . . .

Two consecutive terms are 187 and 204.

When one number
follows another
number, the numbers
are **consecutive**.

So, 200 is not a term in the pattern.
If you try to spend $200, you will
have money left over.

Practice

1. Here is a pattern of linking cubes.

   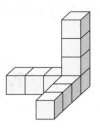

Object 1   Object 2   Object 3   Object 4

The pattern continues. Use linking cubes.
a) Make the next two objects.
b) Copy and complete this table for the first 6 objects.
c) How does the pattern grow?
   Write a pattern rule for the number of cubes.
d) How many cubes will there be in the 10th object?
   How do you know?
e) Will any object have 50 cubes? 51 cubes? How do you know?

Object	Number of Cubes
1	1

2. The pattern in this table continues.

Number of CDs	Cost ($)
1	16
2	32
3	48
4	64
5	

Math Link

Nature

In a beehive, bees make honeycomb to store their honey. The cells in the honeycomb form a pattern.

a) Which of these numbers is the next term in the *Cost* column?
   77, 78, 79, 80, 81
   How do you know?
b) Write a pattern rule for the cost in dollars.
c) Write the next 5 terms in the *Cost* column.
d) How is each term in the *Cost* column different from the term before?
   How is each term different from the following term?

3. Hilary delivers newspapers. Each week she collects $25.

    a) How much money has Hilary collected at the end of 1 week? 2 weeks?

    b) Make a table to show the amounts for the first 8 weeks.

    c) How is each amount different from the amount before?

    d) How much will Hilary collect in total in 3 weeks?

    e) Will Hilary ever collect a total of $240? $250? $260?
       How do you know?

    f) Write a problem you could solve using the table in part b.
      Solve your problem.

4. The sunflower is the only single flower
that grows as high as 300 cm.
Suppose it grows 30 cm each week.
In which week could a sunflower reach a height of 300 cm? Explain.

5. Dave read 40 pages on Monday, 37 pages on Tuesday,
and 34 pages on Wednesday.
This pattern of pages read continued until Dave finished his book.

    a) Which of the numbers below is the number of pages
      Dave read on Thursday? How do you know?
      29, 30, 31, 32, 33

    b) What was the total number of pages Dave read the first 7 days?

    c) Dave finished his book on the day he read 1 page.
      How many pages are in the book?
    Show your work.

6. Look at this shape.

    a) How many triangles are there
      with a side length of 1 unit?
      2 units? 3 units?

    b) How many triangles
      are in this shape?

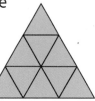

At Home

Reflect

How can using patterns
help you solve problems?
Use an example from this
lesson to explain.

What number patterns
do you see at home?
Look through magazines,
newspapers, and around your
community.
Write about the patterns you see.
How is each term different from the
term before?

LESSON 3

Using a Variable to Describe a Pattern

Explore

You will need green Pattern Blocks
and triangular dot paper.
The side length of the block is shown.

➤ Make an increasing pattern with the blocks.
Draw each figure in the pattern on dot paper.

➤ What is the perimeter of each figure?

➤ Copy and complete this table for the first 3 figures.

Figure Number	Perimeter (units)
1	

➤ Continue the pattern.
Make the next 3 figures.
Draw these figures on dot paper.
Extend the table for these 3 figures.

➤ What patterns do you see in the table?
How is each perimeter different from
the perimeter before?
How is the perimeter related to the
figure number?

Show and Share

Compare your table with that of another pair of students.
Suppose you know the figure number.
What would you do to get the perimeter of the figure?
What is the perimeter of the 100th figure? The 200th figure?

LESSON FOCUS | Describe a pattern using an expression.

13

➤ Here is a pattern of line segments drawn on dot paper.

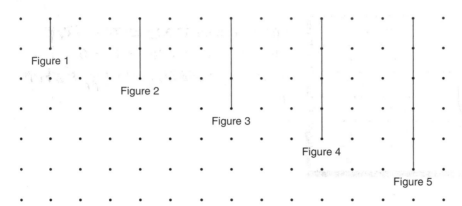

The table shows each figure number and the number of dots on the figure.

Figure Number	Number of Dots
1	2 = 1 + 1
2	3 = 2 + 1
3	4 = 3 + 1
4	5 = 4 + 1
5	6 = 5 + 1

The number of dots is 1 more than the figure number.

We can write each number of dots as this sum: Figure number + 1

We can use a letter, such as f, to represent any figure number.
f is called a **variable**.
Then, the number of dots on Figure f is $f + 1$.
$f + 1$ is an **expression** that represents the pattern in the numbers of dots.

A variable is shown in italics.

We can check that this expression is correct.
For the number of dots on the 6th figure, replace f with 6.
Then, $f + 1 = 6 + 1$
$= 7$
The 6th figure has 7 dots.
We continue the pattern above to verify this.

Figure 6

➤ We can use a variable to write a pattern rule.
Look at this pattern: 7, 8, 9, 10, 11, . . .
Each term is 1 more than the preceding term.
Look for a way to relate the value of a term to its position in the pattern.

Term Position	Term Value
1	$7 = 1 + 6$
2	$8 = 2 + 6$
3	$9 = 3 + 6$
4	$10 = 4 + 6$
5	$11 = 5 + 6$

Let n represent any term position.
Then, the term value is $n + 6$.
So, an expression for the pattern rule
is $n + 6$.

We can check that the expression $n + 6$ is correct.
For the 5th term, replace n with 5.
$$n + 6 = 5 + 6$$
$$= 11$$
This matches the value of the 5th term in the table above.
So, the expression is correct.

Practice

1. For the pattern below:
   a) Copy and complete the table.
   b) Write an expression to represent the
      pattern in the numbers of dots.

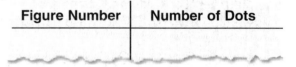

Figure Number	Number of Dots

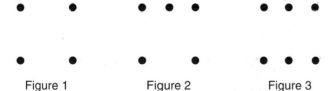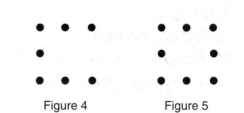

Figure 1   Figure 2   Figure 3   Figure 4   Figure 5

2. For the pattern below:
   a) Copy and complete the table.
   b) Write an expression to represent the
      pattern in the numbers of squares.

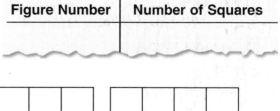

Figure Number	Number of Squares

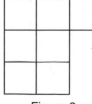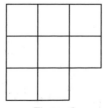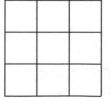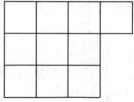

Figure 1   Figure 2   Figure 3   Figure 4   Figure 5

3. For each table, write an expression for the number of dots in any figure. Check that each expression is correct.

a)

Figure Number	Number of Dots
1	5
2	6
3	7
4	8
5	9
6	10

b)

Figure Number	Number of Dots
1	6
2	7
3	8
4	9
5	10
6	11

c)

Figure Number	Number of Dots
1	0
2	1
3	2
4	3
5	4
6	5

4. Use a variable to write a pattern rule for each number pattern.
   a) 2, 3, 4, 5, 6, 7, . . .   b) 10, 11, 12, 13, 14, 15, . . .   c) 8, 9, 10, 11, 12, 13, . . .

5. Find the 100th term in each pattern in question 4.
   Explain how you did this.

6. Write an expression for each number pattern.
   Write the next 5 terms in each pattern.
   Explain how you know the expressions and terms are correct.
   a) 15, 16, 17, 18, 19, . . .   b) 16, 17, 18, 19, 20, . . .
   Show your work.

7. Here are some decreasing patterns.
   Match each pattern with an expression below.
   How can you check that you are correct?
   a) 99, 98, 97, 96, 95, . . .   b) 34, 33, 32, 31, 30, . . .   c) 50, 49, 48, 47, 46, . . .
   A. $51 - t$ B. $35 - t$ C. $100 - t$

8. Use a variable to write a pattern rule for each number pattern.
   a) 10, 9, 8, 7, 6, 5, . . .   b) 40, 39, 38, 37, 36, 35, . . .   c) 1000, 999, 998, 997, 996, . . .
   How is each pattern different from the patterns in question 4?

Reflect

How can using a variable help you represent a pattern?
Use words, numbers, or pictures to explain.

Tic-Tac-Toe Challenge

You will need 1-cm grid paper.
Think about the game Tic-Tac-Toe.
On a 3 by 3 grid, people take turns
to write X or O.
The winner is the person who gets
3 in a row, column, or diagonal.

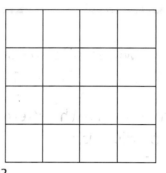

Try Tic-Tac-Toe on a 4 by 4 grid.
Take turns to write X or O in a grid
square until one person gets 3 in a row.

Play the game several times.
Try to find a strategy so the person
who plays first always wins.
Where does that person write her first X or O?

Variation: Play Tic-Tac-Toe on a 4 by 4 grid so the first person to
get 4 in a row *loses*.

Strategies Toolkit

Explore

Two students stretch a piece of modelling clay until it breaks into 2 pieces. This is Round 1.
The students then stretch each new piece until it breaks into 2 pieces. This is Round 2.
This process continues.
How many pieces of clay will there be after Round 8?

Show and Share

Describe the strategy you used to solve the problem.

Connect

Suppose a cow produces her first female calf when she is 2 years of age.
After that, she produces a female calf each year.
Suppose each cow produces her first female calf when she is 2 years of age and no cows die.
How many cows will there be after 5 years?

What do you know?
- Each cow produces a female calf at age 2.
- Every year after that, she produces 1 female calf.
- No cows die.

Think of a strategy to help you solve the problem.
- You can **draw a diagram**.
- Find out how many cows there are after 1 year, then after 2 years, and so on.

Strategies

- Make a table.
- Use a model.
- Draw a diagram.
- Solve a simpler problem.
- Work backward.
- Guess and test.
- Make an organized list.
- Use a pattern.

Copy and continue the diagram.

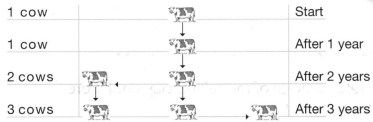

1 cow		Start
1 cow		After 1 year
2 cows		After 2 years
3 cows		After 3 years

After 1 year, there is 1 cow.
After 2 years, there are 2 cows.
After 3 years, there are 3 cows.
How many cows are there
after 5 years?

Check your work.
What pattern do you see in the numbers of cows?

Practice

Choose one of the

Strategies

1. A mouse crawls through this maze.
   The mouse always moves forward.

   a) How many different paths could
   the mouse take from A to B?
   From A to C? From A to D?
   What pattern do you see?

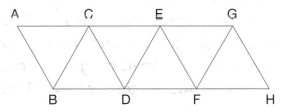

   b) Predict the number of different paths the mouse could take from A to H.

2. Here is a regular pentagon. Copy the pentagon.
   Join each vertex to all other vertices.
   How many different triangles are there?

Reflect

How does drawing a diagram help to solve a problem?
Use words, pictures, and numbers to explain.

Using a Variable to Write an Equation

Which statements below are equations?
How do you know?

$3 + 7 = 10$ $3 + 7 + 10$ $12 = 14 - 2$ $12 - 2 + 14$ $5 - 1 = 2 + 2$

How would you say each equation without using these words:
"plus", "add", "minus", or "take away"?

Explore

You will need index cards and scissors.

➤ Create 4 game cards, each one similar to one of the cards below.
   Use one of $+, -, \times,$ or $\div$ in each equation.

Eight is three more than a number.	$8 = \square + 3$
Two less than a number is nine.	$\triangledown - 2 = 9$
Four times a number is twenty.	$4 \times \lozenge = 20$
Five is thirty divided by a number.	$5 = 30 \div *$

➤ Cut the cards in half, then shuffle them.
   Trade your cards with those of another pair of classmates.
   Match each sentence to its equation.

Show *and* Share

What strategies did you use to write the equations?
How did you decide which symbol to use?
What strategies did you use to match the cards?
For each sentence, how could you write the equation a different way?

Connect

We may be able to write an equation to help us solve a problem.
We use a letter variable to represent what we do not know.

The variable we choose is often the first letter of a word in the problem.

➤ Jean-Luc opened a package of 20 pencils.
He gave out some pencils.
There were 6 pencils left.
How many pencils did Jean-Luc give out?

We use a variable to represent
the number of pencils given out.
Let p represent the number of pencils given out.
Here are 3 equations we can write.

- We know that:
  Total number of pencils = number given out + number left
  One equation is: $20 = p + 6$
- We know that:
  Number left − total number of pencils − number given out
  A second equation is: $6 = 20 - p$
- We know that:
  Number given out = total number of pencils − number left
  A third equation is: $p = 20 - 6$

➤ Marie had 36 e-mails in her inbox.
This was twice as many e-mails as she had last week.
How many e-mails did Marie have last week?

Let e represent the number of e-mails Marie had last week.
Here are 2 equations we can write.

- We know that:
  $2 \times$ number of e-mails last week = number of e-mails this week
  One equation is: $2 \times e = 36$
  Or, $2e = 36$

We write $2 \times e$ as $2e$: that is, we do not write the multiply sign.

- We know that:
  Number of e-mails last week = number of e-mails this week $\div$ 2
  A second equation is: $e = 36 \div 2$

Practice •

1. Which equation below represents this problem? Explain your choice.
   Together, Melissa and Pierre have 15 rare hockey cards.
   Melissa has 9 cards.
   How many cards does Pierre have?
   a) $c = 15 + 9$ **b)** $15 = c + 9$ **c)** $9 = 15 + c$ **d)** $c - 15 = 9$

Write an equation for each of questions 2 to 4.

2. Mary-George has 4 buckets of clams
   for the Long House feast.
   Each bucket contains the same number of clams.
   Altogether, Mary-George has 120 clams.
   How many clams are in each bucket?

3. Lesley read 114 pages of an exciting novel.
   The novel is 204 pages.
   How many more pages does Lesley have to read?

4. The water cooler held 66 cups of water.
   Each minute, 3 cups of water were taken.
   How many minutes did it take for the water cooler to empty?

Write 2 equations for each of questions 5 and 6.

5. Three towers were built. Each tower had the same number of toy blocks.
   Altogether, there were 144 blocks.
   How many blocks were in each tower?

6. Jaipreet picked 30 boxes of blueberries in the bush.
   After she sold some boxes, she had 13 boxes left.
   How many boxes did Jaipreet sell?

7. Write a word problem for which you can write an equation.
   Write as many equations as you can for your problem.
   Explain how you know each equation represents the problem.

Reflect

Look at the questions above.
Explain how you decided whether to use $+$, $-$, $\times$, or $\div$ in an equation.

Solving Equations Involving Addition and Subtraction

How many counters are in the bag?
How do you know?

Explore

➤ Solve this problem:
Rui has $35.
After he spent some money, Rui had $19 left.
How much money did Rui spend?

➤ How many different ways can you solve the problem?
Describe each strategy you used.

Show *and* Share

Share your strategies and solution with another pair of classmates.
If you wrote an equation, did you write the same equation?
If not, is one equation incorrect? Explain.
If you did not write an equation, work together now
to write and solve an equation to solve the problem.

Connect

Wendy washed 72 windows in an apartment building.
She had 98 windows to wash altogether.
How many more windows has Wendy to wash?

Write an equation to solve this problem.
Let *w* represent the number of windows Wendy has still to wash.
We know that:
Total number of windows = windows already washed + windows still to be washed
One equation is:

$$98 = 72 + w$$

LESSON FOCUS | Create and solve equations using addition and subtraction.

23

Here are two ways to solve this equation.

- Guess and test

$98 = 72 + w$
Guess a number for w, then test to see if you are correct.

Guess: $w = 10$
Test: $72 + 10 = 82$ This is too low.

Guess: $w = 20$
Test: $72 + 20 = 92$ This is too low, but closer to the number we want.

Guess: $w = 25$
Test: $72 + 25 = 97$ This is very close.

Guess: $w = 26$
Test: $72 + 26 = 98$
So, $w = 26$

- **By inspection**

$98 = 72 + w$
Which number do we add to 72 to get 98?

We subtract to find out.
The number we add is: $98 - 72 = 26$
So, $w = 26$

Wendy has 26 more windows to wash.

$w = 26$ is the **solution** to the equation.

By *inspection* means I look at, or *inspect*, the equation to try to figure out the number that w represents.

Practice

1. Solve each equation.
   Which strategy will you use?
   a) $20 = c + 1$ **b)** $c + 2 = 20$ **c)** $3 + c = 20$ **d)** $20 = 4 + c$

2. Solve each equation.
   Which strategy will you use?
   a) $10 = n - 1$ **b)** $n - 2 = 10$ **c)** $10 - n = 3$ **d)** $4 = 10 - n$

For each of questions 3 to 7, write an equation.
Solve the equation to solve the problem.

3. Scott and Jamie have a collection of autographed pictures.
   Altogether, they have 36 pictures.
   Scott has 13 pictures.
   How many pictures does Jamie have?

4. The girls' field hockey team has 32 jerseys.
   Some of these jerseys are new. Nineteen jerseys are from last year.
   How many jerseys are new?

5. Mandeep buys a case of 24 cans of juice.
   In one week, Mandeep drinks 11 cans.
   How many cans are left?

6. Sholeh wants to add 40 files to a folder in her laptop computer.
   There is only enough room for 13 files. Sholeh cannot delete any files.
   How many files will not fit?

7. A ribbon is 45 cm long. Adam cuts off a piece.
   The ribbon that is left is 12 cm long.
   How long was the piece Adam cut off?

8. For each equation, write a story problem that could be solved
   by using the equation.
   a) $30 = a + 5$ **b)** $h - 4 = 25$ **c)** $40 - c = 16$ **d)** $35 = d - 11$

9. **a)** Write as many different equations as you can for this problem:
       Sandra and Kirk have 72 linking cubes.
       Kirk has 28 cubes.
       How many cubes does Sandra have?
   b) Solve each equation you wrote in part a.
   c) Solve the problem in part a.
   Show your work.

Reflect

Which method for solving an equation do you find easiest?
Explain your choice.

Solving Equations Involving Multiplication and Division

➤ Solve this problem:

For a school fund-raiser, Yettis is packing boxes
for children in Guyana, South America.
Yettis has 48 notebooks.
She puts 6 notebooks in each box.
How many boxes will have notebooks?

➤ How many different equations can you write to solve the problem?
List each equation.

Show and Share

Share your equations and solution with another pair of classmates.
What types of equations did you write?
What strategies did you use to solve your equations?

Connect

Clive watched the first snow of the season fall outside his window.
Each hour, 3 cm of snow fell.
The total snowfall was 15 cm.
For how many hours did it snow?

Write an equation to solve this problem.
Let t represent the number of hours it snowed.
Here are 3 equations we can write and solve.

➤ Using multiplication
We know that:
Total snowfall = snow that falls in 1 h × number of hours it snowed
One equation is:

$$15 = 3 \times t$$

Or, $\quad 15 = 3t$

3t is a short way to write 3 × t.

To solve this equation, think:

Which number do we multiply 3 by to get 15?

We know that: $3 \times 5 = 15$

So, $t = 5$

➤ Using division
   • We know that:

   Number of hours it snowed = total snowfall ÷ snow that falls in 1 h

   One equation is:

   $$t = 15 \div 3$$

   So, $t = 5$

   • We also know that:

   Snow that falls in 1 h = total snowfall ÷ number of hours it snowed

   Another equation is:

   $$3 = 15 \div t$$

   To solve this equation, think:

   Which number do we divide 15 by to get 3?

   We know that: $15 \div 5 = 3$

   So, $t = 5$

The snow fell for 5 h.

Practice

1. Solve each equation.
   a) $2 \times m = 4$
   b) $2 \times m = 6$
   c) $2 \times m = 8$
   d) $2 \times m = 10$
   e) $3 \times m = 18$
   f) $3 \times m = 21$
   g) $3 \times m = 24$
   h) $3 \times m = 27$

2. Solve each equation.
   a) $20 = 5c$
   b) $2c = 30$
   c) $4c = 44$
   d) $50 = 5c$
   e) $6c = 42$
   f) $56 = 7c$
   g) $8c = 64$
   h) $54 = 9c$

3. Solve each equation.
   a) $n = 16 \div 2$
   b) $30 \div n = 10$
   c) $8 = 48 \div n$
   d) $5 = n \div 6$
   e) $25 \div n = 5$
   f) $6 = 42 \div n$
   g) $n = 72 \div 8$
   h) $n \div 4 = 8$

4. Solve each equation.
   a) $63 \div r = 7$
   b) $21 = 7s$
   c) $t \div 5 = 7$
   d) $36 = 4u$
   e) $49 \div 7 = v$
   f) $5w = 45$
   g) $8 = 40 \div z$
   h) $8n = 80$

For each of questions 5 to 9, write an equation.
Solve the equation to solve the problem.

5. For a traditional burning ceremony, Cam had 22 bundles of cedar logs.
   Each bundle contained 3 logs.
   How many logs did Cam have altogether?

6. Holly made a comic book with 8 pages.
   She had several copies of the book printed.
   Holly paid for 96 pages altogether.
   How many comic books did she print?

7. Starkley used his computer to write and record a drum track.
   Each bar of the song had 4 beats.
   The printout showed 31 bars of music.
   How many beats did Starkley record?

8. Kimberly left Edmonton for a long car trip.
   She travelled 400 km in 5 h.
   About how far did Kimberly travel in 1 h?

9. Teagan picked cranberries for one week.
   Each day, he picked 30 baskets of cranberries.
   How many baskets did Teagan pick in 7 days?

10. For each equation, write a story problem that could be solved
    by using the equation.
    a) $45 = 5n$ **b)** $77 \div 7 = r$ **c)** $6 = 24 \div s$ **d)** $t \div 7 = 8$

11. **a)** Write an equation.
    b) Write a story problem that could be solved by solving the equation.
    c) Solve the equation and the problem.
    d) What other equations could you write to solve the story problem?
    Show your work.

Reflect

When you have a problem that can be solved by dividing,
why can you write at least two equations for the problem?
Use an example to explain.

Match It!

Your teacher will give you copies of Equation Cards and Problem Cards.

You will need scissors.

The goal of the game is to match each Equation Card to a Problem Card, and explain why the match was made.

➤ Cut out the cards.
   Shuffle the cards.
   Place all the cards face up in an array.

➤ Take turns to pick two matching cards.
   Explain how you know the match is correct.
   If the match is not correct, the player returns the cards to the array, and awaits his next turn.

➤ One point is awarded for the correct match.
   One point is awarded for a clear explanation.
   A bonus point is awarded for solving the equation and the problem.

➤ Play until all the cards have been matched,
   or until a player has 10 points.

LESSON

1

1. Write the first 6 terms of each pattern.
   a) Start at 100. Subtract 6 each time.
   b) Start at 10. Alternately, add 5 then subtract 2.

2. For each pattern below:
   • Use counters to show the first 3 terms.
   • Predict the 6th and 7th terms.
   • Use counters to check your predictions.
   • Describe the pattern.
     How is each term different from the term before?
   • Write a pattern rule.
   a) 2, 4, 6, 8, 10, . . .   **b)** 2, 4, 7, 11, 16, . . .   **c)** 2, 4, 5, 7, 8, . . .

2

3. For each pattern below, choose the number that is the next term in the pattern.
   Explain your choice.
   a) 5, 8, 12, 15, 19, . . .
      Which number is the next term: 20, 21, 22, 23, or 24?
   b) 50, 48, 47, 45, 44, . . .
      Which number is the next term: 43, 42, 41, 40, or 39?
   c) 10, 12, 16, 22, 30, . . .
      Which number is the next term: 34, 36, 38, 40, or 42?

4. A magazine costs $4.00.
   a) What is the cost of 2 magazines? 3 magazines? 4 magazines?
      5 magazines? 6 magazines?
      Show your answers in a table.
   b) How much would 98 magazines cost?
   c) How many magazines can you buy with $100?
   d) Suppose you have $50.00.
      Can you buy magazines and have no money left over?
      How do you know?

3

5. Use a variable to write a pattern rule for each number pattern.
   Find the 50th term in each pattern.
   a) 4, 5, 6, 7, 8, . . .
   b) 12, 13, 14, 15, 16, . . .

6. For each hour Riley does chores, her mother increases her earnings by $1 per hour.
This table shows Riley's earnings per hour for the first 3 hours.

Hours Worked	Money Earned per Hour
1	$3
2	$4
3	$5

a) Copy the table.
Extend the table 3 more rows.

b) Use a variable to write an expression for the money earned per hour.

c) Suppose this pattern continues.
How much would Riley earn for the 10th hour she works?

For each of questions 7 to 9, write an equation for the problem, then use the equation to solve the problem.

7. Adala runs 5 km each day.
How far does Adala run in 17 days?

8. Joe is collecting cans of food for the food bank.
On Monday, he had 27 cans.
On Tuesday, he had 53 cans.
How many more cans did Joe have on Tuesday than on Monday?

9. Suri has 75 stickers.
She shares the stickers among her friends.
Each friend has 15 stickers.
How many friends received stickers?

10. For each equation, write a story problem that could be solved by using the equation.
a) $36 = 4n$
b) $4 + n = 36$
c) $36 = n - 4$
d) $n \div 4 = 36$

UNIT

1 Learning Goals

- ☑ use a pattern rule to describe a pattern
- ☑ make predictions about terms in a pattern
- ☑ use a variable to describe a pattern
- ☑ use a variable to write equations
- ☑ solve equations to solve problems

Unit Problem

Charity Fund-raising

Plan an event to raise money for charity.

Include:
- a description of the event
- how much you estimate the costs will be
- how much money you expect to raise
- tables to show any patterns in the money you expect to raise
- a poster to promote your fund-raising event

Check List

Your work should show
- ☑ a detailed plan of the event
- ☑ how you calculate the amount you expect to raise
- ☑ any tables and patterns you used
- ☑ correct math language

Bike-A-Thon

Bake Sale

Pies - $7   Muffins - $2
Cakes - $9   Cookies - $1

Reflect on Your Learning

Write about some of the different equations in the unit, and how you used them to solve problems.

2

Whole Numbers

Languages We Speak

When settlers from Europe arrived in Canada, they met First Nations people who spoke many different Aboriginal languages. Most settlers spoke French or English. These are now the two official languages of Canada. Canadians speak many other languages at home and at work.

Learning Goals

- represent and describe whole numbers to 1 000 000
- use different strategies to estimate sums and differences
- estimate to solve problems

This table shows how many people speak some of the Aboriginal languages in Western and Northern Canada.

	B.C.	Yuk.	Alta.	N.W.T.	Sask.	Man.	Nvt.
Cree	1160	15	15 010	155	22 020	18 090	0
Inuktitut	50	20	100	760	50	70	18 605
Ojibway	275	10	625	65	1 370	8 840	0
Dakota/ Sioux	25	0	2 765	0	350	730	0
Blackfoot	35	10	2 630	0	15	25	0
Salish	2570	10	0	0	0	0	0
South Slave	100	20	250	1005	0	0	0
Dogrib	20	0	10	1830	10	0	0
Chipewyan	10	10	225	300	0	20	10

Adapted from Statistics Canada: Population reporting by Aboriginal identity (2001 Census)

Key Words

expanded form

standard form

front-end rounding

compatible numbers

compensation

- Do you think the numbers in the table are exact or estimates? Explain.
- Why do the numbers have 0 or 5 as the ones digit?
- Which aboriginal language is spoken by the greatest number of people? How do you know?
- In Alberta, do more people speak Dakota/Sioux or Blackfoot? Explain.
- Which language do about 9000 people in Manitoba speak?
- Write a question you could answer using the data in the table.

Numbers to 100 000

About 30 000 people live in Nunavut. How does 30 000 compare with the number of people in your community?

Explore

➤ Use Base Ten Blocks to help you answer each question.

- How many ones are in 10? In 100? In 1000?
- How many tens are in 100? In 1000?
- How many hundreds are in 1000?

➤ How could you make a model to show 10 000? How many of each Base Ten Block would you need if you used only:

- the ones cubes?
- the tens rods?
- the hundreds flats?
- the thousands cubes?

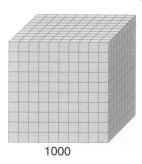
1000

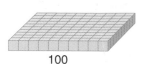
100

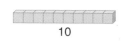
10

1

Show *and* Share

Share your work with another pair of students.
Talk about how the numbers 10, 100, 1000, and 10 000 are related.
Compare your ideas for models of 10 000.
Which model is more efficient?

- Ten thousand is 10 times as great as 1 thousand.

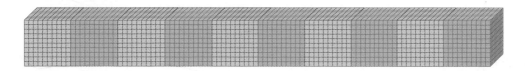

- Ten thousand is 100 times as great as 1 hundred.
  There are 100 hundreds in 10 000.

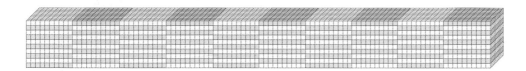

- Ten thousand is 1000 times as great as 1 ten.
  There are 1000 tens in 10 000.

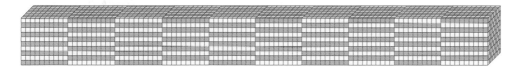

- Ten thousand is 10 000 times as great as 1 one.
  There are 10 000 ones in 10 000.

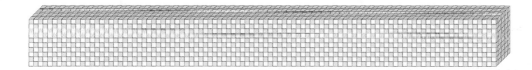

- A place-value chart shows the values of the digits in a number.
  This place-value chart shows the number 33 333.
  As you move to the left on this place-value chart, the value of the digit
  is 10 times as great as the digit before.

Ten Thousands	Thousands	Hundreds	Tens	Ones
3	3	3	3	3

3 ten thousands = 30 thousands   3 hundreds = 30 tens

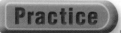

Use Base Ten Blocks if you need them.

1. Your teacher will give you a copy of 100 dots.
   What would:
   • 1000 dots look like?
   • 10 000 dots look like?
   • 50 000 dots look like?

2. Would you rather have one hundred $10 bills or ten $1000 bills?
   Explain your choice.

3. Suppose you were paid $10 an hour.
   a) How many hours would you have to work to earn $500?
   b) How many hours would you have to work to earn $5000?

4. Forty thousand coins were minted.
   How many boxes are needed to store
   the coins if each box contains:
   a) 100 coins?   b) 10 coins?
   c) 10 000 coins?   d) 1000 coins?
   Use numbers, words, or pictures to explain.

5. a) How many tens are in 8000?
   b) How many hundreds are in 8000?
   c) How many thousands are in 8000?

6. a) How many tens are in 20 000?
   b) How many hundreds are in 20 000?
   c) How many thousands are in 20 000?

7. Use only the digits 1, 3, and 5.
   Write a number greater than
   fifteen thousand.

Your World

Statistics Canada publishes data
about people and places.
These data often involve
large numbers.
Use the Internet to find some
of these large numbers.

Reflect

When you see a large number, how can you tell how it compares
to 10, to 100, and to 1000? Use a large number to explain.

Aim for 100 000

You will need:
- a number cube labelled 1 to 6
- a calculator
- a score sheet

The goal of the game is to reach as close to 100 000 as possible.

Your teacher will give each player copies of a score sheet like this:

Roll	Ten Thousands	Thousands	Hundreds	Tens	Ones
1					ones
2					

➤ Players take turns to roll the number cube.
  Each time the cube is rolled, players decide on the place value of the number and record their decision on their score sheet.
  For example, if a 2 is rolled, it can be used to make:
  20 000 or 2000 or 200 or 20 or 2

➤ After 7 rolls, players add the numbers on their score sheets to find the total.
  The player who is closest to 100 000, without going over, scores 1 point.
  Use a calculator to check any sums you need to.

➤ The first player to get 5 points wins.

Exploring One Million

These people are having their heads shaved for charity.
Brown-haired people have about
100 000 hairs on their heads.
About how many people do you
think would have to be shaved
to collect 1 million hairs?

You can use patterns to learn about 1 million.

Words	One Million	One Hundred Thousand	Ten Thousand	One Thousand	One Hundred	Ten	One
Numbers	1 000 000	100 000	10 000	1000	100	10	1
Base Ten Block	?	?	?				

Look at the chart above.

➤ What do you think:
  • the 10 000 block would look like?
  • the 100 000 block would look like?
  • the 1 000 000 block would look like?

➤ Sketch each block.
  How do the lengths, widths, and heights of the blocks compare?
  What patterns do you see?

➤ In the chart, what patterns do you see in the numbers?

Show and Share

Share the patterns you found with another pair of students.
How do the patterns in the chart compare with the patterns
in your sketches of the blocks?

Connect ....

One million is a very large number.
You can visualize 1 million by imagining
a model of a cubic metre.
To fill the cube, you would need
1 million Base Ten unit cubes
or 1000 thousand cubes.

Here are some benchmarks to help
you think about the number 1 million.

1 000 000 = 1000 thousands
$1 000 000 = ten thousand $100 bills
1 000 000 min is about 2 years.
1 000 000¢ = $10 000

Practice ....

Use a calculator when it helps.

1. Have you lived one million hours?
   If your answer is no, have you lived one million minutes?
   Explain your thinking.

2. Suppose you use a calculator to count to 1 000 000.
   How many times will you press the "equals" key if you:
   a) count by 1000s?
   b) count by 10 000s?
   c) count by 100 000s?
   Use a calculator to check.

3. How many $10 bills would it take to make $1 million?

4. How long would a line of 1 million centimetre cubes be?
Give your answer using as many different units as you can.

5. How many days would it take you to spend $1 000 000,
if each day you spend:
- **a)** $100 000?
- **b)** $50 000?
- **c)** $10 000?
- **d)** $1000?
- **e)** $500?
- **f)** $100?

6. Suppose you save $100 a month.
How many months would it take until
you could trade your savings for
1 million pennies?

7. There are 100 pennies in one roll.
How many pennies are there in
- **a)** 5 rolls?
- **b)** 10 rolls?
- **c)** 50 rolls?
- **d)** 100 rolls?
- **e)** 500 rolls?
- **f)** 1000 rolls?

8. How many rolls of pennies do you need, to have one million pennies?

9. Copy and complete.
- **a)** $999\,999 - 1 = \square$
- **b)** $1\,000\,000 - 100\,000 = \square$
- **c)** $800\,000 + \square = 1\,000\,000$
- **d)** $500\,000 \times \square = 1\,000\,000$
- **e)** $250\,000 \times \square = 1\,000\,000$
- **f)** $1\,000\,000 \div 10 = \square$

10. Measure a straw to the nearest centimetre.
Suppose 1 million straws were laid end-to-end.
How far would they stretch?
How many different ways can
you find out?

At Home

Reflect

What do you know about
one million?

Use newspapers and catalogues.
Find items that you could buy to
total $1 million.
Interview a senior or elder.
Find out what could have been
purchased with $1 million fifty
years ago. List the items.

Representing Numbers

Action Comic Sells for Record $350 000

Miro Painting Auctioned for $910 000

Reward of $50 000 Posted

Tsunami Death Toll Over 280 000

Wild B.C. Weather leaves 200 000 Without Power

Where do you see large numbers used?

 **Explore** ··

Large numbers like those above can be difficult to visualize.
You can use place value to help get a better feel for large numbers.
Your teacher will give you a copy of this table.

	350 000	910 000	280 000	50 000	200 000
Ten thousands	35				
Thousands					
Hundreds			2800		
Tens				5000	
Ones					

Complete this table.
What patterns do you see in the completed table?

Show *and* Share

Share the patterns you found with another pair of students.
What other ways can you represent large numbers?

LESSON FOCUS | Represent and describe whole numbers in different ways.

43

Connect

In 2003, there were 656 792 people who attended the Women's World Cup soccer matches.
Here are some different ways to represent that number of people.

- Use a place-value chart to show the number 656 792:

Hundred Thousands	Ten Thousands	Thousands	Hundreds	Tens	Ones
6	5	6	7	9	2

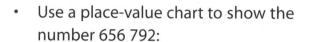

| 600 000 | 50 000 | 6000 | 700 | 90 | 2 |

Every digit has a place value depending on its position.

- Use **expanded form** to write 656 792.
Expanded form shows a number as a sum of the values of all its digits.

656 792 = (6 × 100 000) + (5 × 10 000) + (6 × 1000) + (7 × 100) + (9 × 10) + (2 × 1)

= 600 000 + 50 000 + 6000 + 700 + 90 + 2

- Use words.
656 792 is six hundred fifty-six thousand seven hundred ninety-two.

> We do not use the word "and" when we write or say whole numbers.

- Use **standard form**.
The number 656 792 is written in standard form.
It has space between the thousands digit and the hundreds digit.

> When we write numbers with more than 4 digits in standard form, we put a space between groups of 3 digits.

1. Use a place-value chart to show each number.
   a) 273 190   b) 40 920   c) 738   d) 3789

2. Describe the meaning of each digit in this number:
   There are 25 630 key chains in the world's largest collection.

3. Write each number in standard form.
   a) 600 000 + 20 000 + 50 + 7
   b) nine hundred fifty thousand six
   c) sixty-three thousand five hundred twenty-nine
   d) 500 000 + 80 000 + 6000 + 400 + 20 + 9

   Remember to use correct spacing.

4. The digits in 134 589 are in order from least to greatest.
   Write 5 different 6-digit numbers with their digits in order
   from least to greatest.

5. You will need a calculator.
   a) Key in 3 digits.
      Record the number in the display,
      then write it in expanded form.
   b) Do not clear the display.
      Key in another digit.
      Record the new number,
      then write it in expanded form.
   c) Repeat part b to record a 5-digit number in expanded form.
   d) Repeat part b to record a 6-digit number in expanded form.
   e) What happened to the first digit you keyed in?
      How did its value change as you keyed in more digits?

6. Copy and complete. Replace each □ with >, <, or =.
   How did you decide which symbol to use?
   a) 35 937 □ 35 397   b) 272 456 □ 227 456
   c) 456 123 □ 456 123   d) 975 346 □ 985 346

7. Use the digits 5, 2, 8, 3, 6, 9.
   a) What is the greatest number you can make?
   b) What is the least number you can make?
   c) Write 4 numbers between the numbers you wrote in parts a and b.
   d) Order the numbers in parts a, b, and c from least to greatest.

8. Write each number using words, then in expanded form.

    a) 34 780   **b)** 40 246   **c)** 100 250   **d)** 329 109

9. Write the numbers in each fact as many ways as you can.

    a) The Whistler media room reports that the lifts can carry 59 007 skiers and snowboarders per hour.

    b) 597 204 people voted for mayor in the November 2006 elections.

    c) The 2004 Census found that there were 186 430 children under the age of 4 in Alberta.

10. Write the value of the red digit in each number.

    a) 245 852   **b)** 10 349   **c)** 501 672

    d) 1 000 000   **e)** 982 748   **f)** 34 817

11. Use the data in the table.

Province	Area in Square Kilometres
Alberta	661 848
British Columbia	944 735
Manitoba	647 797
Saskatchewan	651 036

    a) Which is the largest province?

    b) What is its area?

12. Mariette wrote a 6-digit number.
One digit was 0.
The other digits were odd.
No two digits were the same.
The number was the greatest number she could write with these digits.
What number did Mariette write?
How do you know?

13. A student said 84 914 is greater than 311 902 because 8 is greater than 3.
Is the student correct?
How do you know?

14. Count Down to Zero!

 Game

Each of you needs a calculator.
Each of you keys in a 4-digit number.
Do not show your partner your number.
The goal of the game is to get
your partner's number to 0.
Take turns.
Choose a digit, such as 9.
Say to your partner, "Please give me your 9s."
If your partner has that digit in his number,
he has to tell you the number it represents.
For example, if your partner's number is 9209,
he says, "I'll give you nine thousand nine."
You add 9009 to your number.
Your partner subtracts 9009 from his number.
If you choose a digit your partner does not
have in his display, you miss that turn.
Play continues until one of you has
only 0 in the display.

15. What does the zero in each number tell you?

    a) 40 817   **b)** 309 563   **c)** 987 034

16. Use the digits from 1 to 9 only once in each question.

    a) Make a 6-digit number as close to 100 000 as possible.

    b) Make a 6-digit number as close to 500 000 as possible.

    c) Which number did you get closer to? How do you know?

17. Here is part of the expanded form of a number:

    600 000 + 90 000 + 4000 + . . .

a) What might the number be?

b) How many different numbers are possible?
    How do you know?

Reflect

Use numbers, words, or pictures to explain the meaning
of each digit in the number 987 564.

Estimating Sums

Some problems do not need an exact answer. Sometimes you can estimate a sum.

How do you know if $1000 is enough money to buy the TV and the DVD player?

Do you need to add the prices of the items or can you estimate to find out? Explain your answer.

Explore

This chart shows the seating capacity of each NHL Canadian team's home arena.

Team	Seats
Calgary Flames	20 140
Edmonton Oilers	17 100
Montreal Canadiens	21 273
Ottawa Senators	20 004
Toronto Maple Leafs	18 819
Vancouver Canucks	18 630

➤ Suppose a game was sold out in Vancouver and in Calgary. About how many people attended these two games?

➤ The NHL ordered 35 000 pennants to give away for the opening Leafs and Oilers games. The games were sold out. Will there be a pennant for everyone? Explain how you know.

Show and Share

Compare your estimates with those of another pair of classmates.
What strategies did you use to estimate?
When is it better to estimate using a greater number than the given number?

➤ Lori-Ann Muenzer of Edmonton participated in the 2004 Athens Olympic Games. She won Canada's first ever gold medal in cycling.

Lori-Ann was one of 11 090 athletes at the 2004 Athens Olympic Games. There were 10 651 athletes at the 2000 Sydney Olympic Games. About how many athletes attended both Olympic Games?

You know that an exact answer is not required because the question asks "about how many." Estimate: 11 090 + 10 651

- One strategy is to use the front digits to estimate. This strategy is called **front-end rounding**.

  Add the first digits of the numbers:
  11 090 + **1**0 651 is about 10 000 + 10 000 = 20 000

  Then adjust the front-end estimate by looking
  at the first two digits in each number:
  11 090 + **10** 651 is about
  11 000 + 10 000 = 21 000
  Using the first two digits gets you closer to the exact answer.
  There were about 21 000 athletes at the two games.

  Front-end rounding always gives an *underestimate*.

- Another strategy is to use **compatible numbers** to estimate. Compatible numbers are pairs of numbers that are easy to work with. For example, multiples of 10 are compatible numbers. To estimate, replace the actual numbers with numbers that are compatible:
  Write: 11 090 + 10 651
  as: 11 100 + 10 650 = 21 750
  There were about 21 750 athletes at the two games.

  Compatible numbers may give an underestimate or an overestimate. It depends on the numbers you use.

In some situations, I want to overestimate. When I shop, I want to know that I have more than enough money!

➤ You can use front-end rounding when you estimate the sum of more than two numbers. You can also use front-end rounding if the numbers have different numbers of digits.

Here are data for five Summer Olympic Games.

Olympic Games	Number of Athletes
Athens, 2004	11 090
Sydney, 2000	10 651
Atlanta, 1996	10 320
Barcelona, 1992	9 956
Seoul, 1988	8 465

When there are 4-digit and 5-digit numbers in a column, we align the digits. So, the 4-digit numbers have a space between digits too.

About how many athletes were at the five games?

Use front-end rounding to find out:
11 090 + **10** 651 + **10** 320 + **9**956 + **8**465 is about
10 000 + 10 000 + 10 000 + 9000 + 8000 = 47 000
There were about 47 000 athletes at the five games.

We can adjust the estimate by using **compensation**.
11 090 + 10 651 + 10 320 + 9956 + 8465

$\downarrow$ $\downarrow$ $\downarrow$ $\downarrow$ $\downarrow$

11 000 + 11 000 + 10 000 + 10 000 + 8000 = 50 000

$\downarrow$ $\downarrow$ $\downarrow$ $\downarrow$ $\downarrow$

round down   round up   round down   round up   round up or down

If we round one number down, we round the next number up.

When we estimate then compensate, the estimate is closer to the exact value.
There were about 50 000 athletes at the five games.

1. Use the numbers in the box.
   Find pairs of numbers with each sum.
   a) 50   b) 60
   c) 70   d) 80

10	15	20	25
30	35	40	45
50	55	60	65

2. Some compatible numbers have a sum that is a multiple of 10.
   Use your answers to question 1 to list pairs of compatible numbers.

3. Use the numbers in the box.
   a) Find pairs of numbers with a sum
      that is a multiple of 100.
   b) Why are the numbers compatible
      in each pair you listed in part a?

110	230	290	320
460	470	540	650
660	740	820	850

4. Estimate each sum. Explain your strategy.
   a) 6145 + 3007   b) 3654 + 372   c) 500 + 2150
   d) 1999 + 999   e) 4003 + 2968   f) 7741 + 685

5. Estimate to find the sums less than 10 000.
   a) 3099 + 5824   b) 6489 + 3201   c) 4673 + 6595
   d) 9997 + 8743   e) 5063 + 297   f) 9539 + 470

6. Estimate: 32 756 + 16 345
   a) Do you think the exact answer will be less than
      or greater than your estimate?
      Explain your thinking.
   b) How could you use compensation to improve your estimate?

7. The school held a magazine drive.
   The junior classes raised $15 875.
   The intermediate classes raised $19 256.
   a) Did the students beat last year's record of $34 200? Explain.
   b) How could you use compatible numbers to estimate?

8. Use these numbers: 5245, 6020, 7985, 6755, 4850
   Estimate to find which 2 numbers have the sum closest to:
   a) 10 000   b) 15 500
   Which estimation strategies did you use?

9. Write a story problem where you do not need to find
   an exact answer to solve the problem.
   Explain why estimating the sum is a reasonable strategy.

10. These data show how the population of the Yukon Territory has changed over the past 50 years.

Date	Population
1961	14 600
1971	18 400
1981	23 200
1991	27 800
2001	28 700

Use these data to predict the population of Yukon in 2011.
Explain how you estimated to predict.

11. The table shows the number of tickets sold to 5 live shows at a Concert Hall.

Shows	Monday	Tuesday	Wednesday	Thursday	Friday
Tickets Sold	12 900	14 590	26 565	16 750	24 810

a) About how many tickets were sold for the first two shows?

b) About how many tickets were sold on the two days when the greatest and least numbers of tickets were sold?

c) About how many tickets were sold during the week?
What strategies did you use to solve each problem?

12. At the opening baseball game, 16 254 programs were sold.
At the second game, 15 910 programs were sold.
Predict how many programs should be printed for
the third and fourth games.
Explain your thinking.

13. Think of a situation where you would estimate to make a prediction.
Explain how you would estimate.

Reflect

How can you tell if your estimate is greater than or less than the exact sum?

Using Benchmarks to Estimate

About twenty-eight thousand fans are here today.

Why did Melinda use "about twenty-eight thousand" to describe the attendance?
How did she arrive at that number?

Explore

You will need a copy of these number lines.

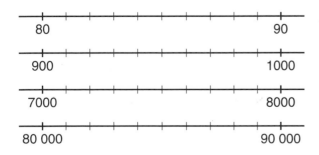

80	90
900	1000
7000	8000
80 000	90 000

➤ Label the first number line with:
- the number that is halfway between the two given numbers
- a number that is closer to the first number than the second number
- a number that is closer to the second number than the first number

➤ Repeat with the other number lines.

LESSON FOCUS | Use benchmarks of tens, hundreds, thousands, and ten thousands.

53

Show *and* Share

Compare the numbers you wrote with those of another pair of classmates.
Talk about how you placed the numbers on the number lines.
Share the strategies you used.

Connect

There were 23 782 people at a lacrosse game.
The number 23 782 is exact.
It is a count of the number of people.
To write an estimate for the number of people,
you can find the closest benchmark.

It is easier
to remember 24 000
than to remember 23 782.

 On this number line labelled in thousands:

23 782 is between 23 000 and 24 000.
It is closer to 24 000.
An estimate for 23 782 is 24 000.

 On this number line labelled in hundreds:

23 782 is between 23 700 and 23 800.
It is closer to 23 800.
A closer estimate for 23 782 is 23 800.

 On this number line labelled in tens:

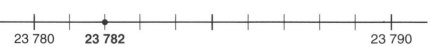

23 782 is between 23 780 and 23 790.
It is closer to 23 780.
An even closer estimate for 23 782 is 23 780.

Sometimes it is important to overestimate.

There are 310 people going to the zoo.
Each school bus holds 50 people.
How many school buses should be ordered?

310 is closest to the benchmark 300.
We would need 6 school buses for 300 children.
But, 10 people would have to stay behind.
It makes sense to overestimate 310 to 350.
Then, we would order 7 school buses.

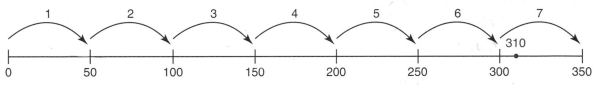

Practice

Use a number line when it helps.

1. The longest country line dance had 6275 people.
   What is the closest benchmark in thousands?

2. Ms. Carr is buying granola bars for her choir.
   There are 72 students in the choir.
   Granola bars come in boxes of 10.
   How many boxes should Ms. Carr buy?
   Explain.

3. Estimate to the closest thousand.
   How did you get each answer?
   a) 2376   b) 47 891   c) 86 300
   d) 4735   e) 1999   f) 3087

4. Estimate to the closest hundred.
   a) 9876   b) 41 509   c) 53 055
   d) 1749   e) 5465   f) 8230

5. Estimate to the closest ten. How did you get each answer?
   a) 2347   b) 6708   c) 78 973   d) 7597

6. Write three numbers for which 300 is an estimate.
   How did you choose the numbers?

7. Write three numbers for which 7000 is an estimate.
   How do you know that the numbers you chose are correct?

8. Explain how you would write an estimate for 32 627 to the closest
   thousand and the closest ten thousand.

9. Liam said, "It's about 3:45. "
   What might the exact time be?
   Give reasons for your answer.

10. Write a number that has the same estimate when using benchmarks
    of thousands and ten thousands.
    Explain how you found the number.

11. a) Give 2 situations in which exact numbers are important.
    b) Give 2 situations in which estimated numbers
       are more appropriate.

12. The number of people who attended
    the baseball game was about 42 000
    when estimated to the closest thousand.
    What was the least possible number of people
    who attended the game? How do you know?

Reflect

When is it important to overestimate?

Estimating Differences

Explore

The first day the ski hills were open,
1368 lift tickets were sold.
The second day, 1155 lift tickets were sold.

About how many more tickets were sold
the first day?
Estimate to find out.
Record your answer.

Show *and* Share

Compare your estimate with that of another pair of students.
How did the strategies you used affect your answers? Explain.

Connect

Here are some students' strategies for estimating a difference.

➤ To estimate: 3818 − 2079,
Alice used front-end rounding.
She subtracted the first digits of the numbers:
3818 − **2**079 is about
3000 − 2000 = 1000

3818 − 2079 is about 1000.

For a closer estimate, Alice looked at the last 3 digits of each number.
818 is about 800.
079 is about 100.
800 − 100 = 700
Alice added 700 to her estimate of 1000: 1000 + 700 = 1700
So, 3818 − 2079 is about 1700.

3818 is closer to 4000 than
to 3000. So, using only the first
digits does not give me a
close estimate.

➤ To estimate: 5849 − 3097,
Brian estimated each number to the closest 1000.
5849 is closer to 6000 than to 5000.
3097 is closer to 3000 than to 4000.
6000 − 3000 = 3000
So, 5849 − 3097 is about 3000.

For a closer estimate, Brian estimated each number to the closest 100.
5849 is closer to 5800 than to 5900.
3097 is closer to 3100 than to 3000.
5800 − 3100 = 2700
So, 5849 − 3097 is about 2700.

➤ Both Marie and Sunil used compatible
numbers to estimate: 4803 − 310
Marie said that 4803 is close to 4810.
Then, 4810 − 310 = 4500

I changed 2 digits in the first number so both numbers have the same last 2 digits.

Sunil said that 310 is close to 303.
Then, 4803 − 303 = 4500

I changed 2 digits in the second number so both numbers have the same last 2 digits.

Both students had the same estimate.
4803 − 310 is about 4500.

Practice

1. Use any strategy you wish to estimate each difference.
   a) 6723 − 985   **b)** 7415 − 4002   **c)** 6345 − 4328
   d) 8640 − 445   **e)** 9876 − 1234   **f)** 8025 − 980

2. Tell if you think each estimate is high or low. How do you know?
   Which estimation strategy do you think was used?
   a) 2593 − 1548 is about 1000   **b)** 9845 − 6050 is about 3800
   c) 7520 − 807 is about 6713   **d)** 6056 − 985 is about 5000

3. Use front-end rounding to estimate each difference.
   a) 2593 − 1590   **b)** 9705 − 562   **c)** 8739 − 6326

4. There are 8625 tickets for the concert.
   Six thousand eight hundred eighty-five tickets have been sold.
   About how many tickets are still for sale?

5. Sandi is in Room 401.

Magazine Sales	Money Collected
Room 401	$2855
Room 402	$980
Room 403	$1900
Room 404	$2595

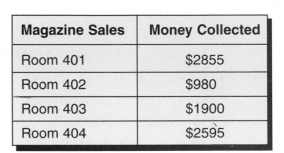

   a) Sandi estimates that her class has collected about $1000 more than Room 403.
   Is her estimate high or low? Explain.

   b) Sandi estimates that Room 404 has collected about $1000 more than Room 403.
   How do you think she estimated?
   How do you think Sandi should have estimated?

   c) What is a good way to estimate the difference between the money collected by Room 402 and Room 403?
   Why do you think so?

6. Two 4-digit numbers have a difference of about 3500. What might the numbers be? How do you know?

7. *Census at School* is a website where students answer surveys and collect data. The table shows the numbers of students in Canada who answered surveys in the past few years.

Year	2003/04	2004/05	2005/06
Number of Students	7683	22 643	31 960

Predict how many students will answer surveys on the site in 2006/07.
Explain how you estimated to predict.

8. Describe a situation when you would estimate a difference rather than find the exact answer to a subtraction problem.
Explain why an estimate is appropriate.

Math Link

Your World

Jeanne Louise Calment of France was the oldest woman ever. She lived from 1875 to 1997.
About how many years did she live?

Reflect

How do you decide which estimation strategy to use when you subtract? Use words and numbers to explain.

Using Estimation to Check Answers

A pedometer records
the number of steps you take.

Explore

Emma wore a pedometer for 2 hours.
She recorded the number of steps each hour.
The first hour, Emma took 1347 steps.
The second hour, she took 984 steps.

➤ In which hour did Emma take
more steps?

➤ How many more steps did Emma
actually take?

➤ Estimate how many more steps
Emma took.

➤ Compare the estimate to the
exact number.
Is the answer reasonable? Explain.

Show *and* Share

Share your work with another pair of students.
Describe and compare the strategies you used
to estimate to check the answer.

The students at Glenville Public School are raising money to build wells in Africa.
The Grade 5 class raised $3432. The Grade 6 class raised $2180.

➤ How much did the two classes raise together?

To find out, add: 2180 + 3432
Here are one student's strategies for adding and estimating.
Nate adds from left to right.

```
  2180
+ 3432
  5000
   500
   110
+    2
  5612
```

> I compensate by rounding one number up and the other number down.

To check this sum is reasonable, Nate uses compensation.
He rounds 2180 *up* to 2200.
He rounds 3432 *down* to 3400.
2200 + 3400 = 5600
Since 5600 is close to 5612, the sum is reasonable.
The two classes together raised $5612.

➤ Which class raised more money?
How much more money did it raise?

Since $3432 is greater than $2180, the Grade 5 class raised more money.
To find out how much more, subtract: 3432 − 2180
Here are one student's strategies for subtracting and estimating.
Abby uses a number line to help her count on to subtract.

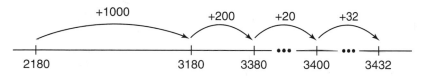

Abby counted on: 1000 + 200 + 20 + 32 = 1252
To check her answer is reasonable,
Abby uses an estimate for the number she subtracts.
2180 is closer to 2200 than to 2100.
3432 − 2200 = 1232
Since 1232 is close to 1252, the answer is reasonable.
The Grade 5 class raised $1252 more than the Grade 6 class.

> Since 2200 > 2180, the estimate is less than the exact answer.

Practice

1. Add. Estimate to check.
   a) 9875 + 5630
   b) 3098 + 840
   c) 5984 + 8408
   d) 8305 + 988

2. Subtract. Estimate to check.
   Is each answer reasonable? How do you know?
   a) 7774 − 1796
   b) 8350 − 2673
   c) 6432 − 2798
   d) 9808 − 1759

3. Estimate to predict which sums are greater than 7000.
   Show how you estimated.
   a) 4176 + 2457
   b) 3872 + 5129
   c) 5839 + 987
   d) 6518 + 2828

4. Estimate to predict which differences are greater than 10 000.
   a) 73 350 − 65 196
   b) 28 645 − 12 550
   c) 35 430 − 29 820

5. Keshav collects stamps.
   He has 3845 Canadian stamps and
   2690 stamps from other countries.
   a) How many stamps does he have altogether?
   b) How do you know your answer is reasonable?

6. Great Slave Lake has an area of 28 568 square kilometres.
   Great Bear Lake has an area of 31 328 square kilometres.
   About how much greater is the area of Great Bear Lake?

7. Taking 10 000 steps a day is a target for healthy living.
   Suppose your pedometer counts 8934 steps in one day.
   About how many more steps do you need to reach the target number?
   Show your work.

8. Carly and Nicole have been saving pennies since they were young.
   Carly has collected 45 880 pennies.
   Nicole has collected 54 250 pennies.
   a) How many more pennies does Nicole have?
   b) Both girls have the same goal of collecting 100 000 pennies.
      How many more pennies does each of them need?
   c) How could you estimate to check your answers are reasonable?
   Show your work.

9. Two games were played in the semi-finals
of a soccer tournament.
The attendance at one game was 18 595.
The attendance at the other game was 19 240.
  a) How many people attended the semi-finals?
  b) Check that your answer is reasonable.

10. Members of the school council have raised $10 500.
They plan to buy sports equipment for $3985 and
library books for $7545.
  a) Use compensation to predict whether the council raised
      enough money to make the purchases.
  b) Check your prediction.

11. A student used a calculator to add: 4370 + 5298
The calculator display showed 48988.
  a) Is the answer reasonable? How could the student find out?
  b) Which numbers do you think the student keyed in? How do you know?

12. The fund-raising committee has a goal of $25 225.
It raised $14 285 at the benefit concert and
$10 975 at the annual spring fair.
Did the committee reach its goal? Explain how you know.

13. Regional Recycling has a target of 24 500 kg of aluminum.
Fairfield delivers 16 650 kg of aluminum.
Westdale delivers 7950 kg of aluminum.
  a) Predict whether Regional Recycling met its goal.
  b) What strategy did you use to predict?
  c) How can you check your prediction?

14. Two 4-digit numbers have a sum of about 9400.
What might the numbers be? How do you know?
Show your thinking.

Reflect

Which is your favourite estimation strategy to check an answer?
Why do you prefer that strategy?

Strategies Toolkit

Explore

Janay lives in Vancouver.
This year, she visited two cities on
two different trips.
Janay flew a total distance of 33 078 km.
Which cities did she visit?

Vancouver
Ottawa: 3568 km
Toronto: 3382 km
London: 7596 km
Paris: 7965 km
Beijing: 8574 km
Honolulu: 4350 km
Cairo: 10840 km
Calcutta: 11492 km

Show *and* Share

Describe the strategy you used to solve this problem.

Connect

The Seven Summits are the highest peaks
on the seven continents.

Summit	Continent	Elevation
Kilimanjaro	Africa	5895 m
Vinson Massif	Antarctica	4892 m
Carstensz Pyramid	Australia	4884 m
Everest	Asia	8848 m
Elbrus	Europe	5642 m
Mount McKinley	North America	6194 m
Aconcagua	South America	6962 m

Strategies

- Make a table.
- Use a model.
- Draw a diagram.
- Solve a simpler problem.
- Work backward.
- Guess and test.
- Make an organized list.
- Use a pattern.

Terrell has climbed two summits for a total climb of 13 156 m.
Which two summits has he climbed?

What do you know?
- Terrell has climbed two summits.
- The total distance in metres he climbed is 13 156.

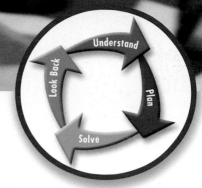

Think of a strategy to help you solve
the problem.

- You can use **guess and test**.
- Estimate which two heights have a sum of 13 156 m.
- Add the two heights to find out the actual distance in metres.

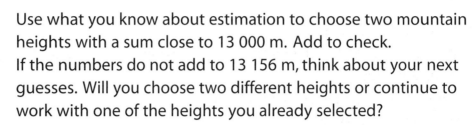

Use what you know about estimation to choose two mountain
heights with a sum close to 13 000 m. Add to check.
If the numbers do not add to 13 156 m, think about your next
guesses. Will you choose two different heights or continue to
work with one of the heights you already selected?

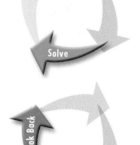

Check your work.
Is the sum of the two heights 13 156 m?
How could you solve this problem another way?

Practice

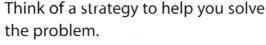

Choose one of the
Strategies

Use the data from *Explore* or *Connect* for these questions.

1. Jay is planning a trip.
   He plans to fly from Vancouver to Cairo with one stop over.
   It is 3511 km by air from London to Cairo.
   It is 9210 km by air from Toronto to Cairo.
   Jay wants to take the shortest route. How should he fly?

2. Kyla has climbed one of the Seven Summits.
   She says after she climbs the next one on her list,
   she will have climbed between 10 000 m and 11 000 m.
   Which of the Seven Summits is Kyla planning to climb next?

Reflect

Choose one *Practice* question. Describe how you solved it.

LESSON

1

1. On a place-value chart, how is:
   a) a 1 in the tens place related to a 1 in the ones place?
   b) a 1 in the thousands place related to a 1 in the tens place?
   c) a 1 in the ten-thousands place related to a 1 in the tens place?

2

2. Copy and complete.
   a) 999 999 + 1 = ☐   **b)** 1 000 000 − 10 000 = ☐
   c) 500 000 + ☐ = 1 000 000   **d)** 990 000 + ☐ = 1 000 000

3

3. Write each number from these headlines in words and in expanded form.
   a) Police Estimate 350 000 at Canada Day Celebrations
   b) 21 273 Attend Each Montreal Hockey Game
   c) Power Still Out at 125,500 Homes

4. Write each number in standard form, then in a place-value chart.
   a) eighty thousand five hundred twenty-seven
   b) 500 000 + 60 000 + 4000 + 300 + 8
   c) 200 000 + 5000 + 70 + 9
   d) four hundred fifty-six thousand two hundred eighty-five

5. Write the value of each underlined digit.
   a) 3<u>4</u>5 123   **b)** 29 0<u>8</u>7   **c)** <u>5</u>09 340
   d) <u>1</u> 000 000   **e)** 6<u>4</u>5 997   **f)** 45 9<u>8</u>5

6. Write 3 numbers that are greater than 365 000 but less than 367 500.
   Write the numbers in order from least to greatest.

4
5

7. Estimate each sum or difference. Explain your strategy.
   a) 1258 + 2835   **b)** 4504 − 945   **c)** 58 349 + 23 890
   d) 45 340 − 29 760   **e)** 35 608 + 8956   **f)** 36 785 − 9245

8. The playground committee plans to rebuild the playground.
   The materials will cost $28 565.
   The labour will cost $15 870.
   The committee has raised $45 000.
   Does the committee have enough money? Explain how you know.

9. Danny and Jake are wearing pedometers for a week.
Danny took 85 678 steps. Jake took 79 876 steps.
  a) About how many steps did the students take in total?
  b) About how many more steps did Danny take?
  Explain your estimation strategies.

5

10. The deepest a submarine has gone is 6526 m below the surface of the ocean.
Use benchmarks to write this distance to the closest:
  a) hundred   **b)** thousand   **c)** ten

7

11. Add or subtract.
How do you know your answers are reasonable?
  a) 45 890 + 28 145   **b)** 56 980 − 4695
  c) 6985 − 4856   **d)** 14 598 + 73 423

4
6
7

12. The students in Room 25 collected 56 789 pop can tabs.
The students in Room 28 collected 62 450 pop can tabs.
  a) Which room collected more tabs? How many more?
  b) How many tabs did the 2 rooms collect in total?
  c) How many more tabs do the students need to collect
    to reach their combined goal of 150 000?
  d) Estimate to check that the answers are reasonable.

13. This chart shows the number of tickets sold at each ride at the Summer Festival.

Ride	Number of Tickets Sold
Ferris Wheel	45 980
Super Loop	38 675
Top Ten	29 675
Roller Rider	42 781

a) Did the Super Loop or the Top Ten ride sell
more tickets? About how many more?
b) Fifty thousand tickets were printed for each ride.
At the end of the festival, about how many
tickets were left for each ride?

UNIT

2 Learning Goals

☑ represent and describe whole
numbers to 1 000 000

☑ use different strategies to
estimate sums and differences

☑ estimate to solve problems

Languages We Speak

This table shows how many people spoke the Aboriginal languages and the top 10 non-official languages in 1971 and in 2001.
In 30 years, there have been many changes in Canada.

Home Language	Number of People, 1971	Number of People, 2001
Aboriginal languages	122 205	181 350
Arabic		209 240
Cantonese		345 730
Chinese	77 890	392 950
German	213 350	220 685
Greek	86 825	
Hungarian	50 670	
Dutch	36 170	
Italian	425 230	371 200
Polish	70 960	163 745
Portuguese	74 760	187 475
Punjabi		280 535
Spanish		258 845
Tagalog		185 420
Ukrainian	144 755	
Yiddish	26 330	

1. Which languages were in the table in 1971 but not in 2001?

2. Which languages have grown in use from 1971 to 2001?

3. Which languages have declined in use from 1971 to 2001?

Check List

Your work should show
- ☑ your thinking in words, pictures, or numbers
- ☑ the strategies you used to estimate
- ☑ how you know your answers are reasonable
- ☑ a clear solution to your problem

4. Tell whether each statement is true or false. Give reasons for your answers.
   a) In 1971, about twice as many people spoke Ukrainian as Chinese.
   b) In 2001, about 2000 more people spoke Tagalog than Polish.
   c) In 2001, about 60 000 more people spoke Aboriginal languages than in 1971.
   d) In 2001, fewer than 350 000 people spoke Italian.
   e) In 2001, more than 479 000 people spoke German or Spanish.

5. Write two other true statements based on the data in the table.

6. a) In 2001, about how many people spoke Polish or Portuguese?
   b) About how many more people spoke Polish in 2001 than in 1971?
   c) About how many more people spoke Portuguese in 2001 than in 1971?

7. Write a problem that someone could solve using the table. Solve your problem and explain your solution.

Reflect on Your Learning

You have learned different ways to estimate.
Which way do you find easiest? Why?
Use examples to show the different types of questions for which you estimate.

UNIT 3

Multiplying and Whole Numbers

On the Dairy Farm

Learning Goals

- find basic multiplication facts to 81 and the related division facts
- use different strategies to estimate products and quotients
- estimate to solve problems
- use different strategies to multiply mentally
- multiply a 2-digit number by a 2-digit number
- divide a 3-digit number by a 1-digit number

Dividing

Key Words

factor

product

dividend

divisor

quotient

multiple

compatible numbers

front-end rounding

partial products

- Hay is one part of a dairy cow's diet.
  70 kg of hay feed 2 cows for 1 week.
  About how much hay does 1 cow eat each week?
  Each day?

- The Allards have 90 dairy cows on their farm.
  Each day, they collect twenty-seven litres of milk
  from 1 cow.
  Estimate the amount of milk produced by 9 cows.

Patterns in Multiplication and Division

What are the related facts for 9 × 8 = 72?
What are the related facts for 8 × 8 = 64?

How do you know how many related facts a multiplication fact has?

> **Factors** are numbers you multiply to get a product. 9 and 8 are *factors* of 72. 72 is the **product.**

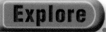

Your teacher will give you a large copy of this multiplication chart.

Use patterns to complete the chart.

How many multiplication facts can you write:

- with 9 as a factor?
- with 10 as a factor?

For each of these multiplication facts, write all the related facts.

×	1	2	3	4	5	6	7	8	9	10
1	1	2	3	4	5	6				
2	2	4	6	8	10	12				
3	3	6	9	12	15	18				
4	4	8	12	16	20	24				
5	5	10	15	20	25	30				
6	6	12	18	24	30	36				
7										
8										
9										
10										

Show *and* Share

Share your work with another pair of students.
What patterns did you use to complete the chart?
How do you know you found all the related facts?
Look at the factors and products for the 9s facts.
What patterns do you see that would help you remember or find out the multiplication facts for 9?

➤ Here are some strategies to help you multiply.

• Skip count up from a known fact.

To find 6 × 8:

Start with: 6 × 6 = 36

Skip count up by 6 to add two more groups of 6.

So, 6 × 8 = 36 + 6 + 6

          = 48

So, 6 × 8 = 48

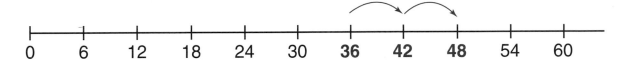

0	6	12	18	24	30	**36**	**42**	**48**	54	60

• Skip count down from a known fact.

To find 6 × 7:

Start with: 7 × 7 = 49

Skip count down by 7 to subtract one group of 7.

So, 6 × 7 = 49 − 7

          = 42

So, 6 × 7 = 42

To find 5 × 7:

Start with: 7 × 7 = 49

Skip count down by 7 to subtract two groups of 7.

So, 5 × 7 = 49 − 7 − 7

          = 35

So, 5 × 7 = 35

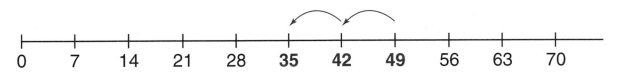

0	7	14	21	28	**35**	**42**	**49**	56	63	70

➤ Here is a strategy for division.
   Use related multiplication facts to find the quotient.
   To find 72 ÷ 8:

Think: 8 times which number is 72?

You know 8 × 9 = 72.
So, 72 ÷ 8 = 9

The **divisor** is 8.

72 ÷ 8 = 9

The **dividend** is 72.   The **quotient** is 9.

➤ Think about multiplying by 0.
For example, 8 × 0 is 8 groups of nothing.
Here are 8 plates with 0 sandwiches on each plate.

So, there are no sandwiches.
8 × 0 = 0

And 0 × 8 is no groups of 8.
So, 0 × 8 = 0

➤ Think about dividing 0 by a number.
For example, to find 0 ÷ 5, think of
the related multiplication fact.

Think: 5 times which number is 0?

5 × □ = 0
You know 5 × 0 = 0
So, 0 ÷ 5 = 0

➤ Think about dividing a number by 0.
For example, to find 5 ÷ 0, think multiplication.

Think: 0 times which number is 5?

0 × □ = 5
There is no number that you can multiply 0 by to get 5.
So, you *cannot* divide a number by 0.

 Practice •

1. Multiply.

   a) 8 × 7   **b)** 0 × 7   **c)** 9 × 3   **d)** 3 × 0

   e) 6 × 6   **f)** 9 × 9   **g)** 8 × 5   **h)** 4 × 8

2. When you multiply a number by 0, why is the product always 0?

3. Find each quotient.
   Write a related multiplication fact for each division statement.
   a) $0 \div 9$ b) $81 \div 9$ c) $45 \div 5$ d) $56 \div 7$

4. Why can you not divide a number by 0?

5. For each set of numbers, write as many related facts as you can.
   a) 9, 7, 63   b) 8, 7, 56   c) 5, 7, 35   d) 6, 9, 54

6. Lani knows that $3 \times 8 = 24$.
   How can she use that fact to find the product 5×8?
   Use numbers, words, or pictures to explain.

7. There are 4 utensils at each place setting on the table.
   There are 7 place settings.
   How many utensils are on the table?

8. Jason knows the product of 5 and 9 is 45.
   How can he use that fact to find the product
   of 4 and 9?

9. There are 6 loot bags for a birthday party.
   There are 42 items to be shared equally among the bags.
   How many items go in each bag?

10. Write a multiplication fact that can help you find each quotient.
    a) $45 \div 9$ b) $42 \div 7$ c) $36 \div 9$ d) $64 \div 8$

11. Éric finds the multiplication facts for 9 by multiplying each number by 10,
    then subtracting the number.
    How does his strategy work?
    Use words, numbers, or pictures to explain.

Reflect

Which facts do you find most difficult to remember?
Which strategies do you use to help you?
Use examples to explain.

Other Strategies for Multiplying and Dividing

You can show every multiplication fact as an array.
Which multiplication facts does this array show?

Explore

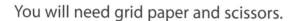

You will need grid paper and scissors.

➤ Use the grid paper.
Draw an array for 8 × 8.
Cut out the array.
Record a multiplication fact
to describe your array.
Record a related division fact.

➤ Cut the array into 2 equal arrays.
Write a multiplication fact
to describe each new array.
Write the related division facts.

➤ Cut the arrays again into 2 equal arrays.
Write the related multiplication and division
facts for each new array.

Show and Share

Share your work with another pair of students.
Are the facts you wrote the same?
If not, who is correct? Or, can both pairs be correct?
What patterns can you find in the facts you recorded?

Doubling and repeated doubling are strategies you can use to multiply.

➤ Begin with a fact you know.

To find another fact, double one factor, then double the product.

You know $2 \times 6 = 12$.
Double the factor 2 to get 4.
Double the product 12 to get 24.
Now you know $4 \times 6 = 24$.

To double a number, add it to itself. Double 12 is $12 + 12 = 24$.

Use $4 \times 6 = 24$.
Double the factor 4 to get 8.
Double the product 24 to get 48.
Now you know $8 \times 6 = 48$.

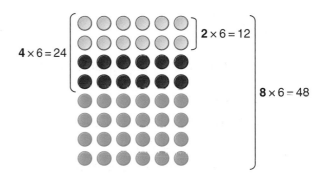

I think of a fact I know. When I double one factor, the product doubles.

➤ Here are two ways to use repeated doubling to find 4×8.

- You know $2 \times 8 = 16$.
  So, $4 \times 8 = 16 + 16$
  $\qquad = 32$

- You know $4 \times 4 = 16$.
  So, $4 \times 8 = 16 + 16$
  $\qquad = 32$

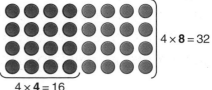

Halving and repeated halving are strategies you can use to divide.

➤ To find: 64 ÷ 4

 4 is 2 × 2;

so, to divide by 4,
I can divide by 2, then divide by 2 again.

64 ÷ 2 = 32
Divide by 2 again.
32 ÷ 2 = 16
So, 64 ÷ 4 = 16

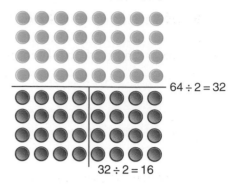

64 ÷ 2 = 32

32 ÷ 2 = 16

➤ To find: 96 ÷ 8

Think: 8 is 4 × 2, and 4 is 2 × 2;

so, to divide by 8, I can divide by 2,
then divide by 2, then divide by 2 again.

96 ÷ 2 = 48
Divide by 2 again.
48 ÷ 2 = 24
Divide by 2 again.
24 ÷ 2 = 12
So, 96 ÷ 8 = 12

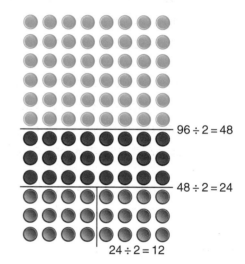

96 ÷ 2 = 48

48 ÷ 2 = 24

24 ÷ 2 = 12

Practice

1. Multiply.
   Then, double one factor and write a new multiplication fact.
   Draw an array to show how you got each fact.
   a) 4 × 8   b) 5 × 7   c) 6 × 4   d) 4 × 4

2. Use doubling to find each product.
   Write the multiplication fact you started with each time.
   Draw an array to show how you found each product.
   a) 8 × 6   b) 9 × 4   c) 7 × 6   d) 8 × 7

3. How can you use 3 × 6 to find 6 × 6?
   Use numbers, words, or pictures to explain.

4. Which multiplication fact could you use to find 6 × 12 by doubling?

5. Use repeated halving to divide.
   a) 36 ÷ 4   **b)** 48 ÷ 4   **c)** 60 ÷ 4   **d)** 72 ÷ 4

6. Choose one division fact from question 5.
   Draw an array to show repeated halving.

7. Divide.
   a) 48 ÷ 8   **b)** 24 ÷ 4   **c)** 78 ÷ 6   **d)** 52 ÷ 4

8. Sixty-four students signed up to attend francophone cultural activities.
   a) How many groups of 8 can the students make?
   b) One-half of the students go to a "cabane à sucre."
      How many students do not go?
   c) The students are divided equally among 4 teachers.
      How many students are with each teacher?

9. Kayla finds the multiplication facts for 8
   by doubling the multiplication facts for 4.
   How does Kayla's strategy work?
   Use words, numbers, or pictures to explain.

10. Sophia has trouble recalling 6 × 8.
   Which strategy would you explain to help her?

11. How can you divide by 2 to find 40 ÷ 8?
   Show all the steps.

12. a) Why can you not use doubling to find these products?
      3 × 5   5 × 9   9 × 7   7 × 5
   b) Which strategy could you use to find each product?
   Find each product and explain the strategy.

Reflect

Which multiplication and division facts can you find:
   • by doubling? By repeated doubling?
   • by halving? By repeated halving?

Use words, numbers, or pictures to explain.

Multiplying with Multiples of 10

Every **multiple** of 10 has 10 as a factor.
These are multiples of 10:

> 100　　1000　　30　　300　　3000

What are some other multiples of 10?

Explore

You will need a calculator and a place-value chart.

➤ Find each product.
Record the products in a place-value chart.

11 × 1	9 × 9	12 × 8
11 × 10	9 × 90	12 × 80
11 × 100	9 × 900	12 × 800
11 × 1000	9 × 9000	12 × 8000

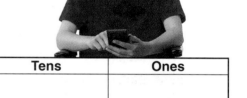

Ten Thousands	Thousands	Hundreds	Tens	Ones

➤ Find each product.
Record the products in a place-value chart.

20 × 9	70 × 7	50 × 6
20 × 90	70 × 70	50 × 60
20 × 900	70 × 700	50 × 600

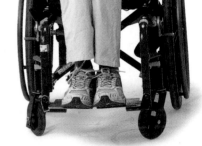

Show *and* Share

Share your work with another pair of students.
Describe any patterns you see.
How can you tell how many digits each product will have?
How can you tell which digits in a product will be 0?

➤ Use place value to multiply by 10, 100, and 1000.
Find each product. Record each product in a place-value chart.

- 25 × 10
  25 × 1 ten = 25 tens
  25 × 1**0** = 25**0**

- 25 × 100
  25 × 1 hundred = 25 hundreds
  25 × 1**00** = 25**00**

- 25 × 1000
  25 × 1 thousand = 25 thousands
  25 × 1**000** = 25 **000**

Product	Ten Thousands	Thousands	Hundreds	Tens	Ones
250			2	5	0
2500		2	5	0	0
25 000	2	5	0	0	0

➤ Use basic facts and place-value patterns
to multiply by multiples of 10, 100, and 1000.
Find each product.

- 3 × 60
  You know 3 × 6 = 18.

  3 × 6 tens = 18 tens   or   3 × **60**   = 3 × **6** × **10**
  3 × **6**0 = **18**0   = 18 × 10
                                                  = 180

- 3 × 600

  3 × 6 hundreds = 18 hundreds   or   3 × **600** = 3 × **6** × **100**
  3 × **6**00 = **18**00   = 18 × 100
                                                   = 1800

- 3 × 6000

  3 × 6 thousands = 18 thousands   or   3 × **6000** = 3 × **6** × **1000**
  3 × **6**000 = **18** 000   = 18 × 1000
                                                    = 18 000

➤ Use what you know about multiplying by multiples of 10, 100, and 1000 to multiply two multiples of 10, 100, and 1000. Find each product.

- 20×30

  2 tens $\times 30 = 60$ tens   or $20 \times 30 = 2 \times 10 \times 3 \times 10$

  $\textbf{20} \times \textbf{30} = \textbf{60}0$ $= 2 \times 3 \times 10 \times 10$

  $= 6 \times 100$

  $= 600$

- 500×40

  5 hundreds $\times 40 = 200$ hundreds or $500 \times 40 = 5 \times 100 \times 4 \times 10$

  $\textbf{5}00 \times \textbf{40} = \textbf{20 0}00$ $= 5 \times 4 \times 100 \times 10$

  $= 20 \times 1000$

  $= 20\ 000$

Practice

1. Multiply.

a) 7×10 **b)** 3×10 **c)** 6×10 **d)** 9×10

   7×100 3×100 6×100 9×100

   7×1000 3×1000 6×1000 9×1000

2. Multiply.

a) 47×10 **b)** 32×10 **c)** 20×10 **d)** 50×10

   47×100 32×100 20×100 50×100

   47×1000 32×1000 20×1000 50×1000

3. Look at the questions and products in questions 1 and 2.
   How can you use mental math to multiply a whole number:
   a) by 10?   **b)** by 100?   **c)** by 1000?

4. Look at the chart below to answer each question.
   How do the digits in a place-value chart move when you multiply
   a whole number:
   a) by 10?   **b)** by 100?   **c)** by 1000?

Ten Thousands	Thousands	Hundreds	Tens	Ones
			3	7
		3	7	0
	3	7	0	0
3	7	0	0	0

5. Use a basic fact and place-value patterns to find each product.

   a) 7 × 80
   7 × 800
   7 × 8000

   b) 5 × 60
   5 × 600
   5 × 6000

   c) 4 × 90
   4 × 900
   4 × 9000

6. Look at the questions and products in question 5.
   How can you use mental math to multiply a whole number by:
   a) a multiple of 10? **b)** a multiple of 100? **c)** a multiple of 1000?

7. Multiply.
   a) 20 × 40   **b)** 30 × 10   **c)** 40 × 70   **d)** 60 × 90
   e) 80 × 50   **f)** 70 × 80   **g)** 50 × 60   **h)** 90 × 30

8. Look at the questions and products in question 7.
   How can you use mental math to multiply two multiples of 10?

9. Michel works in a bank. He receives these deposits.
   How much money is in each deposit?
   a) twelve $10 bills   **b)** sixty $20 bills   **c)** thirty $50 bills
   d) fifteen $100 bills   **e)** twenty $20 bills and ten $50 bills

10. A ruby-throated hummingbird flaps its wings
    about 60 times each second.
    How many times would it flap its wings
    in one minute? In one hour?
    Show your work.

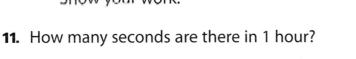

11. How many seconds are there in 1 hour?

12. A student wrote this product: 20 × 500 = 1000
    a) What did the student do wrong?
    b) What is the correct product? How do you know?

13. Write a story problem that can be solved
    by multiplying by a multiple of 1000.
    Solve your problem.

Reflect

How can patterns in the products help you
when you multiply with multiples of 10?
Use words and numbers to explain.

Estimating Products to Solve Problems

Sometimes you don't need an exact answer to solve a problem.

We raised $500. For sure we have enough money to buy 12 sweatshirts for the team!

How do the students know they have enough money?

 Explore

A Grade 5 class has a bake sale to raise money for charity.

The students use a cookie recipe that makes about 36 cookies.
The students bake 12 batches of cookies.
Estimate to find about how many cookies they baked.

Show and Share

Discuss and compare your strategies for estimating
with those of another pair of students.
Did you get the same estimates?
If your answer is no, is one estimate wrong? Explain.
Is one estimate closer than the other? Explain.

There are different ways to estimate products.
Think about the problem and the factors.
Choose a strategy.

➤ You can use **compatible numbers**.
Compatible numbers are close to the actual numbers
and are easy to work with.
Multiples of 10 and of 100 are easy to work with.

• Each bus can seat 48 students.
About how many students can travel on 8 buses?

To estimate: 48 × 8
Think of the multiples of 10 and 100
closest to one or both factors.

Think: 50 × 8 = 400
Or, 48 × 10 = 480
Or, 50 × 10 = 500
About 400 students can travel on 8 buses.

Since 50 > 48, and
10 > 8, all the estimates are
greater than the exact answer. When
you make the factor a greater number,
the estimate is greater than the
exact product. It is an
overestimate.

• During the summer vacation,
Julia delivers 215 flyers each day.
She delivers flyers for 1 week.
About how many flyers does Julia deliver?

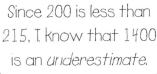

Since 200 is less than
215, I know that 1400
is an *underestimate*.

To estimate: 215 × 7
Think: 200 × 7 = 1400
Julia delivers about 1400 flyers.

➤ You can use compatible numbers and compensation.
A large jug fills 38 glasses of juice.
There are 52 jugs.
About how many glasses can be filled?

To estimate: 38 × 52
Think: 40 × 50 = 2000
About 2000 glasses of juice can be filled.

We round 38 up to 40,
so we round 52 down to 50.
We have *compensated*.

➤ You can use **front-end rounding**.
Use the front digit of each factor.

- There will be 6 performances of the school play.
Fred estimates that about 240 people will come
to each performance.
About how many people will come to the play?

To estimate: 6×240

Think: $6 \times 2$00 $= \mathbf{12}$00

About 1200 people will come to the play.

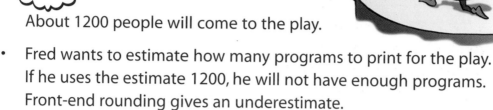

- Fred wants to estimate how many programs to print for the play.
If he uses the estimate 1200, he will not have enough programs.
Front-end rounding gives an underestimate.
To improve the estimate, use a
compatible number *greater* than 240.
6×240 is about 6×250.
Fred knows that 4×25 is 100.
So, 2×25 is 50.
Then, $6 \times 25 = 100 + 50$
$\qquad\qquad = 150$
So, $6 \times 250 = 1500$
Fred should print 1500 programs to make sure he has enough.

*I think about money.
Four quarters make $1,
or 100¢.
So, $4 \times 25 = 100$
2 quarters make 50¢.
So, $2 \times 25 = 50$*

Practice

1. Which compatible numbers would you use to estimate each product?
a) 9×65 **b)** 833×7 **c)** 23×69 **d)** 72×12

2. Estimate each product.
Tell if your estimate is an overestimate, an underestimate,
or why you cannot tell.
a) 28×9 **b)** 74×28 **c)** 467×5 **d)** 8×123

3. Estimate to predict which products are greater than 2000.
Explain your thinking. Which estimation strategies did you use?
a) 289×7 **b)** 95×9 **c)** 48×57 **d)** 375×3

4. Estimate the product of 476 and 8.
Do you think the exact answer will be less than or greater than your estimate?
Explain your thinking.

5. Jack delivers 58 newspapers each day.
About how many papers does Jack deliver
in one week? Show your work.

6. There are 48 chairs in each row.
There are 64 rows of chairs.
About how many people can sit down?
Show your work.

7. Zoé estimated the product 245 × 9.
She wrote these statements about the product.
 • The product is less than 2500.
 • The product is greater than 1800.
How do you think Zoé got each estimated product?
Use words and numbers to explain.

8. The students want to sell about 2000 tickets to a fashion show.
They hope to sell 425 tickets each day.
The students sell tickets for 5 days.
Do you think they will sell enough tickets?
How do you know?

9. The estimated answer to a multiplication question is 4200.
What might the question be?

10. Write a story problem for which an overestimate would be needed.
Solve your problem.
Show your work.

11. Here are 3 students' estimates of the product 93 × 8.
Amal estimated 1000.
Bernard estimated 720.
Chloe estimated 950.
 a) Which estimation strategy do you think each student used? Explain.
 b) Without calculating the exact product, how can you tell
   which estimate is closest to the exact product?

Reflect

Choose a question from *Practice* where you used compensation
in your estimate. Explain why you compensated.

Using Mental Math to Multiply

How many different ways can you find the product 14 × 50?
Record each way.
Use any materials that help.

Show *and* Share

Share your work with another pair of students.
Compare the strategies you used to find the product.

Connect

You know the basic multiplication facts.
Sometimes you can use them to multiply in your head.
The strategy you use can depend on the factors.

Here are some strategies for multiplying mentally.

➤ You can break the number into smaller parts.
  Multiply: 15 × 7

  Think of an array for 15 × 7.

  The product 15 × 7 is equal to
  the sum of the products
  10 × 7 and 5 × 7.

  $15 \times 7 = (10 \times 7) + (5 \times 7)$
  $= 70 + 35$
  $= 105$
  So, 15 × 7 = 105

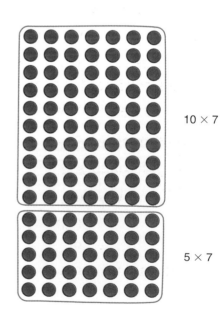

10 × 7

5 × 7

➤ You can use halving and doubling.

• Multiply: 14×5

14 rows of 5   are the same as   7 rows of 10

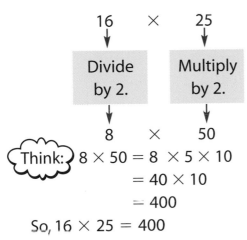

$$14 \times 5$$

7 is half   10 is
of 14   double 5

Think: $7 \times 10 = 70$

So, $14 \times 5 = 70$

• Multiply: 16×25
Use the strategy of halving and doubling.
Look for a factor that doubles to make a multiple of 10.

16	×	25
Divide by 2.		Multiply by 2.
8	×	50

To halve is to divide by 2.
To double is to multiply by 2.

Think: $8 \times 50 = 8 \times 5 \times 10$
$= 40 \times 10$
$= 400$

So, $16 \times 25 = 400$

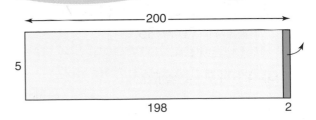

➤ When one factor is close to a multiple of 10 or 100,
you can use compatible numbers and then compensate.

Jane has 198 packs of baseball cards.
There are 5 cards in each pack.
How many cards does Jane have?

Multiply: 198×5

Think: $198 = 200 - 2$

200 is 2 more packs of 5, so to
compensate, subtract
$2 \times 5 = 10$.

So, $198 \times 5 = (200 \times 5) - (2 \times 5)$
$= 1000 - 10$
$= 990$

Jane has 990 cards.

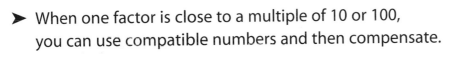

Practice

Use mental math.

1. Which product does each diagram represent?
   Use the diagram to find the product.

   a)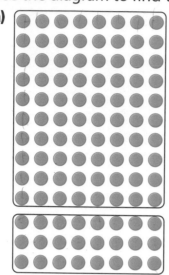

   b)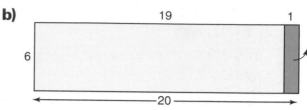

2. Multiply. Picture an array each time.
   a) 18×5
   b) 23×7
   c) 6×31
   d) 4×23
   e) 8×44
   f) 9×29
   g) 2×78
   h) 82×3

3. Eighteen students went on a fishing trip.
   Each student had 6 worms as bait.
   How many worms were there altogether?

4. To find 28×25, a student wrote this:
   $$28 \times 25 = 7 \times 4 \times 25$$
   $$= 7 \times 100$$
   $$= 700$$
   Explain the student's strategy.

5. Multiply. Explain how you could use halving and doubling.
   a) 12×50
   b) 12×25
   c) 24×25
   d) 24×50
   e) 46×25
   f) 23×25
   g) 46×50
   h) 23×50

6. Jamal bought thirty-eight 50¢ stamps.
   What was the cost before tax?

7. Multiply. Use mental math. Explain your strategy.
   a) 6×199
   b) 7×302
   c) 3×498
   d) 5×310
   e) 3×503
   f) 101×4
   g) 4×210
   h) 197×5

8. **Who Has the Greater Product?**

   You will need a set of digit cards from 0 to 9.
   The goal is to arrange 4 digits to make
   a multiplication problem with the greatest product.
   Each player copies and completes the multiplication grid.
   Take turns drawing one card.
   As each card is selected, each player writes that digit
   in any box on her or his grid.
   Continue until all the boxes have been filled.
   Multiply.
   The player with the greater product scores a point.
   The first player to score 5 points wins.

9. List the strategies you used to play the game
   Who Has the Greater Product?

10. Use mental math.
    Find the product of 48 × 50 two different ways.
    Describe the strategies you used.

11. A theatre has 32 rows of seats.
    Each row has 25 seats.
    How many seats are there in the theatre?

12. Copy the multiplication frame at the right.
    Arrange the digits 2, 3, 4, and 5 to make the greatest product.
    Use each digit only once.
    How did you decide how to arrange the digits?

13. Write a multiplication problem that can be solved
    using mental math. Solve the problem.
    Which strategy did you use? Why?

Reflect

Which of these mental math strategies do you find easiest?
Tell why.
   • breaking the number into parts
   • halving and doubling
   • compatible numbers and compensation

LESSON 6

Multiplying 2-Digit Numbers

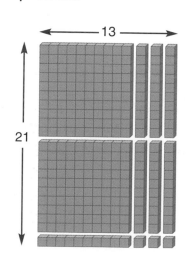

Explore

How many different ways can you find the product 14 × 23? Show your work for each strategy you use.

Show *and* Share

Share your strategies with another pair of students.
If you used a strategy they did not use, explain your strategy to them.

Connect

Multiply: 21 × 13
Here are three strategies students used to find the product.

➤ Rami modelled the problem with Base Ten Blocks.
The array is a rectangle.
Its area is 21 × 13.

Rami sees there are:
- 2 hundreds or 200
- 7 tens or 70
- 3 ones or 3

200 + 70 + 3 = 273

LESSON FOCUS | Use different strategies to multiply two numbers.

➤ Keisha used grid paper.
She drew an array with 13 rows and 21 squares in each row.

$20 \times 10 = 200$

$1 \times 10 = 10$

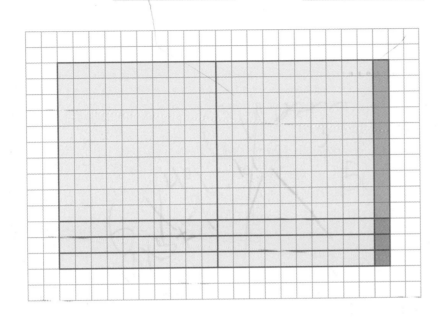

Keisha recorded her
work like this:

```
    21
  × 13
   200
    10
    60
  +  3
   273
```

$20 \times 3 = 60$

$1 \times 3 = 3$

So, $21 \times 13 = 273$

➤ Samuel drew a diagram similar to Keisha's array.

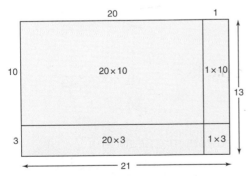

I get *partial products*
by multiplying each number
in the first expanded form
by each number in the
second expanded form.

Samuel wrote each factor in expanded form.
Then he wrote 4 **partial products**.
Samuel wrote: $21 \times 13 = (20 + 1) \times (10 + 3)$
$= (20 \times 10) + (20 \times 3) + (1 \times 10) + (1 \times 3)$
$= 200 + 60 + 10 + 3$
$= 273$

So, $21 \times 13 = 273$

The students estimated to check that the product is reasonable.
They wrote compatible numbers:

13×21 is about $15 \times 20 = 15 \times 2 \times 10$

$$= 30 \times 10$$
$$= 300$$

Since the estimate, 300, is close to the answer, 273,
the answer is reasonable.

Practice

1. Sketch a diagram to find 28×16.
   Show how the diagram helps you find the product.

2. Multiply. Use a different method to check.
   What do you notice about the products in each pair?

   a)   34   26   b)   45   23   c)   19   54
        $\times\,26$ $\times\,34$ $\times\,23$ $\times\,45$ $\times\,54$ $\times\,19$

3. Write each product in expanded form.
   Then find the product.
   a) 23×32 b) 39×13 c) 51×37 d) 44×54

4. Multiply.
   Which strategy did you use each time?
   a) 35×52 b) 65×30 c) 48×25 d) 41×74
   e) 92×43 f) 14×75 g) 20×54 h) 25×16

5. Find each product.
   Which strategy did you use each time?
   a) 46×64 b) 23×50 c) 61×11 d) 17×33
   e) 29×41 f) 68×12 g) 80×16 h) 16×77

6. Can you use mental math to find any of the products in question 5?
   Explain how you know.

7. To multiply 14×32, one student wrote this:

   ```
      14
   × 32
   ─────
      28
   +420
   ─────
     448
   ```

   Explain the student's strategy.

8. Find the product 25 × 25.
How can you use the product 25 × 25 to help find each product?
a) 25 × 26   **b)** 24 × 25   **c)** 50 × 25   **d)** 75 × 25

9. Jordan tiled a wall.
His wall has 27 rows each with 27 tiles.
Sharma tiled a different wall.
Her wall has 26 rows of 29 tiles.
a) Whose wall has more tiles?
b) How many more tiles does it have?
Show the strategies you used.

10. Which multiplication facts can you use to find 45 × 23?
How do you know?
Show your work.

11. Estimate to predict which products are greater than 3000.
Find each product greater than 3000.
a) 58 × 39   **b)** 75 × 58   **c)** 82 × 85   **d)** 30 × 75

12. Anjotie has 24 kayaks. She rents out a kayak for $14 per hour.
All the kayaks are rented for 8 hours.
How much money will Anjotie get?
Show the strategy you used.

13. Erica earns $9 per hour. She works 32 hours per week.
Estimate, then calculate, how much Erica earns in 2 weeks.

14. Suppose you wanted to arrange 4 different digits
to make the greatest product.
Which arrangement would you use? Why?

a) □□□
   × □

b)   □□
   × □□

At Home

Reflect

Which strategy for multiplying
did you find the easiest?
Use words, numbers, or pictures
to explain.

Measure the length and
width of a magazine to the
closest centimetre. Find
the area of the cover of the
magazine.

Multiplication Tic-Tac-Toe

You will need 20 each of two colours of counters and 2 paper clips.
Your teacher will give you a copy of the game board
and the factor list.

The object of the game is
to be the first player to place
3 counters in a row.
The row can be horizontal,
vertical, or diagonal.

➤ Each player chooses a
  different colour.
➤ Player 1 chooses
  any two factors in the
  factor list.
  He marks the factors
  with paper clips.
➤ Player 1 multiplies
  the factors.
  He finds the product
  on the game board and
  covers it with a coloured marker.
  If the product appears more than once on the game board,
  he chooses which one to cover.
➤ Player 2 may move only one of the paper clips on the factor list.
  She finds the product of the factors.
  She finds the product on the game board and covers it with a marker.
➤ Players continue to take turns.
  Each player may move only one paper clip per turn.
➤ The first player to place 3 counters in a row wins.

Share your strategies for playing the game.
Talk about how you found products that you did not know automatically.

Variation:
Play 4-in-a-Row.

Estimating Quotients to Solve Problems

Explore

The LeBlanc family drove 675 km in 8 hours.
The family drove the same distance
each hour.
Estimate to find about how far the
family drove in one hour.

Show *and* Share

Share your results with another pair of students.
Describe the strategies you used to estimate.
Did you get the same distance?
If not, is any distance wrong? Explain.

Connect

Here are some strategies you can use to estimate quotients.

➤ $873 are to be shared among 9 people.
About how much will each person get?

Estimate: 873 ÷ 9
Look for compatible numbers.
873 is close to 900.

9 hundreds ÷ 9 = 1 hundred
            = 100

Each person will get about $100.

This is an overestimate
because 900 > 873.

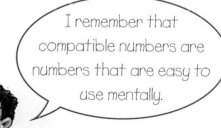

I remember that
compatible numbers are
numbers that are easy to
use mentally.

➤ There are 258 grapefruit.
Each fruit basket will have 4 grapefruit.
About how many fruit baskets can be made?

Because I used a number less than 258, I know that my estimate is an underestimate.

Estimate: 258 ÷ 4

Use front-end rounding.

258 ÷ 4 is about 200 ÷ 4.

Think: 20 ÷ 4 = 5, so **20**0 ÷ **4** = **5**0

This estimate is low.

To get a closer estimate,

look at the first 2 digits of the dividend: **25**8 ÷ **4**

Think: Which division fact is closest to 25 ÷ 4?

You know that 24 ÷ 4 = 6, so 25 ÷ 4 is close to 6.

So, 258 ÷ 4 is about 240 ÷ 4 = 60

About 60 fruit baskets can be made.

Practice

1. Which compatible numbers would you use to estimate each quotient? Why did you choose those numbers?
   a) 238 ÷ 3   b) 193 ÷ 2   c) 742 ÷ 5   d) 384 ÷ 4

2. Estimate each quotient. Which strategies did you use?
   a) 325 ÷ 3   b) 283 ÷ 2   c) 361 ÷ 4   d) 199 ÷ 5
   e) 486 ÷ 5   f) 768 ÷ 7   g) 476 ÷ 8   h) 927 ÷ 9

3. Nine hundred seventy-five maple taffy candies are shared equally among 9 students. About how many candies will each student get?

4. Nine hundred thirty bottles are placed in cartons of 6. About how many cartons are there?

5. Eight hundred twenty-eight pencils are packaged in boxes of 8. About how many boxes are there?

6. In the photographs section of the yearbook, there are 8 student photos per page. About how many pages are needed for 654 photos?

7. Kris has 862 game tokens. He plans to share them among 9 people. About how many tokens will each person get? How did you find out?

8. Martin estimated 365 ÷ 4. He wrote these statements:
   • The quotient has 2 digits.
   • The quotient is greater than 80.
   How might Martin have made his estimate? Use words and numbers to explain.

9. The Grade 5 class organized a walk to raise funds for a charity. Nine students walked a total distance of 130 km.
   a) About how far did each student walk?
   b) What assumptions did you make?

10. One toonie is about 3 cm wide. Toonies are placed in a row 448 cm long.
   a) About how many toonies are in the row?
   b) What is the approximate value of the toonies?

11. Geri is organizing school supplies. She counted 248 pencils. Geri decided to put 6 pencils in each packet. About how many packets did she make?

12. Four elephants eat a total mass of 890 kg of food in one day.
   a) About how much food does one elephant eat?
   b) What assumptions did you make?

Reflect

When might you want to estimate to find an approximate quotient? Use an example to explain.

Dividing a 3-Digit Number by a 1-Digit Number

**Explore**

Each sheet of this photo album holds 8 photos.
Evan has 325 photos.
How many sheets does he need?
How many different ways can you find out?
Show your work for each strategy you use.

Show and Share

Share your strategies with another pair of students.

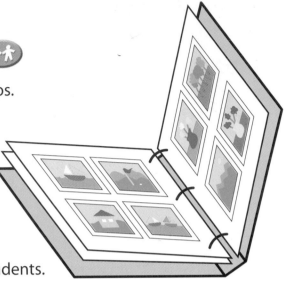

Connect

Three children share $1.25 equally. How much does each child get?

Change $1.25 to 125¢.
To find out how much each child gets, divide: 125 ÷ 3
Here are two strategies students used to find the quotient.

➤ Emma used Base Ten Blocks.

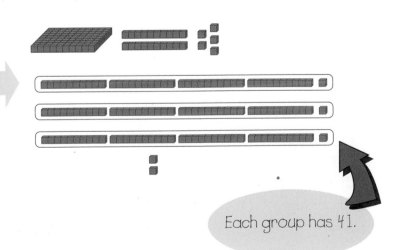

She traded the hundred flat for 10 rods.

Emma then arranged the 12 rods and 5 unit cubes into 3 equal groups.

There are 2 cubes left over.

So, 125 ÷ 3 = 41 R2

Each group has 41.

➤ Amil uses repeated subtraction to divide.
He subtracts multiples of the divisor.
Multiples of 3 are: 3, 6, 9, 12, 15, 18, 21, 24, 27, 30, 33, …
Write 125 ÷ 3 as 3)125.
Choose any multiple of 3 less than 125.
Start with 30. Subtract 30.

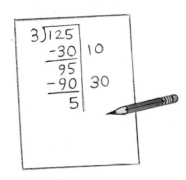

30 is a multiple of 3.
When I subtract 30, I am subtracting 3 ten times.
So, I write 10 at the side.

Then subtract 90.

90 is a multiple of 3.
When I subtract 90, I am subtracting 3 thirty times. So, I write 30 at the side.

Then subtract 3.

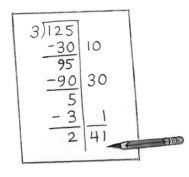

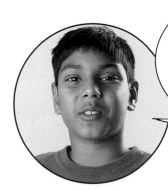

When I subtract 3, I write 1 at the side, because 3 × 1 = 3.
I add the numbers at the side.
3)125 is 41 with 2 left over.

125 ÷ 3 = 41 R2
Each child gets 41¢. There are 2¢ left over.
We ignore the remainder because each child must have the same amount.

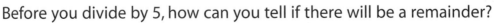
Use Base Ten Blocks when they help.

1. Divide.
   a) 794 ÷ 2   **b)** 263 ÷ 9   **c)** 410 ÷ 4   **d)** 314 ÷ 6

2. Divide. Use Base Ten Blocks, then record your answer.
   a) 145 ÷ 5   **b)** 189 ÷ 2   **c)** 272 ÷ 8   **d)** 230 ÷ 6
   e) 344 ÷ 8   **f)** 420 ÷ 7   **g)** 245 ÷ 9   **h)** 328 ÷ 4

3. Janelle has a book with 246 pages.
   She has to read it in 6 days.
   Janelle plans to read the same number of pages each day.
   How many pages does she need to read daily?

4. Divide. Which strategy did you use each time?
   a) 4)484   **b)** 3)651   **c)** 6)670   **d)** 5)715
   e) 375 ÷ 8   **f)** 274 ÷ 6   **g)** 434 ÷ 7   **h)** 853 ÷ 4

5. A baker made 615 loaves of bread in 5 days.
   She made the same number of loaves each day.
   How many loaves did the baker make each day?

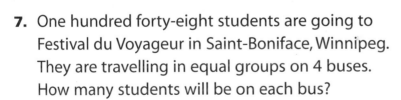

6. Divide.
   a) 250 ÷ 5   **b)** 146 ÷ 5
   c) 165 ÷ 5   **d)** 324 ÷ 5
   e) 480 ÷ 5   **f)** 487 ÷ 5
   g) 495 ÷ 5   **h)** 139 ÷ 5
   Before you divide by 5, how can you tell if there will be a remainder?

7. One hundred forty-eight students are going to
   Festival du Voyageur in Saint-Boniface, Winnipeg.
   They are travelling in equal groups on 4 buses.
   How many students will be on each bus?

8. Write a story problem that can be solved
   by finding 342 ÷ 3.
   Trade problems with a classmate.
   Solve your classmate's problem.

9. Without dividing, how can you tell if 415 ÷ 5 has a 3-digit answer or a 2-digit answer? Show your work.

10. Alex is putting his 246 sports cards into an album. He will mount 8 cards on each page.
   a) How many pages will Alex need?
   b) Explain why you need to think about the remainder.

11. Each student needs a notebook.
   There are 148 students.
   There are 8 notebooks in each packet.
   a) How many packets are needed?
   b) What does the remainder tell you?

12. Two hundred sixty-five slices of tourtière were ordered for a Taste of Québec Day. There are 8 slices in one tourtière.
   a) How many tourtières does the school need to order?
   b) How many more slices could be sold before the school needs to order another tourtière?
   c) Suppose the school sold 10 slices less than were ordered. How would that change the number of tourtières needed? Explain your thinking.

13. When you divide a 3-digit number by a 1-digit number, will the answer ever be a 1-digit number? Explain how you know.

14. Kendra has twice as many building blocks as Janet.
   Janet has twice as many as Fariah.
   Fariah has 57 blocks.
   The girls use all the blocks to build 3 identical towers.
   How many blocks are in each tower? How do you know?

Reflect

When is the remainder in a division problem ignored?
When does the remainder indicate that
the quotient should be rounded up?
Use words and numbers to explain an example of each problem.

Other Strategies for Dividing Whole Numbers

A tire factory makes
824 tires a day.
A new car needs
a set of 4 tires.
How many sets of tires
are made each day?

Show *and* Share

Share your strategy with that
of another pair of students.
Which strategy do you prefer?
Why?

Some vehicles have 5 tires in a set.
How many sets of 5 tires can be made with 728 tires?

To find out, divide: $5\overline{)728}$

➤ Estimate.
Think of a multiple of 10 that is easy
to divide by 5.
728 is about 750.
750 ÷ 5 = 75 tens ÷ 5
      = 15 tens
      = 150
So, 728 ÷ 5 is about 150.

➤ Use Base Ten Blocks and place value to divide: 728 ÷ 5

Divide 7 hundreds into 5 equal groups.

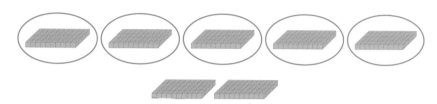

```
    h t o
    1
5 )7 2 8
  -5
    2
```

There are 1 hundred in each group, with 2 hundreds left over.

Trade the 2 hundred flats for 20 ten rods.
There are now 22 ten rods.

Divide the 22 ten rods among the 5 equal groups.
There are now 1 hundred 4 tens in each group, with 2 tens left over.

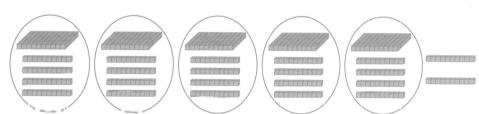

```
    h  t o
    1  4
5 )7  2 8
  -5  ↓
    2  2
  -2  0
       2
```

Trade the 2 ten rods for 20 unit cubes.
There are now 28 unit cubes.

Divide the 28 cubes among the 5 equal groups.
There are now 1 hundred 4 tens 5 ones in each group,
with 3 ones left over.

```
    h  t  o
    1  4  5
5 )7  2  8
  -5  ↓
    2  2
  -2  0  ↓
       2  8
      -2  5
          3
```

There are 145 in each group, with 3 left over.
So, 728 ÷ 5 = 145 R3

➤ Use mental math.

Divide: $728 \div 5$

Break 728 into numbers you can divide easily by 5.

$728 = 500 + 200 + 28$

$500 \div 5 = 50$ tens $\div 5$ $200 \div 5 = 20$ tens $\div 5$ $28 \div 5 = 5$ R3

         $= 10$ tens $= 4$ tens

         $= 100$ $= 40$

So, $728 \div 5 = 100 + 40 + 5$ R3

              $= 145$ R3

One hundred forty-five sets of tires can be made.
There will be 3 tires left over.

To check, multiply 145 by 5, then add 3.

$145 \times 5 = 725$

$725 + 3 = 728$ ⟵ Since this is the dividend, the answer is correct.

Practice

1. Find each quotient. Estimate first. Show your work.

     a) $9\overline{)540}$ **b)** $3\overline{)720}$ **c)** $5\overline{)255}$ **d)** $8\overline{)168}$

     e) $4\overline{)268}$ **f)** $7\overline{)112}$ **g)** $6\overline{)704}$ **h)** $2\overline{)173}$

     i) $9\overline{)398}$ **j)** $4\overline{)600}$ **k)** $3\overline{)299}$ **l)** $3\overline{)212}$

2. Divide. Check by multiplying. Show your work.

     a) $925 \div 6$ **b)** $537 \div 9$ **c)** $588 \div 7$ **d)** $831 \div 4$

     e) $108 \div 4$ **f)** $311 \div 6$ **g)** $284 \div 5$ **h)** $606 \div 9$

     i) $667 \div 7$ **j)** $424 \div 8$ **k)** $903 \div 8$ **l)** $418 \div 6$

3. Look at your answers for question 2.
Which quotients had 3 digits? Which had 2 digits?
How can you tell how many digits
the quotient will have before you divide?

4. Most minivans have 3 wiper blades.
How many sets of 3 blades can be made from 342 blades?

5. Gabi has 629 pennies.
She wants to give 90¢ to each of 7 friends.
Can she do it? Explain.

6. Zoomin' Inc. makes skateboards.
   In 5 days, 980 skateboards were made.
   The same number of skateboards was made each day.
   How many skateboards were made each day?
   How can you check?

7. Write a division problem that can be solved by dividing
   a 3-digit number by a 1-digit number.
   Trade problems with a classmate.
   Solve your classmate's problem.

8. Troy is planning a family reunion.
   He estimates that 250 people will attend.
   Troy plans one hot dog per person.
   Hot dogs come in packages of 6 or 8.
   Which type of package should Troy buy?
   Justify your answer.

9. The Grades 5 and 6 classes get together for a 5-a-side soccer
   tournament. There are 133 students.
   a) How many students will not be on a team?
      Justify your answer.
   b) Soccer can also be played with 4, 6, or 7 people on a team.
      Which size team would provide for the fewest students not
      on a team?
      Justify your answer.

10. Use each of these digits once: 8, 6, 1
    Arrange the digits to make a 3-digit number.
    How many different 3-digit numbers can you make
    that have no remainder when divided by 7?
    How do you know you have found all of them?

Reflect

Which strategy for dividing did you find most difficult to use?
Talk to a classmate about the strategy.
Write what you learned about the strategy.

Target No Remainder!

You will need:
* a spinner with 6 equal sectors, labelled 4 to 9
* 3 number cubes, each labelled 1 to 6

The goal of the game is to get the least remainder.

Take turns.
On your turn, roll all 3 number cubes and spin the pointer.
Arrange the numbers rolled on the number cubes
to make a 3-digit number.
Divide the 3-digit number by the number
on the spinner.
Record the remainder.
This is your score for this turn.
At the end of the game, total your score.
The player with the lesser total wins.

Solving Problems

You have used addition, subtraction, multiplication, and division
to solve problems with whole numbers.

In this lesson, you will solve problems with more than one step.

Explore

Rhianna mows lawns and shovels driveways.
Last year, she earned $1252.
She mowed 93 lawns for $8 each.
How much money did she earn
from shovelling driveways?

Show *and* Share

Share your work with another pair of students.
Compare your answers and
the strategies you used to find them.
What did you need to calculate before
you could find how much Rhianna earned
from shovelling driveways? Explain.

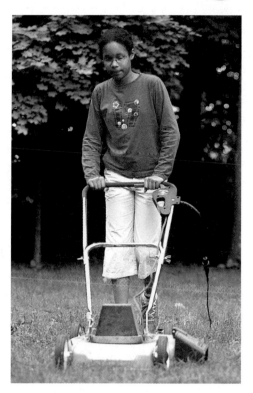

Connect

➤ Robert spent $1478 on stamps and coins for his collection.
   He bought 14 stamps for $37 each.
   How much did Robert spend on coins?

   To find the amount Robert spent on coins,
   we first need to find out how much he spent
   on stamps.

Multiply: 14×37
Use expanded form, then partial products.

$$14 \times 37 = (10 + 4) \times (30 + 7)$$
$$= (10 \times 30) + (10 \times 7) + (4 \times 30) + (4 \times 7)$$
$$= 300 + 70 + 120 + 28$$
$$= 370 + 148$$
$$= 518$$

	30	7
10	10×30	10×7
4	4×30	4×7

Robert spent $518 on stamps.

Find how much Robert spent on coins.
Subtract the amount he spent on stamps
from the total amount he spent.
Subtract: $1478 - 518$

$$1478 - 518 = 960$$

Robert spent $960 on coins.

➤ Mackenzie uses 16 m of fabric to make 4 outfits
from one pattern.
How much fabric would she need to make 9 outfits
from the same pattern?

To find the amount of fabric she needs for 9 outfits,
we first need to know how much fabric she needs for 1 outfit.
Divide: $16 \div 4 = 4$

Mackenzie needs 4 m of fabric to make 1 outfit.
Multiply the amount of fabric needed for 1 outfit
by the number of outfits, 9.
$$4 \times 9 = 36$$

Mackenzie needs 36 m of fabric to make 9 outfits from the pattern.

Practice

1. Campbell bought 48 hardcover books. Each book cost $35.
   a) How much did Campbell spend on books?
   b) Write a story problem that uses your answer to part a.
      Trade problems with a classmate.
      Solve your classmate's problem.
   c) Compare your problem to your classmate's problem.

2. For each problem, describe what you need to find before you can solve the problem.

    a) At Sam's Office Supply, a package of 3 colour inkjet cartridges costs $216.
    At Ink World, the same brand of cartridge costs $79 each.
    How much more does a colour cartridge cost at Ink World?

    b) Karen booked the computer for 2 hours.
    She spent 75 minutes typing a report
    and 32 minutes checking her work.
    How much computer time does Karen have left?

3. The Lakeland District choir stood in rows of 12 for a performance.
The people in 2 rows carried red streamers.
The people in 4 rows carried yellow streamers.
The people in 3 rows carried purple streamers.
How many people are in the choir?

4. Pierre-Luc runs 2 m every second.
    A cheetah runs 29 m every second.
    a) How much farther than Pierre-Luc will the cheetah run in 9 seconds?
    b) Explain how you solved the problem.

5. Kamil played a game 3 times.
His first score was 1063 points.
His second score was 129 points lower.
His third score was 251 points higher than his second score.
How many points did Kamil score in his third game?

6. Three people are sharing the costs for a barbecue equally.
Alison buys the meat for $157.
Brent buys the pop and juice for $124.
Ahmed buys the salads, buns, and desserts for $136.
How much should each person pay? Justify your answer.

Reflect

What clues do you use to find out if you need to add, subtract, multiply, or divide to solve a problem?

Explore •

Samrina organized a team to participate
in a 325-km bike relay.
Half the team members ride 25 km.
The rest ride 40 km.
Including Samrina, how many people
are on Samrina's team?

Show *and* Share

Describe the strategy you used to solve the problem.
How could you solve the problem a different way?

Connect •

Mr. Tremblay bought resource books for $28 each
and bookshelves for $84 each.
He spent $616 on 12 items.
How many of each item did Mr. Tremblay buy?

Understand

What do you know?
- Resource books cost $28 each.
- Bookshelves cost $84 each.
- The total number of books
  and bookshelves is 12.
- The total cost is $616.

Plan

Think of a strategy to help you solve
the problem.
You could **make an organized list** in a table.
- Choose a number for the bookshelves bought
  and another number for the books bought.
- Find the total cost of bookshelves and books.

Strategies

- **Make a table.**
- **Use a model.**
- **Draw a diagram.**
- **Solve a simpler problem.**
- **Work backward.**
- **Guess and test.**
- **Make an organized list.**
- **Use a pattern.**
- **Draw a graph.**

Find the cost of 1 bookshelf.
Find the cost of 11 books.
Record the costs in an organized list.
Find the total cost. Is it $616?
If not, find the cost of 2 bookshelves and 10 books.
Continue until the total cost is $616.

Number of Bookshelves	Cost ($)	Number of Books	Cost ($)	Total Cost ($)
1	84	11	308	392

Check your work.
Is the total number of books and bookshelves 12?
Is the total cost of books and bookshelves $616?

Practice

Choose one of the

Strategies

1. Colin's grandma gave him $100.
   He bought a game for $61.
   He wants to buy another game that costs $47.
   a) Does Colin have enough money? How do you know?
   b) If your answer to part a is yes, how much will Colin have left after he buys the game?
   If your answer to part a is no, how much more money does Colin need?

2. Together, two bicycles cost $300.
   One bicycle costs $40 more than the other.
   What is the cost of the cheaper bicycle?

Reflect

When is "make an organized list" a useful strategy for solving problems?

LESSON

1

1. Write as many related facts as possible for each set of numbers.
   a) 9, 9, 81   b) 7, 9, 63   c) 0, 0, 8   d) 6, 9, 54

2. Write a multiplication fact that can help you find each quotient.
   a) $54 \div 6$ b) $48 \div 6$ c) $27 \div 9$ d) $40 \div 8$

3. Léa knows the product of 8 and 9 is 72.
   How can she use that fact to find the product of 7 and 9?

2

4. How can you use 5×10 to find 9×5? Explain your strategy.

5. How can you use 4×7 to find 8×7? Explain your strategy.

6. How can you use repeated halving to find $68 \div 4$?

7. Sami bought 8 paperback books for $6 each, including tax.
   a) How much did the books cost?
   b) How could you use repeated doubling to find out?

3

8. Multiply. How can you use what you know about basic facts to help you?
   a) 8×7000 b) 50×90 c) 8×500 d) 60×60

4

9. Which compatible numbers would you use to estimate each product?
   a) 9×73 b) 810×4 c) 39×52 d) 126×8

10. Estimate each product.
    Tell whether your estimate is an overestimate, an underestimate,
    or why you cannot tell.
    a) 89×9 b) 54×38 c) 785×6 d) 7×456

11. Raffi's stamp album has 35 pages.
    There are 48 stamps on each page.
    About how many stamps are in Raffi's album?

5

12. Use mental math to multiply. Explain your strategy each time.
    a) 32×25 b) 50×78 c) 699×6 d) 5×92

6
8

13. Multiply or divide.
   a) 32 × 65   **b)** 760 ÷ 8   **c)** 80 × 56   **d)** 188 ÷ 6

6

14. Jacob has ninety-seven $20 bills.
How much money does he have?

15. Sandra bought 17 CDs for $23 each.
How much did she spend on CDs?

7

16. There are 265 students in Mountview Elementary School.
There are 9 classes. About how many students are in each class?

8

17. Divide, then check.
   a) 5)625   **b)** 338 ÷ 2   **c)** 4)750   **d)** 382 ÷ 8

9

18. Use mental math or place value to divide.
   a) 635 ÷ 5   **b)** 738 ÷ 9   **c)** 444 ÷ 6   **d)** 576 ÷ 8

19. Bedding plants are sold in trays of 6.
How many trays are needed to hold 340 plants?

10

20. At Mary's Market, you can buy
6 boxwood plants for $354.
At Green Gardens, the same size
of boxwood plant costs $53.
Which store has the better price
on boxwood plants?
How do you know?

21. An apartment building has 32 one-bedroom
apartments, 24 two-bedroom apartments,
and 16 three-bedroom apartments.
How many bedrooms are in the building?

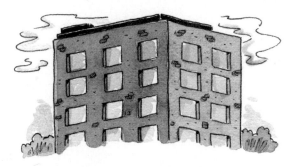

UNIT

3 Learning Goals

☑ find basic multiplication facts
to 81 and the related division
facts

☑ use different strategies
to estimate products and
quotients

☑ estimate to solve problems

☑ use different strategies
to multiply mentally

☑ multiply a 2-digit number by a
2-digit number

☑ divide a 3-digit number
by a 1-digit number

On the Dairy Farm

Silage is made from green corn plants. The whole plant is harvested, chopped, and fermented in a storage silo.

Haylage is hay that has been cut, chopped, and stored moist.

Each day, a cow eats:
- 5 kg of hay
- 9 kg of haylage
- 9 kg of corn silage
- 10 kg of dairy ration

A cow also needs minerals and salt, and eighty to one hundred sixty litres of water each day.

Check List

Your work should show

☑ that you can choose the correct operation to solve problems

☑ all calculations in detail

☑ a challenging story problem using whole numbers

☑ a clear explanation of how you solved your story problem

1. Amy has 43 dairy cows on her farm.
   How many kilograms of feed will she use each day?

2. Simon has 72 hectares of field on his farm.
   He plans to use 4 parts to plant hay, 1 part to plant corn, and 1 part as cow pasture.
   How many hectares of field will he use for each purpose?

   1 hectare is equal to 10 000 m².

3. The Allards can milk 14 cows at a time in their milking parlour.
   It takes a milking machine about 5 minutes to milk a cow.
   About how long will it take the machines to milk all 90 cows?

4. Write a story problem about a dairy farm.
   Solve your problem.
   How did you solve the problem?

Reflect on Your Learning

Choose one strategy for multiplication and one for division.
Use an example to show when you might use each strategy.

UNIT

1

1. The first 2 terms of a pattern are 3 and 5.
   Write 5 different patterns that start with these 2 terms.
   List the first 6 terms for each pattern.
   Write each pattern rule.

2. Choose one pattern from question 1.
   Use counters to show the pattern.
   Sketch the counters you used.

3. Here is a pattern made with square tiles.
   The side length of each square is 1 unit.
   The pattern continues.

     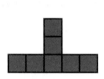   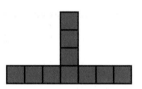

Frame 1   Frame 2   Frame 3

   a) Find the perimeter of each frame.
      Record the frame number and the perimeter in a table.
   b) Predict the perimeter of Frame 12. How did you do this?
   c) Does any frame have a perimeter of 40 units? 50 units?
      How do you know?

Frame number	Perimeter (units)

4. Solve each equation.
   a) $16 + n = 20$ b) $16 - m = 5$ c) $16 = 2e$ d) $16 = r \div 2$

5. For each equation in question 4, write a story problem
   you could use the equation to solve.

2

6. a) How many tens are in 6000?   b) How many hundreds are in 6000?
   c) How many thousands are in 6000?

7. a) Write this number in standard form: 900 000 + 60 000 + 300 + 5
   b) Write this number in words: 805 601
   c) Write this number in expanded form: 710 543

8. Use the 2 digits of your age and the 4 digits of the year you were born.
    a) Write the greatest number with those 6 digits.
    b) Write the least number with those 6 digits.
    c) Write 3 numbers between the numbers you wrote in parts a and b.

9. Estimate to find the differences that are less than 2000.
    a) 5697 − 3748   **b)** 9876 − 6789   **c)** 4005 − 2010   **d)** 8332 − 7441

10. Janelle is travelling with her family.
She keeps a record of how far she travels each day.
Here is Janelle's data for one week.

Day	Mon.	Tues.	Wed.	Thurs.	Fri.	Sat.	Sun.
Distance (km)	658	132	754	37	458	207	856

    a) Estimate how far Janelle travelled at the weekend.
       Which strategy did you use?
    b) Estimate how far Janelle travelled on Wednesday, Thursday, and Friday.
       Did you use a different strategy this time? If so, explain why.

11. Suppose you know that 2 × 4 = 8.
Which other facts can you find by repeated doubling?

12. In a parking lot, there are 59 rows of parking spaces.
There are 25 spaces in each row.
About how many cars can park in the lot? Show your work.

13. Draw a diagram to help find each product.
    a) 304 × 5   **b)** 297 × 8

14. Estimate each quotient. Which strategy did you use each time?
    a) 136 ÷ 3   **b)** 250 ÷ 6   **c)** 387 ÷ 9   **d)** 507 ÷ 7

15. For a school fund-raiser, Kyle helped his dad bake 456 cookies in
3 days. They baked the same number of cookies each day.
    a) How many cookies did Kyle and his dad bake each day?
    b) Kyle wraps cookies in packages of 5 cookies to sell.
       How many packages can he make? Explain your answer.

Measurement

At the Zoo

DEPTH AT THIS POINT 2.6 m

GASOLINE CAPACITY 20 000 L

BITOWN 20
ULVILLE 55

OVERPASS CLEARANCE 8.4 m

50 km/h

COMMERCIAL PROPERTY FOR SALE
500 m by 300 m

Learning Goals

- measure length in millimetres
- select referents for units of measure
- relate units of measure
- draw different rectangles for a given perimeter or area
- estimate and measure volume
- estimate and measure capacity

millimetre (mm)

referent

perimeter

area

volume

cubic centimetre (cm³)

dimensions

cubic metre (m³)

capacity

litre (L)

millilitre (mL)

displacement

- Which measurements can you find in this picture?
- Which measurements describe length? Height? Width?
- What does "500 m by 300 m" on the property for sale sign mean?
- Do you think the property for sale is larger or smaller than your school's property?
- What does "Capacity 20 000 L" on the gasoline truck mean?
- Which unit would you use to measure the perimeter of the apple orchard? The length of the rhinoceros? The length of a seal's whiskers? The area of the petting zoo?

Measuring Length

This ruler shows centimetres.

This ruler shows centimetres and **millimetres**.
We use the symbol **mm** for millimetres.

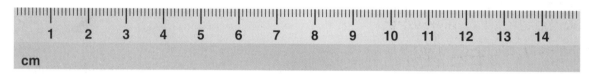

How many millimetres are in 1 cm?

Explore

You will need a ruler and a metre stick or tape measure
marked in centimetres and millimetres.
Have a scavenger hunt.

➤ Estimate to find an object whose length fits each description:
  • about 25 mm
  • about 80 mm
  • about 250 mm
  • between 500 and 1000 mm
  • shorter than 10 mm

➤ Measure to check your estimate.
  Record your results in a table.

Given measurement	Object	Actual measurement
about 25 mm	an eraser	30 mm

Show *and* Share

Share your strategies for estimating with other students.
Record your strategies in a class list.

Connect . . . .

You can use millimetres to measure
the length, width, height, or thickness
of small objects.
A dime is about 1 mm thick.

↓ **1 mm**
↑

You can use the
thickness of a dime as a
referent for 1 mm. A referent
is used to estimate
a measure.

This pine needle is about 6 cm long.
To be more precise,
you read the length in millimetres.
The pine needle is 62 mm long.

One millimetre is one-tenth of
a centimetre.
So, you can also read the length of
the pine needle in centimetres.
The pine needle is 6.2 cm long.
You say: 6 and 2 tenths centimetres

Centimetres and millimetres are related.

A referent for 1 cm is the width of my little finger. There are 10 mm in 1 cm.

So, that means 1 mm is $\frac{1}{10}$ of a centimetre, or 0.1 cm.

Metres and centimetres are related.

A referent for 1 m is the width of the classroom door. There are 100 cm in 1 m.

So, that means 1 cm is $\frac{1}{100}$ of a metre, or 0.01 m.

Metres and millimetres are related.

And there are 1000 mm in 1 m.

Use a ruler or metre stick when it helps.

1. Copy and complete each table.

a)
cm	1	2	3	4	5	6	7	8	9	10	11	12
mm	10	20										

b)
mm	1	2	3	4	5	6	7	8	9	10	11	12
cm	0.1	0.2										

c)
m	1	2	3	4	5	6	7	8	9	10	11	12
mm	1000	2000										

2. What patterns do you see in each table in question 1?

3. Copy and complete. How can you use a ruler to help you?
   a) 8 cm = ☐ mm   b) 20 cm = ☐ mm   c) 63 cm = ☐ mm

4. Copy and complete.
   a) 60 mm = ☐ cm   b) 40 mm = ☐ cm   c) 100 mm = ☐ cm

5. Copy and complete.
   a) 2000 mm = ☐ m   b) 6000 mm = ☐ m   c) 9000 mm = ☐ m
   d) 5 m = ☐ mm   e) 2 m = ☐ mm   f) 8 m = ☐ mm

6. Name another referent for each unit of measure. Explain each choice.
   a) 1 mm   b) 1 cm   c) 1 m

7. Draw each item. Measure its length in millimetres.
   a) a pencil   b) a needle

8. Draw a picture of each thing. Use grid paper when it helps.
   a) a feather 15 cm long   b) an insect 14 mm long
   c) a label 6 cm long and 4 cm wide   d) a flower 10 cm tall

9. Use a ruler to draw each item.
   Write each measure.
   Trade pictures with a classmate.
   Check your classmate's measures.
   a) a worm 8.5 cm long   b) a straw 13.8 cm long

10. Which items would you measure in millimetres?
Which units would you use to measure the other items?
Explain your choice.
   a) the length of a driveway
   b) the length of the sash of a "Coureur de bois"
   c) the depth of a footprint in the sand
   d) the width of a baby's finger

11. a) How are millimetres and centimetres related?
   b) How are millimetres and metres related?

12. Which is longer? How do you know?
   a) 6 cm or 80 mm   **b)** 25 cm or 200 mm   **c)** 9 m or 7000 mm

13. Suppose you found a leaf that was 88 mm long.
   a) Is its length closer to 8 cm or 9 cm? How do you know?
   b) What other way could you write the length of the leaf?
   Show your work.

14. Which unit would you use to measure each item?
Explain your choice.
   a) the height of a house   **b)** the length of an eyelash
   c) the width of a calculator   **d)** the thickness of a bannock

15. Nicole drew a line longer than 8 cm but shorter than 99 mm.
How long might the line be? How do you know?

16. Estimate the length of each line segment in millimetres. Then measure
and record the actual length in millimetres and in centimetres.
   a) ────────────────────   **b)** ──────────────

At Home

Reflect

Name 2 items whose length, width,
height, or thickness you would
measure in millimetres. Explain
why you would use millimetres
and not any other unit.

Measure the height of a relative.
Draw a picture.
Write the height using as many
different units as you can.
Round when you need to.

Strategies Toolkit

Explore •

Ernesto made a 1-m square garden this year.
He plans to enlarge the garden. Ernesto will increase
each of the four side lengths by 2 m each year.
What will the perimeter and the area of
Ernesto's garden be in 6 years?

Show *and* Share

Describe the strategy you used to solve the problem.

Connect •

Helen raises Angora rabbits.
When Helen got her first pair of rabbits,
she built a 2-m by 1-m pen for them.
As Helen's rabbit population grew, she increased
the size of the pen by doubling the length and the width.
What were the perimeter and area of Helen's pen
after she increased its size 5 times?

Strategies

- **Make a table.**
- **Use a model.**
- **Draw a diagram.**
- **Solve a simpler problem.**
- **Work backward.**
- **Guess and test.**
- **Make an organized list.**
- **Use a pattern.**

What do you know?
- Helen's first pen measured 2 m by 1 m.
- She increased the size of the pen by doubling the length and width.
- She did this 5 times.

Think of a strategy to help you solve the problem.
- You can **use a pattern**, then **make a table**.
- Use Colour Tiles to model each pen.
- List the dimensions, the perimeter, and the area of each pen.

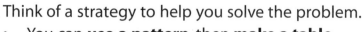

Record your list in the table.

	Length	Width	Perimeter	Area
Original Pen	2 m	1 m	6 m	2 m²
First Increase	4 m	2 m	12 m	8 m²
Second Increase				

Look for patterns.
Continue the patterns to find
the perimeter and the area after 5 increases.

Check your work.
What pattern rules created the patterns in your table?

Practice

Choose one of the

Strategies

1. Harold is designing a patio with congruent
   square concrete tiles. He has 72 tiles.
   Use grid paper to model all the possible rectangular patios
   Harold could build. Label the dimensions in units.
   Which patio has the greatest perimeter? The least perimeter?

2. Suppose you have a 7-cm by 5-cm rectangle.
   You increase the length by 1 cm and decrease the width by 1 cm.
   You continue to do this.
   What happens to the perimeter of the rectangle? The area?
   Explain why this happens.

Reflect

How does using a pattern or making a table help you solve a problem?
Use pictures, words, or numbers to explain.

Exploring Rectangles with Equal Perimeters

What is the perimeter of this rectangle?
What is its area?
How do you know?

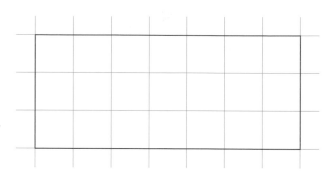

Explore

You will need a geoboard, geobands, and 1-cm grid paper.

Simon wants to build a rectangular pen in
his backyard for his potbelly pig, Smiley.
Simon has 22 m of wire mesh for a fence to enclose the pen.
Simon wants the greatest possible area for the pen.

➤ Use a geoboard to make models of all possible
rectangles. Draw each model on grid paper.

➤ Find the area of each pen.

➤ Write the perimeter of each pen.

➤ Record your work in a table.

➤ Find the pen with the greatest area.

Show and Share

Share your work with another
pair of students.
What do you notice about the
shape of the rectangle with the
greatest area?
What do you notice about the width of the rectangle with the least area?

Length	Width	Area	Perimeter

Rectangles with equal perimeters can have different areas.
Each rectangle below has perimeter 18 cm.

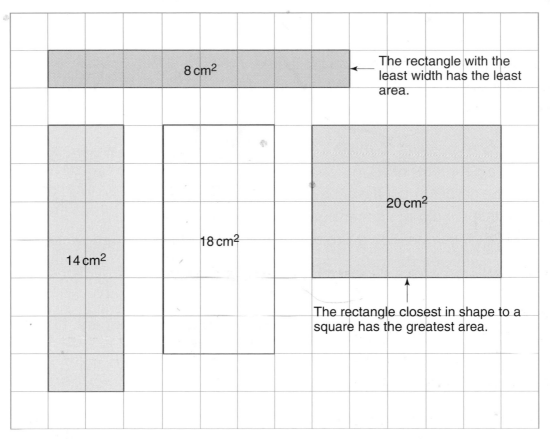

8 cm²

The rectangle with the least width has the least area.

14 cm²

18 cm²

20 cm²

The rectangle closest in shape to a square has the greatest area.

Practice

1. Copy each rectangle onto 1-cm grid paper. For each rectangle:
   - Find the perimeter.
   - Draw a rectangle with the same perimeter but greater area.
   - Draw a rectangle with the same perimeter but lesser area.
   - Find the area of each rectangle you draw.

   a) 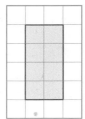   **b)** 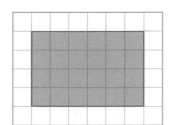   **c)**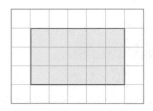

2. Use 1-cm grid paper.
   Draw all possible rectangles with each perimeter.
   Find the area of each rectangle.
   a) 16 cm   **b)** 20 cm   **c)** 14 cm

3. Draw 2 different rectangles with each perimeter below.
   One rectangle has the least area.
   The other rectangle has the greatest area.
   Find the area of each rectangle you draw. Use a geoboard to help you.
   a) 10 cm   **b)** 12 cm   **c)** 8 cm

4. Suppose you want to make a rectangular garden
   with a perimeter of 24 m.
   a) The garden must have the greatest possible area.
      What should the dimensions of the garden be?
   b) Which garden would you design if you do not like garden work?
      Explain your design.
   Show your work.

5. Describe a situation where both area and perimeter are important.

6. Use a geoboard to make a rectangle with each perimeter and area.
   Record your work on dot paper.
   a) perimeter 24 units and area 32 square units
   b) perimeter 14 units and area 10 square units
   c) perimeter 8 units and area 4 square units

7. Xavier has 16 m of fencing to put around his square flower garden.
   a) What are the side lengths of Xavier's garden? How do you know?
   b) What is the area of his garden?

8. Sarah has 100 cm of trim for each rectangular placemat she is making.
   a) List the lengths and widths of 6 possible placemats.
   b) Which placemat in part a would be the best size?
      Give reasons for your choice.

Reflect

Write a letter to a friend to explain the difference between
area and perimeter.

Who Can Fill the Page?

You will need 2 sheets of 1-cm grid paper,
and a number cube labelled 1 to 6.
The goal of the game is to cover the grid paper with rectangles.

➤ Each of you has a sheet of grid paper.
   Take turns to roll the number cube twice.
   Multiply the numbers.
   The product is the perimeter of a rectangle in centimetres.

➤ On the grid lines, draw as many different rectangles as you
   can with that perimeter. The rectangles must not overlap.
   If it is not possible to draw a rectangle, roll again.

➤ Play then passes to your partner.

➤ The first person to cover her grid paper with rectangles
   is the winner.

Exploring Rectangles with Equal Areas

Explore

You will need Colour Tiles or congruent squares, and 1-cm grid paper.
The Magic Carpet Store has donated 36 congruent squares of carpeting to Ms. Hannibal's Grade 5 class.
The students plan to place the squares together to make a rectangular carpet for their reading nook.

➤ Use the squares.
   Find all the possible rectangles the class can make.
➤ Draw each rectangle on grid paper.
➤ Record the measurements of each rectangle in a table.
   Look for patterns in your table.

Length	Width	Perimeter	Area
36 units	1 unit	74 units	36 square units

Show *and* Share

How are all the rectangles you made the same?
How are the rectangles different?
What patterns did you find in the table?
Which rectangle do you think the class will use? Explain your choice.

Rectangles with equal areas can have different perimeters.
Each rectangle below has area 16 cm^2.

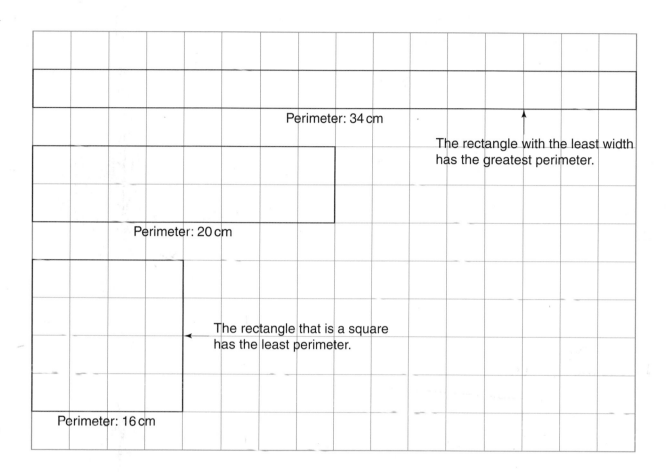

Perimeter: 34 cm

The rectangle with the least width has the greatest perimeter.

Perimeter: 20 cm

The rectangle that is a square has the least perimeter.

Perimeter: 16 cm

Practice

Use Colour Tiles or congruent squares when they help.

1. Use 1-cm grid paper.
Draw all the possible rectangles with each area.

a) 8 cm^2 **b)** 15 cm^2 **c)** 20 cm^2 **d)** 14 cm^2

2. This table shows the measures of some of the floors of rectangular dog pens you can build with 48 congruent concrete squares.

Length (units)	Width (units)	Perimeter (units)
48	1	
24	2	

a) Copy and extend the table.
   Use whole numbers only.
b) Which pen would take the most fencing?
c) Which pen would you build? Explain.

3. The area of a rectangular garden plot is 64 m².

a) What is the greatest perimeter the garden could have?
b) What is the least perimeter?
c) Why might a person make the garden with the least perimeter?

Show your work.

4. Use 1-cm grid paper.
   Draw a rectangle with each area and perimeter.
   a) area 20 cm² and perimeter 18 cm
   b) area 18 cm² and perimeter 22 cm
   c) area 2 cm² and perimeter 6 cm
   d) area 12 cm² and perimeter 26 cm

5. Salvio wants to make a rectangular pumpkin patch with an area of 30 m².
   a) Use grid paper. Sketch all the possible rectangles.
   b) Find and record the perimeter of each rectangle.
   c) Why might Salvio make the patch with the greatest perimeter?

6. How do the length and width of a rectangle relate to its area?
   Draw a diagram to illustrate your answer.

 Reflect

Suppose you know the area of a rectangle.
Can you find its perimeter? Explain.

Exploring Volume

How could you find out how much space
there is inside this shoe box?

Explore

You will need an empty box and collections
of items like those shown here.

➤ Choose a bag of items.
Estimate how many of the items
will fill the box.
Fill the box.
Record your work.

➤ Choose another bag and repeat
the activity.

Show *and* Share

Share your work with another group of students.
Talk about how you estimated.
Which item or items more accurately measure
how much space is inside your box? Why?

The amount of space inside an object is a measure of the **volume** of the object.

You can find the volume of a box by filling it with identical items, then counting them.

➤ This box holds 144 sticks of chalk.
   It has a volume of about 144 sticks of chalk.

> We use "about" to describe the volume because the items do not fill the space.

➤ This box holds 24 oranges.
   It has a volume of about 24 oranges.

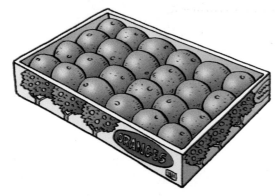

➤ This box holds 80 sugar cubes.
   It has a volume of 80 sugar cubes.

> The sugar cubes fill the box without leaving any spaces.

136

1. Find a small box.
   Estimate its volume in orange Pattern Blocks.
   Fill the box to check your estimate.
   Record your work.

2. Find a small cup.
   Estimate its volume in acorns.
   Fill the cup to check your estimate.
   Record your work.

3. Suppose you filled the cup in question 2 with dried blueberries.
   Do you think you would need more dried blueberries or
   more acorns to fill the cup?
   Explain your choice.

4. Which item in each set would you use to get the best measure
   of the volume of a tissue box? Explain each choice.
   a) golf balls, acorns, or sugar cubes
   b) lima beans, Snap Cubes, or yellow Pattern Blocks

5. The volume of one box is about 8 tennis balls.
   The volume of another box is about 4 tennis balls.
   What can you say about the size of the second box compared to the first box?

6. What is the volume of each object?

   a)

   b)

   c)

Reflect

Think of the items you have used to find volume.
Which item do you think gives the best estimate?
Explain why you think so.

Measuring Volume in Cubic Centimetres

Explore ·

You will need a copy of these nets, scissors, tape, and centimetre cubes.

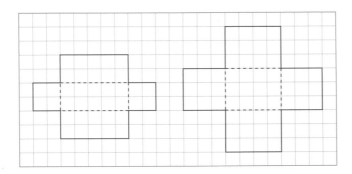

➤ Cut out each net.
Fold and tape four of the faces to make
an open box.

➤ Estimate how many centimetre cubes
each box can hold.

➤ Fill each box to check your estimate.
Record your results in a table.

Show *and* Share

Share your results with another pair
of students.
What strategies did you use to estimate
the volume of each box?
Is there another way, besides counting
every cube, to find how many cubes fill
each box? Explain.

A centimetre cube has a volume of one **cubic centimetre** (1 **cm³**).

The length of each edge of this centimetre cube is 1 cm.

We can use cubic centimetres to measure volume.

➤ This box holds 4 rows of 6 cubes, or 24 cubes.
The volume of this box is 24 cubic centimetres, or 24 cm³.

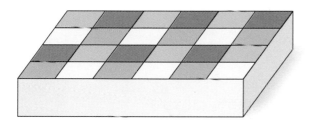

➤ This box holds 2 layers of cubes.
There are 2 rows of 4 cubes, or 8 cubes in each layer.
So, the volume of this box is 16 cubic centimetres, or 16 cm³.

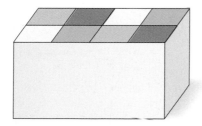

➤ The volume of an object is also the space it occupies.
This object has 8 cubes in the bottom layer
and 3 cubes in the top layer.
The volume of this object is 11 cubic centimetres,
or 11 cm³.

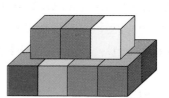

You will need centimetre cubes.

1. Make each object with centimetre cubes.
   Find the volume of each object.
   Order the objects from least to greatest volume.

   a)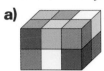

   b)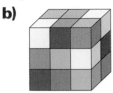

   c)

   d)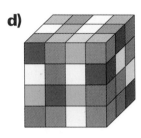

   e)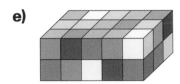

   f)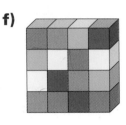

2. Make each object with centimetre cubes.
   Find each volume.

   a)

   b)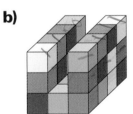

   c)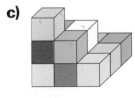

   d)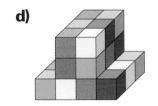

   e)

   f)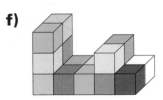

3. Look at the objects in question 2.
   Order the objects from least to greatest volume.

4. **a)** Name a referent for 1 cm^3. Explain your choice.
   b) Find 3 small boxes.
      Use your referent to estimate the volume of each box.
      Explain how you did this.

5. Find a small box that you think has a volume of about 24 cm^3.
   Determine the actual volume of the box.

140

6. Each box below was made by folding 1-cm grid paper.
Find the volume of each box.
Explain how you found each volume.

a)

b)

c)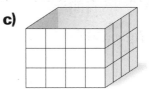

7. Each Pattern Block is 1 cm high. Use a referent for 1 cm³ to estimate the volume of each Pattern Block. Explain how you did this.

8. Ogi says that he can find the volume of this box using only a few centimetre cubes. How do you think Ogi will do this?

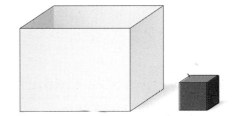

9. A box has a volume of 20 cm³.
The box is 2 cm tall.
   a) How many centimetre cubes will fit in one layer in the bottom of the box? How do you know?
   b) How long and how wide might the box be? Try to give as many answers as possible.

10. Describe a strategy you could use to estimate, then find the volume of this textbook.
What problems might you have finding the volume?
Compare your strategy with that of a classmate.

11. Use a referent for 1 cm³ to estimate the volume of a pen. Explain how you did this.

Reflect

Suppose you need to estimate the volume of a lunchbox.
Would you visualize centimetre cubes or your referent for 1 cm³?
Explain your choice.

Constructing Rectangular Prisms with a Given Volume

This rectangular prism is made with centimetre cubes.
What is its length? Width? Height?
What is the volume of the rectangular prism?

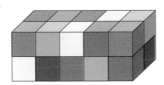

Length, width, and height are **dimensions** of the rectangular prism.

Explore

You will need centimetre cubes.

➤ Construct as many different rectangular prisms as you can, each with a volume of 24 cubic centimetres.

➤ Record your work in a table.

Length	Width	Height	Volume
24 cm	1 cm	1 cm	24 cm³

Show and Share

Share your work with another pair of students.
How do you know you have found all the possible rectangular prisms?

Connect

➤ Suppose you have 11 centimetre cubes.
You can make only 1 rectangular prism with all 11 cubes.
The volume of this rectangular prism is 11 cm³.

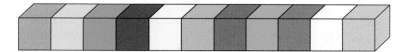

➤ Suppose you have 12 centimetre cubes.
You can make 4 different rectangular prisms with 12 cubes.
The volume of each rectangular prism is 12 cm³.

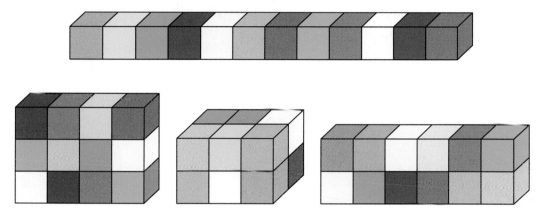

Practice

Use centimetre cubes.

1. These rectangular prisms are made with centimetre cubes.
Find the volume of each prism.

a)    b) 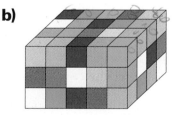   c)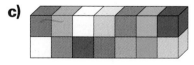

2. Build a rectangular prism with each volume.
Record your work in a table.
   a) 9 cm³   b) 36 cm³
   c) 13 cm³   d) 15 cm³

Volume	Length	Width	Height
9 cm³			

3. Build all the possible rectangular prisms with a volume of 16 cm³.
Record your work in a table.

4. Build a rectangular prism
with each set of dimensions
shown in the table.
Find the volume of each prism.

	Length (cm)	Width (cm)	Height (cm)	Volume (cm³)
a)	8	3	2	
b)	3	4	2	
c)	7	3	1	

5. **a)** How many different rectangular prisms can be made with
18 centimetre cubes? Write the dimensions of each prism.
   b) Suppose the number of centimetre cubes were doubled.
How many different prisms could be made?
Write their dimensions.

6. Suppose you have 100 centimetre cubes.
How many larger cubes can you make using any number
of the centimetre cubes?
Record your work in a table.
What patterns do you see?

7. **a)** Anjana used centimetre cubes to build a rectangular prism
with a volume of 26 cm³.
What might the dimensions of Anjana's prism be?
Give as many answers as you can.
   b) Build a rectangular prism with one-half the volume
of Anjana's prism. Record its dimensions.
How many different prisms can you build? Explain.

8. Suppose you want to build a rectangular prism with
50 centimetre cubes. You put 10 cubes in the bottom layer.
   a) How many layers of cubes will you need?
   b) What are the dimensions of the prism?

Reflect

How can you tell if you can build only one rectangular prism
with a given number of centimetre cubes?
Use examples to explain.

Measuring Volume in Cubic Metres

Explore

You will need metre sticks, newspapers, tape, and a calculator.

➤ Create 12 rolled-up newspapers, each 1 m long.
Arrange 4 rolls to show a square metre.
Connect the remaining rolls to build a skeleton of a cube
with an edge length of 1 m.

➤ Compare the size of the cube to the size of your classroom.
About how many of your cubes would it take to fill your classroom?

Show *and* Share

Share your estimate with another group of students.
Talk about the strategies you used to make your estimate.

The cube you built in *Explore* has edge lengths of 1 m.
The cube has a volume of one **cubic metre** (1 **m³**).

We use cubic metres to measure the volumes of large objects.

➤ This stack of hay bales has bales with edge lengths of 1 m.
There are 2 layers of 6 bales, or 12 bales.
The stack has a volume of 12 m³.

➤ This wooden crate has a volume of 1 m³.

Six of these crates can fit in the back of this pick-up truck.
The back of the truck has a volume of 6 m³.

1. **a)** Name a referent you could use for a volume of one cubic metre. Explain your choice.
   b) Use your referent to estimate the volume of each object.
   • a telephone booth • your bedroom • an elevator

2. Which unit – cubic centimetre or cubic metre – is represented by each referent?
   a) a sugar cube **b)** a playpen
   c) a Base Ten unit cube **d)** a dog cage

3. Suppose you have to measure the volume of each item below. Would you use cubic centimetres or cubic metres?
   a) a refrigerator **b)** the cargo space in a truck
   c) a tissue box **d)** the gym

4. Each rectangular prism is built with 1-m cubes. Find the volume of each prism.

   a)  **b)** 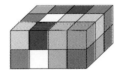 **c)**

   d)  **e)** 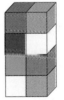 **f)**

5. Marianne stacks crates.
   Each crate has a volume of 1 m³.
   Marianne makes 4 layers, with 12 crates in each layer.
   a) What is the volume of the stack of crates?
   b) How many rows of crates could be in each layer? How many crates could be in each row?

Reflect

Name 2 objects that might be measured in cubic metres. Explain your choices.

Exploring Capacity: The Litre

Camille carries a drinking bottle when she hikes.
The bottle holds one **litre** of water.
We use the symbol **L** for litres.

Explore

You will need some containers and sand.

➤ Look at the container
   that holds one litre.
   Choose another container.
   Estimate whether it holds
   less than one litre,
   more than one litre,
   or about one litre.
   Check your estimate.
   Record your work.
   Repeat this activity with
   other containers.

➤ Choose a large container.
   Estimate its capacity in litres.
   Record your estimate.
   Check your estimate.
   Record your work.

Show *and* Share

Discuss the strategies you used to make your estimates.
Can containers of different shapes hold about the same amount?
Do you drink more or less than one litre of liquids in a day?

When you fill a container with liquid to find out how much it holds, you measure its **capacity**.

This carton has a capacity of one litre.
You write: 1 L
The carton holds one litre of juice.
One litre fills about 4 glasses.

Here are some other things that are measured in litres.

I use a 1-L milk carton to estimate capacity. I think this bowl holds about 4L.

Practice •

1. Which containers hold less than one litre?

a)   b)   c)   d)

2. Choose the better estimate. How do you know?

a) 5 L or 210 L   b) 9 L or 1 L   c) 2 L or 26 L

d) 1 L or 17 L   e) 4 L or 25 L   f) 1 L or 6 L

3. Order these containers from least to greatest capacity.

4. a) Name a referent you could use for a capacity of one litre.
      Explain your choice.
   b) Find 3 containers that you think have capacities greater than one litre.
      Use your referent to estimate the capacity of each container.
   c) Find the capacity of each container. Explain your strategy.

5. Suppose you estimate that you made about 1 L of lemonade.
   How can you check your estimate if you do not have a 1-L container?
   Show your work.

6. Suppose you make 4 L of apple juice.
   About how many glasses can you fill?
   Explain how you know.

7. Each person at a barbecue was served 1 glass of juice.
   Fifteen litres of juice were served.
   About how many people were at the barbecue?
   Explain how you got your answer.

8. The doctor told Jia she should drink
   8 glasses of water a day.
   About how many litres should Jia drink
   in one week? Explain.

9. Raphie wants to give each of his
   20 guests a glass of fruit punch.
   How many litres of punch should he make?
   How do you know?

Reflect

Use words, pictures, or numbers to explain what *capacity* means.

Exploring Capacity: The Millilitre

This is Chef Alexia's favourite soup recipe.
She serves it piping hot with sour cream.
Each item in the recipe is measured in litres
or **millilitres**.
We use the symbol **mL** for millilitres.

Blueberry Soup
Water   1 L
Blueberries   500 mL
Sugar   50 mL
Cornstarch   15 mL
Cinnamon   2 mL
Lemon Juice   5 mL

Explore

You will need some containers and water.

➤ Look at the measuring cups marked
  in millilitres.
  Choose a container.
  Use the measuring cups to
  estimate the capacity of
  the container in millilitres.
  Check your estimate.
  Record your work.
  Repeat this activity with
  other containers.

➤ Look at a 1-L container.
  Estimate how many
  millilitres it holds.
  Check your estimate.

LESSON FOCUS | Estimate and measure capacity in millilitres.

Show *and* Share

Compare your estimates with those of others in your group.
Explain your strategy for checking your estimates.
Tell what things are measured in millilitres.

Connect

The millilitre (mL) is a small unit of capacity.

This eyedropper has a capacity of 1 mL.
It holds about 10 drops.

A hollow centimetre cube
holds 1 mL of liquid.
I use this as a referent
to estimate capacity in millilitres.

This measuring jug has a capacity of 500 mL.
It holds 500 mL of water.

It takes 2 of those measuring
jugs to fill the one-litre mug.

But 500 mL + 500 mL = 1000 mL
so, I can say that 1 L = 1000 mL

Use measuring cups when they help.

1. a) Name a referent you could use for a capacity of one millilitre.
      Explain your choice.
   b) Find 3 containers whose capacities you would measure in millilitres.
      Use your referent to estimate the capacity of each container.
   c) Find the capacity of each container. Explain your strategy.

2. Choose the better estimate.
   a) 5 mL or 100 mL
   b) 15 mL or 250 mL
   c) 20 mL or 300 mL

  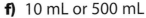

   d) 75 mL or 15 mL
   e) 250 mL or 900 mL
   f) 10 mL or 500 mL

3. Choose the better estimate for each. Explain.
   a) 4 mL or 4 L
   b) 10 mL or 1 L
   c) 100 mL or 2 L

   d) 100 mL or 1 L
   e) 6 mL or 6 L
   f) 50 mL or 7 L

4. Which capacity unit – millilitre or litre – is represented by
   each referent?
   a) an eyedropper
   b) a teaspoon
   c) a water bottle

5. Which unit would you use to measure each capacity:
   millilitre or litre? Explain your choice.

   a)

   b)

   c)

6. Which measure is closest to 1 L? How do you know?

   400 mL   889 mL   799 mL   850 mL

7. Copy and complete.

   a) 1 L = ☐ mL   b) 2 L = ☐ mL   c) 3 L = ☐ mL
   d) 4000 mL = ☐ L   e) 5000 mL = ☐ L   f) 6000 mL = ☐ L

8. James drank 400 mL of water in the morning and 500 mL in the afternoon.
   Did James drink more than or less than 1 L?
   How do you know?

9. Alexis drank one-half of 1 L of water.
   How many millilitres of water does Alexis have left?
   How do you know?

Math Link

Science

The body of a human adult has about 5 L of blood.
A mosquito's bite removes about $\frac{1}{200}$ of a millilitre
of blood!

Reflect

You have learned two units for measuring capacity.
How do you know which unit to use when you measure
the capacity of a container?

11

Relating Capacity and Volume

The capacity of this graduated cylinder is 500 mL.
If we pour in 400 mL of water,
we can say the volume of water is 400 mL.
That is, we can measure the volume of water
in millilitres.

Explore

You will need centimetre cubes, a 500-mL graduated cylinder, and water.

➤ Pour 400 mL of water into a
  500-mL graduated cylinder.
  Record the volume of water in a table.
  Place 10 cubes in the cylinder.
  Record the number of cubes added
  and the new volume, in millilitres.
  Calculate and record the change in volume.
➤ Add 10 more cubes.
  Record the new volume.
  Continue to add groups of 10 cubes.
  Each time, record the volume and the
  change in volume.
➤ Describe any patterns you see in the table.
➤ Look at your results.
  When you added 10 cubes, how did
  the volume in the cylinder change?
  How many millilitres equal 10 cm³?

Number of Cubes Added	Volume (mL)	Change in Volume (mL)
0	400	–
10		

Show and Share

Share the patterns you found with another group of students.
How could you use water in a graduated cylinder to find the volume of a stone?

The volume of an object can be measured in cubic centimetres or millilitres.

$1 \text{ cm}^3 = 1 \text{ mL}$

➤ Here is another way to find the volume of an object.
You can use **displacement** of water to find the volume of this triangular prism.

I can't use unit cubes to find the volume of this prism.

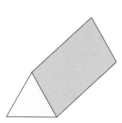

Mark the water level in a container.

Totally submerge the prism. Mark the new water level.

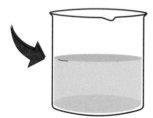

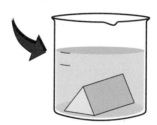

Remove the prism.
Fill the container to the upper mark.
Record the volume of water added, in millilitres.

Convert the volume in millilitres to cubic centimetres.

I added 15 mL of water, so the volume of the triangular prism is 15 cm³.

The volume of the triangular prism is 15 cm³.

You will need a container, water, and a graduated cylinder.

1. Collect 4 small solid objects.
   a) Estimate the volume of each object.
   b) Find each volume.
   c) Order the objects from least to greatest volume.

2. Use modelling clay to build a solid.
   Try to make a solid with a volume of 250 cm³.
   a) Find the volume of your solid.
   b) How close is the volume to 250 cm³?

3. Choose two different solids from the classroom.
   Look for solids with about the same volume.
   a) Explain why you chose the solids you did.
   b) Find the volume of each solid in cubic centimetres.

4. a) What is the volume of 100 centimetre cubes?
   b) Put 100 centimetre cubes into an empty graduated cylinder.
      Read the number of millilitres from the scale.
   c) Compare your answers to parts a and b.
      Explain any differences.

5. You will need 50 counters.
   a) Predict the volume of 50 counters in cubic centimetres.
   b) Find the volume of 50 counters.
   c) How does your estimate compare to the volume?

6. Describe how you could find each measure:
   a) the volume of one dime in cubic centimetres
   b) the volume of a toy car in millilitres

One dime is very small. Think how you could measure more than one dime.

Reflect

Explain how you can use displacement of water to measure the volume of an object.

LESSON

1

1. Use a referent. Estimate the length, width, and height of your desk or table.
   Record each estimate in millimetres, centimetres, and metres.

2. Use a ruler. Draw each item.
   a) a stick 14 cm long   **b)** a pin 15 mm long   **c)** a pencil 16.2 cm long

3. Copy and complete.
   a) 3 m = ☐ mm   **b)** 4000 mm = ☐ m   **c)** 2 m = ☐ mm
   d) 5000 mm = ☐ m   **e)** 10 m = ☐ mm   **f)** 7000 mm = ☐ m

3
4

4. Use 1-cm grid paper.
   a) Draw 3 different rectangles with perimeter 20 cm.
   b) Draw 3 different rectangles with area 20 cm².

5. Use 1-cm grid paper.
   Draw a rectangle with area 36 cm² and perimeter 30 cm.

6. The area of a rectangular garden is 48 m².
   a) What is the greatest perimeter the garden could have?
   b) What shape would the garden with the least perimeter have? Explain.
   c) Why might a person choose to build the garden with the least perimeter?

5

7. Find a small container in the classroom.
   Choose some identical items that will fill the container.
   a) Estimate how many items will fill the container.
   b) Measure the volume of the container with the items you chose.

6

8. Use centimetre cubes to make each object below.
   Find the volume of each object.
   Which object has the greatest volume?

   a)
   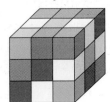

   b)
   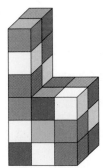

   c)
   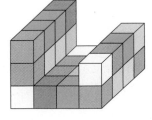

9. Make each rectangular prism with centimetre cubes.
   Find the volume of each prism.

   a)    **b)**    **c)**

7

10. Use centimetre cubes.
    Build a rectangular prism with each volume.
    Record the dimensions of each prism in a table.
    a) 12 cm³   **b)** 24 cm³   **c)** 11 cm³

11. Use centimetre cubes.
    Build all the possible rectangular prisms with volume 18 cm³.
    Record the dimensions of each prism in a table.

8

12. Describe a referent for one cubic metre.
    Name 2 objects that might be
    measured in cubic metres.
    Explain how you could use your referent to estimate each volume.

9 10

13. Choose the better estimate for each capacity.
    a) 15 mL or 500 mL   **b)** 10 L or 1000 mL

    c) 400 mL or 2 L   **d)** 2000 mL or 200 L

14. Order these capacities from greatest to least:
    2 L   1500 mL   4 L   1980 mL

11

15. How could you find the volume of a lacrosse ball?
    Use pictures and words to explain.

UNIT

4   Learning Goals

- ✔ measure length in millimetres
- ✔ select referents for units of measure
- ✔ relate units of measure
- ✔ draw different rectangles for a given perimeter or area
- ✔ estimate and measure volume
- ✔ estimate and measure capacity

Check List

Your work should show

☑ a map of the petting zoo on grid paper, with each section outlined and labelled

☑ the dimensions, perimeter, and area of each section and how you found them

☑ a different rectangle for each region

☑ that the size of a region reflects the size of the animal

NO *HORSING* AROUND - *PONY* UP TO THAT PAPER N' *GIDDY-UP!*

PUT SOME *FUEL* IN THAT *MULE!*

GET SOME *OINK* IN THAT *PEN* N' LET'S GO!

DON'T *MONKEY* AROUND!

HOP TO IT!

Reflect on Your Learning

You have learned about units of measure for dimensions, perimeter, area, volume, and capacity.
Write a sentence to describe where you could use each unit outside the classroom.

Rep-Tiles

You will need Pattern Blocks.

Part 1

A **rep-tile** is a polygon that can be copied and arranged to form a larger polygon with the same shape.

These are rep-tiles: These are not rep-tiles:

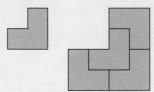

➤ Which Pattern Blocks are rep-tiles?
  How did you find out?

Part 2

Choose a block that is a rep-tile.
Do not use orange or green blocks.
Build an increasing pattern.
Record the pattern.
➤ Choose one Pattern Block that is a rep-tile.
  This is Frame 1.
➤ Now take several of the same type of block.
  Arrange the blocks to form a polygon with
  the same shape.
  This is Frame 2.

➤ Continue to arrange blocks to make
larger polygons with the same shape.
The next largest polygon is Frame 3.

➤ Suppose the side length of the green Pattern Block is 1 unit.
Find the perimeter of each polygon.

➤ Suppose the area of the green Pattern Block is 1 square unit.
Find the area of each polygon.
Copy and complete the table.

Frame	Number of Blocks	Perimeter	Area
1	1		
2			

Part 3

➤ What patterns can you find in the table?

➤ How many blocks would you need to build Frame 7?
How do you know?

➤ Predict the area and the perimeter of the polygon in Frame 9.
How did you make your prediction?

Display Your Work

Record your work.
Describe the patterns you found.

Take It Further

Draw a large polygon you think
is a rep-tile.
Trace several copies.
Cut them out.
Try to arrange the copies
to make a larger polygon with
the same shape.
If your polygon is a rep-tile,
explain why it works.
If it is not, describe how you
could change it to make it work.

Fractions and

In the Garden

Brian and Samantha are planning a garden.
What fraction of the garden
will they plant with flowers?
Vegetables?

Learning Goals

- create sets of equivalent fractions
- compare fractions with like and unlike denominators
- describe and represent decimals to thousandths
- relate decimals to fractions
- compare and order decimals to thousandths
- add and subtract decimals to thousandths

Flower seeds
10 packs for $1.50
Zucchini seeds
$1.09 per pack
Tomato plants
$0.85 each
Pumpkin seeds
$0.99 per package

Roses Zucchini Pumpkin

Decimals

- What is the total cost of 1 pack of zucchini seeds and 1 pack of pumpkin seeds?
- Samantha paid for these seeds with a $5 bill. About how much change would she get?
- About how much will 10 packs of flower seeds and 1 pack of zucchini seeds cost? How could you find the exact amount?

Equivalent Fractions

1

$\frac{6}{12}$ of the stickers are left.

$\frac{1}{2}$ of the stickers are left.

Who is correct?

 **Explore** •

You will need red and yellow Colour Tiles or congruent squares, and 2-cm grid paper.

➤ Outline this rectangle on 2-cm grid paper.
   Place the tiles on the rectangle so that:
   • $\frac{1}{6}$ of the rectangle is red.
   • The rest of the rectangle is yellow.
   Record your work on the rectangle.

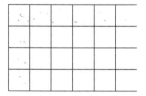

➤ How many ways can you describe the fraction
   of the rectangle that is red? Yellow?
   Record each way.

➤ Find a way to write a fraction that names the same
   amount as each fraction below.
   Write to explain what you did.
   $\frac{1}{3}$ $\frac{8}{10}$ $\frac{5}{8}$ $\frac{6}{12}$

Show *and* Share

Share your work with another pair of students.
Compare the fractions you wrote for each colour.
How did you know which fractions to write?
Describe any patterns you see in the fractions for each colour.

This rectangle was made with Colour Tiles.

What fraction of the rectangle is green?
How many different fractions can you write
to describe the green part?

➤ There are 12 tiles.
6 tiles are green.
$\frac{6}{12}$ of the rectangle is green.

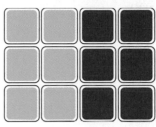

➤ There are 6 groups of 2 tiles.
3 groups are green.
$\frac{3}{6}$ of the rectangle is green.

➤ There are 4 groups of 3 tiles.
2 groups are green.
$\frac{2}{4}$ of the rectangle is green.

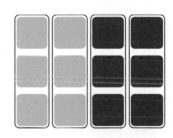

➤ There are 2 groups of 6 tiles.
1 group is green.
$\frac{1}{2}$ of the rectangle is green.

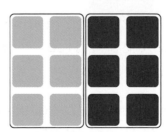

$\frac{1}{2}$, $\frac{2}{4}$, $\frac{3}{6}$, and $\frac{6}{12}$ name the same amount.

They are **equivalent fractions**.

➤ There are patterns in the equivalent fractions.

The numerators are multiples of the least numerator, 1.

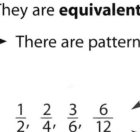

$\frac{1}{2}, \quad \frac{2}{4}, \quad \frac{3}{6}, \quad \frac{6}{12}$

The denominators are multiples of the least denominator, 2.

➤ We can use a set model to find equivalent fractions.

Look at the fraction of each set that is red.

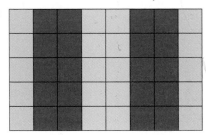

When you multiply or divide the numerator and the denominator of a fraction by the same number, you do not change the value of the fraction.

So, $\frac{3}{4}$, $\frac{6}{8}$, and $\frac{30}{40}$ are equivalent fractions.

The number you multiply or divide by cannot be 0.

Practice

Use Colour Tiles or grid paper when they help.

1. What fraction of each rectangle is blue? Red? Green?
   For each colour, write as many different fractions as you can.

   a)
   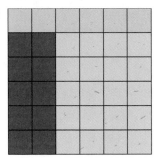

   b)

2. Find as many equivalent fractions as you can for each picture.
   What patterns do you see?

   a)
   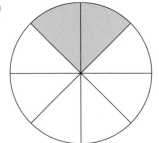

   b)

   c)
   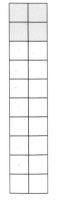

3. Use the patterns you found in question 2.
   Write a rule you can use to find equivalent fractions.
   How can you show your rule is correct?

4. Use a 30-cm ruler.
   How many equivalent fractions can you find for $\frac{20}{30}$?
   Explain how you found the fractions.

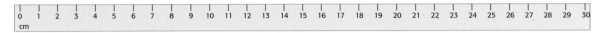

5. Use the strips below. Write 2 fractions that are equivalent to $\frac{2}{5}$.
   Explain how you did it.

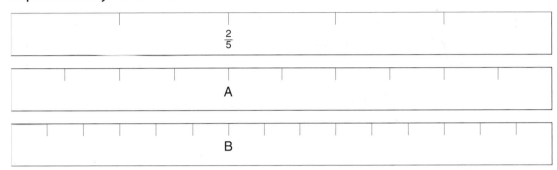

$\frac{2}{5}$

A

B

6. Draw a picture to show each pair of equivalent fractions.
   a) $\frac{1}{4}, \frac{3}{12}$ b) $\frac{2}{3}, \frac{8}{12}$ c) $\frac{3}{5}, \frac{12}{20}$ d) $\frac{18}{24}, \frac{3}{4}$

7. Use tiles or counters to write 3 equivalent fractions for each fraction.
   a) $\frac{1}{2}$ b) $\frac{5}{6}$ c) $\frac{20}{50}$ d) $\frac{4}{5}$ e) $\frac{20}{30}$ f) $\frac{25}{35}$

8. Use counters or draw a picture to find pairs of fractions that are equivalent.
   a) $\frac{1}{6}$ and $\frac{6}{36}$ b) $\frac{12}{15}$ and $\frac{3}{5}$ c) $\frac{6}{16}$ and $\frac{3}{4}$ d) $\frac{8}{14}$ and $\frac{4}{7}$

9. Roxanne cut a pizza into 8 equal slices. She ate 2 slices.
   a) Write 2 equivalent fractions to describe how much pizza Roxanne ate.
   b) Write 2 equivalent fractions to describe how much pizza was left.
   Show your work.

10. For each fraction, identify the equivalent fractions.
    Explain how you know the fractions are equivalent.
    a) $\frac{3}{4}$: $\frac{8}{12}, \frac{6}{8}, \frac{6}{9}, \frac{9}{12}$ b) $\frac{4}{10}$: $\frac{6}{15}, \frac{10}{25}, \frac{2}{5}, \frac{8}{15}$

Reflect

Use numbers, pictures, or words to explain
what it means when fractions are equivalent.

Comparing and Ordering Fractions

I have three-quarters of a dollar.

I have three-fifths of a dollar.

Who has more money?
How do you know?

Explore

Use any of these materials:
counters, tiles, fraction circles, ruler, number line, grid paper

Compare each pair of fractions.
Which fraction in each pair is greater?
How do you know?
Record your work.

$\frac{1}{2}$ and $\frac{1}{3}$ $\frac{6}{12}$ and $\frac{3}{4}$

$\frac{5}{6}$ and $\frac{19}{24}$ $\frac{3}{8}$ and $\frac{2}{8}$

$\frac{6}{8}$ and $\frac{3}{4}$ $\frac{2}{6}$ and $\frac{2}{3}$

Show and Share

Show your work to another pair of students.
Talk about why you chose a particular material to compare fractions.
Try to find a way to compare $\frac{5}{8}$ and $\frac{3}{4}$ without using any materials.

Connect

Here are four strategies to compare and order fractions.

➤ To order $\frac{3}{4}$, $\frac{3}{5}$, and $\frac{5}{8}$ from least to greatest:
Fold or measure, then colour, equal strips of paper; one strip for each fraction.

The least fraction is the shortest coloured strip.
The order from least to greatest is: $\frac{3}{5}$, $\frac{5}{8}$, $\frac{3}{4}$

➤ To compare $\frac{3}{4}$ and $\frac{5}{8}$:
Use fraction circles.

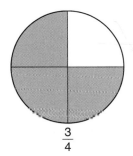   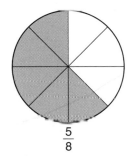

$\frac{3}{4}$ cover more of the circle than $\frac{5}{8}$ do.
So, $\frac{3}{4} > \frac{5}{8}$

➤ To order $\frac{1}{2}$, $\frac{3}{4}$, $\frac{1}{4}$, and $\frac{5}{8}$ from least to greatest:
Draw a number line from 0 to 1.
Divide the number line to show halves,
fourths, and eighths.
Mark and label $\frac{1}{2}$, $\frac{3}{4}$, $\frac{1}{4}$, and $\frac{5}{8}$.

The fractions increase from left to right.

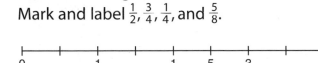

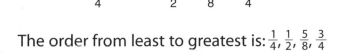

The order from least to greatest is: $\frac{1}{4}$, $\frac{1}{2}$, $\frac{5}{8}$, $\frac{3}{4}$

➤ To compare $\frac{2}{3}$ and $\frac{3}{5}$:

List equivalent fractions until the numerators
or the denominators are the same.

$\frac{2}{3} = \frac{4}{6} = \frac{6}{9} = \frac{8}{12} = \frac{10}{15} = \frac{12}{18} \cdots$

$\frac{3}{5} = \frac{6}{10} = \frac{9}{15} = \frac{12}{20} = \frac{15}{25} \cdots$

When the numerators are the same, the greater fraction has the lesser denominator.

Since $\frac{6}{9} > \frac{6}{10}$, then $\frac{2}{3} > \frac{3}{5}$

Or, since $\frac{10}{15} > \frac{9}{15}$, then $\frac{2}{3} > \frac{3}{5}$

When the denominators are the same, the greater fraction has the greater numerator.

Practice

1. Compare the fractions in each pair.
   a) $\frac{3}{5}$ and $\frac{2}{5}$ b) $\frac{5}{8}$ and $\frac{7}{8}$ c) $\frac{4}{10}$ and $\frac{7}{10}$
   Use counters to show how you know you are correct.

2. Compare the fractions in each pair. Which strategies did you use?
   a) $\frac{4}{9}$ and $\frac{3}{6}$ b) $\frac{2}{3}$ and $\frac{4}{6}$ c) $\frac{8}{9}$ and $\frac{2}{3}$

3. Use three equal strips of paper.
   Show halves on one strip.
   Show tenths on another strip.
   Show fifths on the third strip.
   Use the strips to order these
   fractions from least to greatest:
   $\frac{1}{2}, \frac{7}{10}, \frac{4}{5}$

4. Use three equal strips of paper.
   Mark each strip with
   appropriate fractions.
   Use the strips to order these fractions from least to greatest:
   $\frac{5}{6}, \frac{2}{3}, \frac{7}{12}$

5. Draw a number line like the one below.

   0 ────────────────────────────────── 1

   Divide the number line to show twelfths, sixths, and quarters.
   Use the number line to order these fractions from least to greatest:
   $\frac{11}{12}, \frac{4}{6}, \frac{3}{4}, \frac{7}{12}, \frac{5}{6}$

6. Use a number line to order these fractions from greatest to least:
$\frac{3}{5}$ $\frac{8}{10}$ $\frac{1}{2}$ $\frac{6}{10}$ $\frac{2}{5}$
Explain the strategy you used.

7. Use equivalent fractions to compare the fractions in each pair.
a) $\frac{4}{5}$ and $\frac{6}{10}$ **b)** $\frac{1}{4}$ and $\frac{2}{6}$ **c)** $\frac{3}{5}$ and $\frac{9}{15}$

8. Use grid paper.
Draw pictures to represent 3 fractions that are greater than $\frac{3}{5}$.
Each fraction should have a different denominator.
How do you know that each fraction is greater than $\frac{3}{5}$?

9. A quilt has 20 patches.
One-quarter of the patches are yellow,
$\frac{3}{5}$ are green, and the rest are red.
What colour are the greatest number
of patches?
The least number of patches?
Show how you know.

10. Jessica and Ramon each has the same length of ribbon.
Jessica cut her ribbon into eighths.
Ramon cut his ribbon into twelfths.
Jessica sold 6 pieces and Ramon sold 8.
Who sold the greater length of ribbon?
How did you find out?

11. Which is greater, $\frac{2}{3}$ or $\frac{2}{5}$?
How do you know?

12. Compare the fractions in each pair.
Copy each statement. Write $>$, $<$, or $=$.
How did you decide which symbol to choose?
a) $\frac{4}{5} \square \frac{4}{10}$ **b)** $\frac{3}{8} \square \frac{2}{8}$ **c)** $\frac{2}{3} \square \frac{4}{6}$ **d)** $\frac{1}{4} \square \frac{1}{3}$

Reflect

You have learned 4 strategies for comparing fractions.
Which strategy do you find easiest? Explain why.

Strategies Toolkit

Explore

You will need Pattern Blocks.
Make a quadrilateral that
is $\frac{3}{4}$ red and $\frac{1}{4}$ blue.
Can you do this in more
than one way? Explain.

Show *and* Share

Describe the strategy you
used to solve this problem.

Connect

Use Pattern Blocks.
Make the smallest triangle you can that is
$\frac{3}{16}$ green, $\frac{3}{16}$ red, $\frac{1}{4}$ blue, and $\frac{3}{8}$ yellow.

How many blocks of each colour will you need?

Strategies

- **Make a table.**
- **Use a model.**
- **Draw a diagram.**
- **Solve a simpler problem.**
- **Work backward.**
- **Guess and test.**
- **Make an organized list.**
- **Use a pattern.**

What do you know?

- Use Pattern Blocks to build a triangle.
- $\frac{3}{16}$ of the triangle is green.
- $\frac{3}{16}$ of the triangle is red.
- $\frac{1}{4}$ of the triangle is blue.
- $\frac{3}{8}$ of the triangle is yellow.

Think of a strategy to help you solve the problem.

- You can **use a model**.

Use Pattern Blocks to build the triangle.
$\frac{3}{16}$ of the triangle is to be green.
How many green blocks could you use?
How many blocks of each colour do you need
to build the triangle?

Check your work.
Is $\frac{3}{16}$ of the triangle green?
Is $\frac{3}{16}$ of the triangle red?
Is $\frac{1}{4}$ of the triangle blue?
Is $\frac{3}{8}$ of the triangle yellow?

Practice

Choose one of the

Strategies

1. Brenna cuts wood for a fire. She can cut a log into thirds in 10 min.
   How long would it take Brenna to cut a similar log into sixths?

2. One-fourth of a 10-m by 10-m rectangular garden is planted with corn.
   Two-tenths of the garden is planted with squash.
   Thirty-five hundredths of the garden is planted with beans.
   The rest is planted with flowers.
   What fraction of the garden is planted with flowers?

3. A snail is trying to reach a leaf 8 m away.
   The snail crawls 4 m on the first day.
   Each day after that, it crawls one-half as far as the previous day.
   After 4 days, will the snail reach the leaf? How do you know?

Reflect

How can using a model help you to solve
problems with fractions?
Use words, pictures, or numbers to explain.

Relating Fractions to Decimals

What fraction of the garden is planted with each vegetable? How many different ways can you write each fraction?

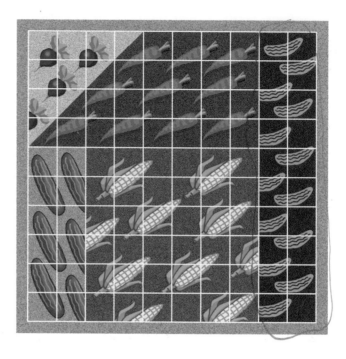

Explore

You will need Base Ten Blocks and grid paper.

Use rods and unit cubes to design a vegetable garden.
Use a flat to represent the whole garden.
Each vegetable is in a separate region of the garden.
The garden must have:
- more carrots than corn
- more onions than potatoes
- all of the land planted with one of these vegetables

Record your vegetable garden design on grid paper.

➤ Write the fraction of your garden planted with each vegetable in as many ways as you can.

➤ How many ways can you use a decimal to describe the fraction of the garden that is planted with each kind of vegetable? Record each way.

Show *and* Share

Share your results with another pair of students.
How did you find the fractions and decimals?
Which fractions and decimals name the same amount?
How do you know?

Connect

➤ This is Jake and Willa's design of a flower garden.
$\frac{25}{100}$, or $\frac{1}{4}$ of the garden is planted with roses.
$\frac{25}{100}$, or $\frac{1}{4}$ of the garden is planted with tulips.
$\frac{30}{100}$, or $\frac{3}{10}$ of the garden is planted with lilies.
$\frac{20}{100}$, or $\frac{2}{10}$ of the garden is planted with daisies.

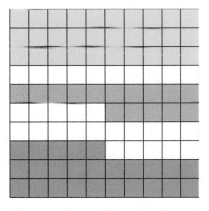

➤ You can write fractions with denominators of 10 and 100 as decimals.
$\frac{3}{10}$ is 3 tenths, or 0.3.
$\frac{15}{100}$ is 15 hundredths, or 0.15.
$\frac{25}{100}$ is 25 hundredths, or 0.25.

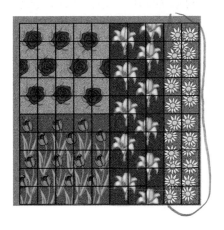

➤ You can use money to write some fractions as decimals.

$\frac{4}{10}$ of a dollar is $0.40.

$\frac{3}{4}$ of a dollar is $0.75.

➤ For some fractions, we can write an equivalent fraction with a denominator of 10 or 100. We can then write the fraction as a decimal.

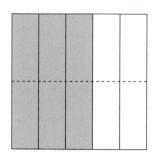

$$\overset{\times 2}{\underset{\times 2}{\frac{3}{5} = \frac{6}{10}}}$$

$\frac{3}{5}$ is equivalent to $\frac{6}{10}$.

$\frac{6}{10}$ is 6 tenths, or 0.6.

So, $\frac{3}{5}$ and 0.6 are equivalent.

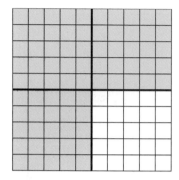

$$\overset{\times 25}{\underset{\times 25}{\frac{3}{4} = \frac{75}{100}}}$$

$\frac{3}{4}$ is equivalent to $\frac{75}{100}$.

$\frac{75}{100}$ is 75 hundredths, or 0.75.

So, $\frac{3}{4}$ and 0.75 are equivalent.

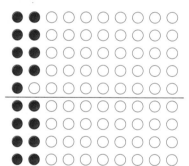

$$\overset{\times 2}{\underset{\times 2}{\frac{9}{50} = \frac{18}{100}}}$$

$\frac{9}{50}$ is equivalent to $\frac{18}{100}$.

$\frac{18}{100}$ is 18 hundredths, or 0.18.

So, $\frac{9}{50}$ and 0.18 are equivalent.

Practice

1. Write a fraction and a decimal to describe:
   • the shaded part of each picture
   • the white part of each picture

   a)

   b)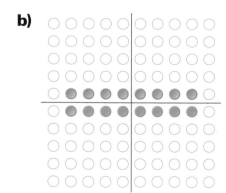

2. Use Base Ten Blocks to show each decimal.
   Sketch the blocks you used.
   a) 0.3   **b)** 0.07   **c)** 0.8   **d)** 0.34

3. Write each decimal in question 2 as a fraction.

4. Shade a hundredths grid to show each decimal.
   Then write an equivalent decimal.
   a) 0.8   **b)** 0.40   **c)** 0.90   **d)** 0.2

5. Write each fraction as a decimal.
   a) $\frac{37}{100}$ **b)** $\frac{5}{10}$ **c)** $\frac{9}{100}$ **d)** $\frac{30}{100}$

6. Write each amount of money as a fraction of a dollar,
   then as a decimal.
   a) 20¢   **b)** 5¢   **c)** 25¢   **d)** 61¢   **e)** 95¢

7. Vijay has $\frac{1}{20}$ of a dollar in his pocket.
   What coins might he have?

8. Use Base Ten Blocks and a grid to represent each fraction.
   Then write each fraction as a decimal.
   a) $\frac{1}{2}$ **b)** $\frac{7}{25}$ **c)** $\frac{9}{10}$ **d)** $\frac{3}{5}$

9. Represent each fraction on a hundredths grid.
   Then write each fraction as a decimal.
   a) $\frac{1}{4}$ **b)** $\frac{4}{5}$ **c)** $\frac{3}{50}$ **d)** $\frac{11}{20}$

10. Use counters to represent each fraction.
    Then write each fraction as a decimal.
    a) $\frac{4}{25}$ **b)** $\frac{3}{4}$ **c)** $\frac{2}{5}$ **d)** $\frac{7}{20}$

11. Do $\frac{3}{5}$ and 0.35 name the same amount?
    Use pictures and words to explain how you know.

Reflect

Which fractions can you write easily as decimals? Why?
Use examples in your explanation.

Fraction and Decimal Benchmarks

Explore

Your teacher will give you a large copy of these number lines.

➤ The number lines are incomplete.
Label the lines with the missing fractions.

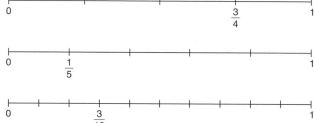

➤ Which fraction in each pair is greater?
How do you know?

$\frac{7}{10}$ or $\frac{3}{4}$ $\frac{5}{10}$ or $\frac{2}{5}$

$\frac{1}{2}$ or $\frac{6}{10}$ $\frac{2}{10}$ or $\frac{1}{4}$

➤ Suppose the number lines were labelled with decimals rather than fractions.
Which decimal would replace each of these numbers?

0      $\frac{9}{10}$ $\frac{3}{5}$ $\frac{1}{2}$ 1 $\frac{1}{4}$

Show *and* Share

Share your work with another pair of students.
How did you know on which number line to place each fraction?
How did you decide which fraction was greater?
How did you change each number to a decimal?

Connect

You can use benchmarks to compare and order decimals.
We can rename the benchmarks 0, $\frac{1}{2}$, and 1 as decimals.

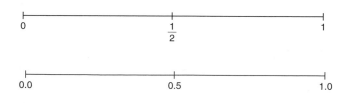

$\frac{1}{2} = \frac{5}{10}$

$\frac{5}{10} = 0.5$

➤ Which decimal is greater, 0.25 or 0.7?

0.25 is between 0.0 and 0.50.
0.7 is between 0.5 and 1.0.

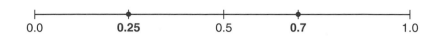

0.5 = 0.50

So, 0.7 > 0.25

➤ Order 0.7, 0.9, and 0.32 from least to greatest.

Use equivalent decimals.
0.0 = 0.00   0.5 = 0.50   0.7 = 0.70   0.9 = 0.90   1.0 = 1.00

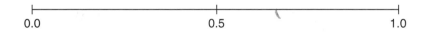

0.32 is greater than 0.00 and less than 0.50.
Both 0.70 and 0.90 are greater than 0.50 and less than 1.00,
but 0.70 < 0.90.

From least to greatest: 0.32, 0.7, 0.9

Practice

Use copies of this number line to help you order decimals in questions 1 to 3.

0.0   0.5   1.0

1. Order the decimals in each set from least to greatest.
   a) 0.7, 0.3, 0.6   b) 0.1, 0.8, 0.4   c) 0.75, 0.30, 0.50   d) 0.80, 0.20, 0.10

2. Use a number line and decimal benchmarks to compare the numbers
   in each pair.
   a) $\frac{7}{10}$ and 0.9   b) $\frac{4}{5}$ and 0.6   c) $\frac{1}{4}$ and 0.2

3. Order 0.70, 0.80, and 0.25 from greatest to least.
   Show your work.

4. Write a decimal for each picture.
Which decimal benchmark is each decimal closest to?
Order the three decimals from least to greatest.

a)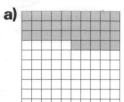

b)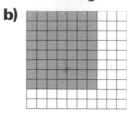

c)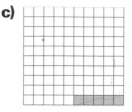

5. Order the decimals in each set from least to greatest.
Think about equivalent decimals when you need to.

a) 0.5, 0.60, 0.75   **b)** 0.39, 0.7, 0.1   **c)** 0.02, 0.4, 0.20   **d)** 0.10, 0.6, 0.15

6. Copy and complete. Use <, >, or =.

a) 0.20 ☐ 0.2   **b)** 0.7 ☐ 0.74   **c)** 0.35 ☐ 0.1

7. Use the data in the table.
a) Which frog made the longest jump?
b) Which frog made the shortest jump?
c) Which frog's jump was longer than Skeeter's but shorter than Squiggy's?

Frog Jumping Contest

Frog	Distance (m)
Charger	0.76
Skeeter	0.89
Speedy	0.90
Squiggy	0.98
Bubbles	0.91

8. a) Copy and complete the table.
b) Order the decimals in the table from least to greatest.

Decimal	Lower Benchmark	Upper Benchmark	Nearest Benchmark
0.21			
0.09			
0.99			
0.80			

Reflect

Describe how using benchmarks can help you to compare and order decimals.

Exploring Thousandths

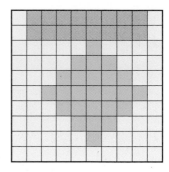

This design contains 100 small square tiles.
What fraction of the design does each colour represent?

Explore

You will need Base Ten Blocks and coloured pencils.
Your teacher will give you several copies of the grid below.

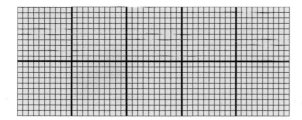

Each grid has 1000 congruent squares.

➤ Use Base Ten Blocks to model
  each number.
  Each time, use the fewest
  blocks possible.

$\frac{700}{1000}$ $\frac{3}{10}$ $\frac{41}{1000}$ $\frac{70}{100}$

$\frac{732}{1000}$ $\frac{62}{1000}$ $\frac{300}{1000}$

➤ Colour grids to show each number.
  Write each number in words.

Show *and* Share

Share your work with another pair of students.
How did you decide what each type of Base Ten Block represents? Explain.
For which pairs of numbers did you use the same blocks? Why?

➤ We can show numbers with **thousandths** in different ways.

Base Ten Blocks  Place-value chart

Ones	Tenths	Hundredths	Thousandths
0	3	4	5

Notation

$\frac{345}{1000} = 0.345$

three hundred forty-five thousandths

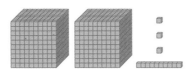

Ones	Tenths	Hundredths	Thousandths
2	0	1	3

2.013

two and thirteen thousandths

Ones	Tenths	Hundredths	Thousandths
0	0	0	8

$\frac{8}{1000} = 0.008$

eight thousandths

➤ We can write some fractions with denominator 1000.

$\overset{\times 5}{\overset{\times 100}{\frac{1}{2} = \frac{5}{10} = \frac{500}{1000}}}$
$\times 5 \quad \times 100$

$\overset{\times 2}{\overset{\times 100}{\frac{2}{5} = \frac{4}{10} = \frac{400}{1000}}}$
$\times 2 \quad \times 100$

$\frac{1}{2}$ is equivalent to $\frac{5}{10}$.

$\frac{5}{10}$ is equivalent to $\frac{500}{1000}$.

$\frac{500}{1000}$ is 0.500,
so $\frac{1}{2}$ is equivalent to 0.500.

$\frac{2}{5}$ is equivalent to $\frac{4}{10}$.

$\frac{4}{10}$ is equivalent to $\frac{400}{1000}$.

$\frac{400}{1000}$ is 0.400,
so, $\frac{2}{5}$ is equivalent to 0.400.

➤ We can write a decimal in expanded form to show the value of each digit.
3.248 = 3 ones + 2 tenths + 4 hundredths + 8 thousandths
= 3 + 0.2 + 0.04 + 0.008

➤ This thousandths grid represents 1 whole.
  It contains 1000 congruent squares.

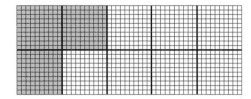

Each small square is one-thousandth of the grid.

300 small squares are $\frac{300}{1000}$, or 0.300.

30 rows of 10 small squares are $\frac{30}{100}$, or 0.30.

3 large squares are $\frac{3}{10}$, or 0.3.

300 small squares = 30 rows of 10 small squares = 3 large squares

So, 0.300 = 0.30 = 0.3

0.300, 0.30, and 0.3 name the same amount.

They are **equivalent decimals**.

Practice

You may use Base Ten Blocks or thousandths grids to model numbers.

1. Write a decimal for each picture.

   a) 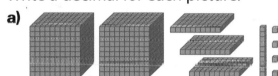   b)

   c) 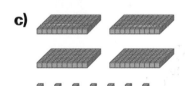   d)

2. Colour a thousandths grid to show each decimal.
   Then write the decimal as a fraction.
   a) 0.358   **b)** 0.209   **c)** 0.001   **d)** 0.048

3. Use the data in the table.
   Write the number that has:
   a) a 5 in the tenths place
   b) a 2 in the thousandths place
   c) a 6 in the hundredths place
   d) a 6 in the ones place
   e) a 5 in the thousandths place
   f) a 0 in the tenths place

Creature	Length (cm)
Praying Mantis	7.620
Garden Spider	2.412
Dust Mite	0.015
Walking Stick Insect	7.564
Desert Tarantula	6.943

4. Shade a thousandths grid to show each decimal.
Then write an equivalent decimal.
 a) 0.070 **b)** 0.300 **c)** 0.010 **d)** 0.900

5. Write two equivalent decimals for each decimal.
Explain how you knew which decimals to write.
 a) 0.9 **b)** 0.7 **c)** 0.1 **d)** 0.3

6. Write an equivalent decimal for each decimal.
 a) 0.31 **b)** 0.29 **c)** 0.87 **d)** 0.55
What is the same about all the decimals you wrote?

7. Record each number in expanded form.
 a) 573 thousandths **b)** 86.093 **c)** 6 and 240 thousandths
 d) 292.73 **e)** 0.124 **f)** 0.107

8. Write each fraction as a decimal.
 a) $\frac{341}{1000}$ **b)** $\frac{16}{1000}$ **c)** $\frac{3}{1000}$ **d)** $\frac{24}{1000}$

9. Write each fraction in question 8 in words.

10. Describe the value of each digit in each decimal.
 a) 2.369 **b)** 0.042 **c)** 1.23

11. Use each of the digits 0, 2, 5, and 8 once.
Make a number that is less than 5 but greater than 1.
Find as many numbers as you can.
Explain the strategies you used.

At this speed, the cockroach travels 5.407 km in one hour.

12. The fastest-moving insect on land is a cockroach.
It has a record speed of 5.407 km/h.
Write this number as many ways as you can.

13. Earth revolves around the sun about every three hundred
sixty-five and two hundred fifty-six thousandths days.
Write this number as a decimal.

Reflect

How are 0.5, 0.50, and 0.500 alike?
How are they different?

Comparing and Ordering Decimals

Mount Logan in the Yukon Territory is the highest mountain in Canada.
It is 5.959 km high!

Explore

This table shows the heights
of the highest mountains
in some Canadian provinces
and a territory.

Use any materials or strategies
you wish.
Order the heights from least
to greatest.

Province/Territory	Mountain	Height (km)
Alberta	Columbia	3.747
British Columbia	Fairweather	4.663
Manitoba	Baldy	0.832
New Brunswick	Carleton	0.817
Newfoundland and Labrador	Caubvick	1.652
Nunavut	Barbeau Peak	2.616

Show and Share

Share your results with another pair of students.
Explain the strategies you used to order the heights.
An unnamed peak in the Northwest Territories is 2.773 km high.
Where does this height fit in your ordered list?
Explain why it fits there.

Many organisms are too small to be seen with the naked eye. Scientists use a microscope to study them.
Here are the lengths of 4 micro-organisms.

Micro-organism	Length (mm)
Tardigrade	0.15
Euglena	0.139
Vorticella	0.11
Paramecium	0.125

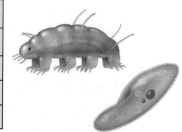

Here are three ways to order the lengths from greatest to least.

➤ Use place value. Write each decimal in a place-value chart.

	Ones	Tenths	Hundredths	Thousandths
Tardigrade	0	1	5	0
Euglena	0	1	3	9
Vorticella	0	1	1	0
Paramecium	0	1	2	5

Compare the ones. All four numbers have 0 ones.
Compare the tenths. All four numbers have 1 tenth.
Compare the hundredths. 5 hundredths is the greatest number of hundredths, then 3 hundredths, 2 hundredths, and 1 hundredth.

The numbers in order from greatest to least are: 0.15, 0.139, 0.125, 0.11

➤ Use equivalent decimals.
Write each decimal in thousandths.
0.15 is 0.150, or 150 thousandths.
0.139 is 139 thousandths.
0.11 is 0.110, or 110 thousandths.
0.125 is 125 thousandths.

Compare the numbers of thousandths.
From greatest to least: 0.150, 0.139, 0.125, 0.110

➤ Use a number line.
0.15, 0.139, 0.11, and 0.125 are between 0.1 and 0.2.
Use equivalent decimals.
So, label the endpoints of the number line 0.10 and 0.20.
Divide the interval between 0.10 and 0.20 to show hundredths.

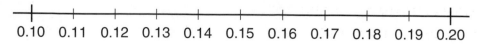

0.10 0.11 0.12 0.13 0.14 0.15 0.16 0.17 0.18 0.19 0.20

Divide the hundredths to show thousandths.
Mark a dot for each number.

0.11   0.125   0.139   0.15

0.10   0.11   0.12   0.13   0.14   0.15   0.16   0.17   0.18   0.19   0.20

The farther to the right on the number line, the greater a number is.
So, reading the numbers from right to left gives the lengths
from greatest to least.

The lengths from greatest to least are: 0.15 mm, 0.139 mm, 0.125 mm, 0.11 mm

Practice

1. Use place value.
   Order the decimals in each set from least to greatest.
   a) 0.8, 0.3, 0.7   **b)** 0.5, 0.2, 0.1   **c)** 0.4, 0.7, 0.6
   d) 0.12, 0.99, 0.81   **e)** 0.73, 0.19, 0.42   **f)** 0.88, 0.98, 0.89
   g) 0.529, 0.592, 0.925   **h)** 0.125, 0.118, 0.181   **i)** 0.354, 0.500, 0.345

2. Copy and complete. Use >, <, or =.
   a) 0.2 ☐ 0.4   **b)** 0.06 ☐ 0.01   **c)** 0.694 ☐ 0.690
   d) 0.9 ☐ 0.90   **e)** 0.745 ☐ 0.75   **f)** 0.624 ☐ 0.8

3. Use equivalent decimals.
   Order the decimals in each set from least to greatest.
   a) 0.576, 0.02, 0.009, 0.1, 0.002   **b)** 0.06, 0.278, 0.003, 0.15, 0.7

4. Order the numbers from least to greatest.
   a) 24.3, 24.7, 24.1   **b)** 0.59, 0.95, 0.57   **c)** 1.76, 1.63, 1.78

5. Order the numbers from greatest to least.
   a) 0.571, 3.53, 0.538   **b)** 1.002, 1.35, 1.267   **c)** 15.2, 15.012, 16

6. Write a number between 6.73 and 6.741.
   How did you choose the number?

7. Lian's paper airplane flew 4.247 m and Maude's flew 4.25 m.
   Whose plane flew farther? Show how you know.

8. Write two numbers between 1.51 and 1.52.
   How did you choose the numbers?

9. This table shows the results of a watermelon seed-spitting contest.
   a) Whose seed went the greatest distance?
   b) Whose seed went the least distance?
   c) Whose seed went farther than Poppy's but not as far as Luis'?
   d) Order the distances from greatest to least.

Name	Distance (m)
Vladimir	2.357
Abu	2.4
Poppy	2.35
Suki	1.943
Cy	1.7
Luis	2.438

10. Use the graph.
    The masses in grams of the hummingbird eggs, in no specific order, are:
    0.482, 0.44, 0.32, 0.56, 0.374
    What is the mass of the egg of:
    a) the Costa's hummingbird?
    b) the bee hummingbird?
    c) the black-chinned hummingbird?

Masses of Some Hummingbird Eggs

11. Which number is closest to 6? Explain how you know.
    5.014, 6.4, 6.002, or 5.91

12. Copy each statement.
    Write a decimal with thousandths to make each statement true.
    a) 0.43 > □
    b) 5.7 < □
    c) 32.002 > □
    d) 2.31 < □
    e) 21.24 > □
    f) 0.1 > □

13. Grady is 1.35 m tall. His sister is 1.7 m tall.
    Grady's mother is 1.59 m tall.
    a) Who is the tallest?
    b) Who is the shortest?
    c) Do you think Grady is older or younger than his sister? Explain.

14. Order these numbers on a number line: 1.27, 1.284, 1.236, 1.2, 1.279

Reflect

A student says that 7.52 is to the left of 7.516 on a number line because 52 is less than 516. Is the student correct? Explain your answer.

Using Decimals to Relate Units of Measure

Each of you will need string, scissors, a ruler, and a metre stick or measuring tape.

➤ Cut off a piece of string you think will fit each description:
  • between 1 m and 2 m long
  • between 50 cm and 100 cm long
  • shorter than 10 cm
➤ Trade strings with your partner.
  Measure your partner's strings to the nearest centimetre.
  Then record each measurement in metres, centimetres, and millimetres.

Show and Share

Share your measurements with your partner.
Explain how you changed centimetres to the other units of length.
How did you use decimals to record some of your measures?

Connect

Here are some relationships among the units you use to measure length.

➤ You can read the length of this humming bird in several ways.

The bird is 9 cm long.

Since 1 cm is 0.01 m, then 9 cm is 0.09 m. The bird is 0.09 m long.

Since 1 cm is 10 mm, then 9 cm is 90 mm. The bird is 90 mm long.

LESSON FOCUS | Describe the length of an object in different units.

191

1 mm = 0.1 cm	1 cm = 10 mm	1 m = 1000 mm
1 mm = 0.001 m	1 cm = 0.01 m	1 m = 100 cm

➤ Change 2 m to millimetres.
   1 m = 1000 mm
   So, 2 m = 2 × 1000 mm
           = 2000 mm

➤ Change 23 mm to metres.
   1000 mm = 1 m
   So, 1 mm = $\frac{1}{1000}$ m = 0.001 m
   Then, 23 mm = $\frac{23}{1000}$ m = 0.023 m

➤ Change 12 mm to centimetres.
   10 mm = 1 cm
   So, 1 mm = $\frac{1}{10}$ cm = 0.1 cm
   Then, 12 mm = $\frac{12}{10}$ cm = 1.2 cm

➤ Change 23 cm to metres.
   100 cm = 1 m
   So, 1 cm = $\frac{1}{100}$ m = 0.01 m
   Then, 23 cm = $\frac{23}{100}$ m = 0.23 m

Practice

Use metre sticks when they help.

1. Measure each line segment. Write its length 3 ways.
   a) •————————————————•

   b) •——————————————————————————•

2. The northern pike can grow
   to a length of about 1 m.
   Write this length in millimetres
   and in centimetres.

3. Copy and complete.
   a) 9 m = ☐ cm   b) 15 mm = ☐ cm   c) 5 m = ☐ mm
   d) 17 cm = ☐ m   e) 45 m = ☐ cm   f) 45 cm = ☐ m

4. How many 1-cm cubes do you need to draw
   a line segment of each length?
   a) 50 mm   b) 1 m   c) 21 m   d) 70 mm

5. Record each measure in millimetres and metres.
   a) 24 cm   b) 17 cm   c) 80 cm   d) 145 cm

6. Record each measure in millimetres and centimetres.
   a) 3 m
   b) 0.5 m
   c) 0.4 m
   d) 0.9 m

7. Draw a feather of each length.
   Then write each length in 2 different units.
   a) 50 mm
   b) 3 cm
   c) 11 cm
   d) 0.07 m

8. Copy and complete. Use =, <, or >. Explain how you know.
   a) 5.56 m ☐ 70 cm
   b) 250 cm ☐ 1.46 m
   c) 16 mm ☐ 1.6 cm
   d) 3000 mm ☐ 2.8 m
   e) 5.3 m ☐ 53 cm
   f) 2.90 m ☐ 227 cm

9. The right whale can grow to a length of 18 m.
   The sperm whale can grow to a length of 1770 cm.
   Which whale can grow to the greater length?
   How do you know?

10. Jackie is 123 cm tall.
    Suppose she wants to know her height in metres.
    How will the number that represents her height
    in metres compare to the number that represents
    her height in centimetres? Explain how you know.

11. Jo-el is 1.21 m tall, Raynen is 1.03 m tall,
    and Keena is 131 cm tall.
    a) Order the students from shortest to tallest.
    b) Who is tallest? By how much?
    Show your work.

12. Hannah-Li plans to measure the width
    of the classroom door in millimetres
    and centimetres. Which will be greater:
    the number that represents the width in
    millimetres or the number that represents
    the width in centimetres? How do you know?

Reflect

Explain how to change a measurement from one unit
to another.
Give examples to support your answer.

Relating Fractions and Decimals to Division

Explore

Javier has 11 apples to share equally with a friend. How many apples will each person get?

Try to do this 2 different ways.
How will you record your answer?

Show *and* Share

Share your answer with another pair of classmates. Compare strategies for solving the problem and writing the answer.

Connect

Helena has 8 doughnuts to share equally among 5 people. How much will each person get?

Here are two ways to solve the problem.

➤ Use pictures.

Each person has 1 doughnut. There are 3 left over.
Divide each leftover doughnut in fifths.

There are 15 fifths.
Each person gets 3 fifths of a leftover doughnut.

each person gets 1 doughnut and $\frac{3}{5}$ more.

LESSON FOCUS | Relate fractions and decimals to division.

Since $\frac{3}{5} = \frac{6}{10}$ and $\frac{6}{10} = 0.6$, we can also say that each person gets 1 doughnut and 0.6 of a doughnut, or 1.6 doughnuts.

➤ Divide.
Eight doughnuts shared equally among 5 people is written as $8 \div 5$.

$$5\overline{)8}^{\,1\text{ R3}}$$

There is a remainder of 3.

The 3 left over are shared equally among 5 people.

This can be written as $3 \div 5$, or $\frac{3}{5}$.

We write 1 R3 as 1 and $\frac{3}{5}$ more.

Any division statement can be written as a fraction.

$3 \div 5 = \frac{3}{5}$

Practice

1. Write each division statement as a fraction.
   a) $2 \div 4$ **b)** $3 \div 8$ **c)** $4 \div 10$ **d)** $5 \div 12$

2. Write each division statement as a fraction.
   a) $15 \div 6$ **b)** $12 \div 5$ **c)** $16 \div 8$ **d)** $17 \div 10$

3. Write each fraction as a division statement.
   a) $\frac{2}{3}$ **b)** $\frac{4}{9}$ **c)** $\frac{1}{8}$ **d)** $\frac{3}{4}$

4. Write each fraction as a division statement.
   a) $\frac{10}{4}$ **b)** $\frac{14}{5}$ **c)** $\frac{20}{6}$ **d)** $\frac{12}{7}$

5. Divide.
   Show each remainder as a fraction.
   a) $7 \div 4$ **b)** $8 \div 3$ **c)** $24 \div 7$ **d)** $230 \div 8$

6. Divide.
   Show each answer as a decimal.
   a) $35 \div 2$ **b)** $193 \div 5$ **c)** $17 \div 5$ **d)** $299 \div 2$

The speech bubble reads: $\frac{3}{5}$ means $3 \div 5$.

7. Wenchun can make 4 origami swans from one sheet of paper.
   a) How many sheets of paper will she need to make 45 swans?
   b) Write the remainder in 2 different ways.

8. Jimmy has 79 m of string.
   He plans to make 5 kites.
   How much string is available for each kite?
   Write the answer as a decimal.

9. Two people share a gift of $125 equally.
   How much does each person get?

10. Mario cycled 17 km from his home to visit a friend.
   He left home at 9 A.M.
   Mario arrived at his friend's home at 11 A.M.
   He cycled the same distance each hour.
   How far did he cycle each hour?
   Write the answer as a decimal.

11. Janine made 4 pizzas for her party.
   She invited 8 friends.
   How much pizza did Janine think each person would eat? Explain.

12. A 4-kg bag of peaches costs $10.
   What does 1 kg of peaches cost?

13. Teagan bought 250 cm of leather cord to make necklaces.
   He wants to make 8 necklaces, all the same length.
   How much cord will Teagan use for each necklace?

Reflect

One student wrote $\frac{9}{4}$ as 2 R1.
A second student wrote $\frac{9}{4}$ as 2.25.
A third student wrote $\frac{9}{4}$ as 2 and $\frac{1}{4}$ more.
Use pictures, numbers, or words to explain why each student is correct.

Estimating Sums and Differences

Use the data in the table, taken from *Guinness World Records 2007*.

➤ Take turns to choose 2 fruits and estimate their combined mass. Tell your partner your estimate. Have your partner guess which 2 fruits you chose. If your partner guesses incorrectly, try to provide a closer estimate. Continue with different pairs of fruit.

➤ Repeat the activity.
This time, estimate the difference in masses of 2 fruits.

Most Massive Fruits on Record

Fruit	Mass (kg)
Apple	1.843
Grapefruit	3.065
Lemon	5.265
Mango	2.466
Peach	0.725
Strawberry	0.231

Show *and* Share

Discuss the strategies you used to estimate the sums and differences. Which strategies gave the closest estimate?

Connect

According to *Guinness World Records 2007*, the most massive head of garlic had a mass of 1.191 kg. The most massive potato had a mass of 3.487 kg.

➤ Here are two ways to estimate the combined mass of these vegetables:
Estimate: 1.191 + 3.487

• Write each decimal to the nearest whole number.
$1 + 3 = 4$
So, 1.191 kg + 3.487 kg is about 4 kg.

• Write only 1 decimal to the nearest whole number.
$1 + 3.487 = 4.487$
So, 1.191 kg + 3.487 kg is about 4.487 kg.

> $1.191 + 3.487 = 4.678$
> So, writing only one decimal to the nearest whole number gave the estimate closer to the actual sum.

➤ Here are two ways to estimate the difference in the masses of the potato and the garlic.
Estimate: 3.487 − 1.191

- Write the decimal being subtracted to the nearest whole number.
  3.487 − 1 = 2.487
  So, 3.487 kg − 1.191 kg is about 2.487 kg.

- Write both decimals to the nearest whole number.
  3 − 1 = 2
  So, 3.487 kg − 1.191 kg is about 2 kg.

The exact difference is:

3.487 − 1.191 = 2.296

For these numbers, writing the decimal being subtracted to the nearest whole number gave the estimate closer to the actual difference.

Practice

1. Estimate each sum. Explain your strategies.
   a) 7.36 + 2.23   b) 1.689 + 3.128
   c) 2.014 + 3.213   d) 4.405 + 2.167
   e) 3.8 + 2.6   f) 5.278 + 0.732
   g) 6.112 + 7.351   h) 6.204 + 3.009
   i) 5.641 + 1.318   j) 4.219 + 8.604

2. Estimate each difference. Explain your strategies.
   a) 4.255 − 1.386   b) 6.593 − 4.991
   c) 8.737 − 5.837   d) 0.456 − 0.214
   e) 4.32 − 1.245   f) 3.104 − 0.8

3. The tallest woman on record was 2.483 m tall.
   The shortest woman on record was 0.61 m tall.
   Estimate the difference in their heights.
   Show your work.

4. Choose the closer estimate. Explain your choice.
   a) 2.225 + 6.95   8 or 9   b) 83.1 − 34.016   50 or 60
   c) 58.37 − 22.845   35 or 30   d) 19.531 + 16.8   35 or 36

5. A grand piano has a mass of 396.696 kg.
   An upright piano has a mass of 267.728 kg.
   a) Could both pianos be put in a freight elevator
      with a mass limit of 650 kg? Explain how you know.
   b) About how much over or under the 650-kg
      limit is the combined mass of the two pianos?

6. Mount Everest is 8.850 km high.
   Mount Logan is 5.959 km high.
   What is the approximate difference in their heights?

7. The reticulated python is the world's longest snake.
   The thread snake is the world's shortest snake.
   A reptile centre has a 6.248-m reticulated python
   and a 0.108-m thread snake.
   Estimate the difference in the lengths of these snakes.

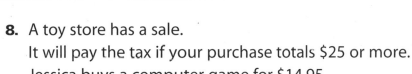

8. A toy store has a sale.
   It will pay the tax if your purchase totals $25 or more.
   Jessica buys a computer game for $14.95
   and some batteries for $7.99.
   About how much more would she need to spend
   and not pay the tax?

9. Tyrel and Jordana estimated the sum of 2.853 + 0.986.
   Tyrel's estimate was 3.8 and Jordana's was 3.853.
   a) Explain how Tyrel and Jordana may have estimated.
   b) Whose estimate was closer to the actual sum?
      How do you know?

At Home

Reflect

Which method for estimating
do you find easiest?
Explain why it is easiest for you.

Talk with family members to find
out when they estimate sums
or differences.
What strategies do they use?
Write about what you find out.

Adding Decimals

I have $5.65.

I have $4.81.

Suppose the students combine their money.
Do they have enough to buy a CD for $10.41? How could you find out?

Explore

Lindy rides her scooter to school.
Lindy's mass, including her helmet, is 28.75 kg.
The mass of her backpack is 2.18 kg.
➤ About what mass is Lindy's scooter carrying?
➤ Find the total mass the scooter is carrying.
Use any materials you think will help.
Record your work.

Show *and* Share

Share your results with another pair of classmates.
Discuss the strategies you used to estimate the mass,
and to find the mass.
Were some of the strategies better than others? How?
Explain.

Julio rides his bike to school.
Julio's mass is 26.79 kg.
The mass of his backpack is 2.60 kg.
What total mass is Julio's bike carrying?

Add: 26.79 + 2.60
Here are 3 different strategies students used to find 26.79 + 2.60.

➤ Sidney used Base Ten Blocks on a place-value mat.
She modelled each number with blocks.
Sidney then traded 10 tenths for 1 one.

represents 10.

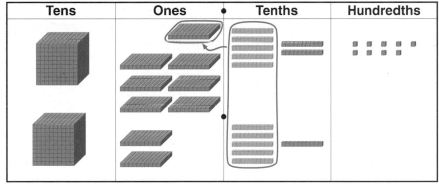

$$\begin{array}{r} \overset{1}{2}6.79 \\ +\ \ 2.60 \\ \hline .39 \end{array}$$

Sidney then counted the ones and counted the tens.

$$\begin{array}{r} \overset{1}{2}6.79 \\ +\ \ 2.60 \\ \hline 29.39 \end{array}$$

➤ Ben added from left to right.
He added whole numbers, then estimated to place
the decimal point.

$$
\begin{array}{r}
2679 \\
+\ 260 \\
\hline
2000 \\
800 \\
130 \\
+\ \ \ \ \ 9 \\
\hline
2939
\end{array}
$$

Since 26.79 + 2.60 is about 20 + 2 = 22,
Ben placed the decimal point in the sum
so the whole number part is a number
close to 22; that is, 29.

So, 26.79 + 2.60 = 29.39

➤ Katy also added from left to right, but she added decimals.
She aligned the decimals as Sidney aligned the blocks on the
place-value mat.

$$
\begin{array}{r}
26.79 \\
+\ \ 2.60 \\
\hline
20.00 \\
8.00 \\
1.30 \\
+\ \ 0.09 \\
\hline
29.39
\end{array}
$$

So, 26.79 + 2.60 = 29.39

Julio's bike is carrying a total mass of 29.39 kg.

Practice

1. Use Base Ten Blocks to add.

a)
$$
\begin{array}{r}
4.6 \\
+\ 2.3 \\
\hline
\end{array}
$$

b)
$$
\begin{array}{r}
9.5 \\
+\ 5.4 \\
\hline
\end{array}
$$

c)
$$
\begin{array}{r}
6.25 \\
+\ 3.92 \\
\hline
\end{array}
$$

d)
$$
\begin{array}{r}
5.24 \\
+\ 6.99 \\
\hline
\end{array}
$$

2. Add. Estimate to check.

a) 27.39 + 48.91　　b) 58.09 + 6.40　　c) $31.74 + $2.86

3. Add. Think about equivalent decimals
when you need to.

a) 7.56 + 4.8　　　b) 7.6 + 3.85

c) 0.3 + 4.71　　　d) 0.62 + 0.9

e) 20.48 + 9　　　f) 10 + 3.7

To add 7.56 + 4.8, I know
4.8 is equivalent to 4.80.
So, I write a 0 after 4.8
to show place value.

4. Paul bought a piece of ribbon 4.9 m long.
He cut it into 2 pieces.
What lengths could the 2 pieces be?
How many different answers can you find?

5. Lesley bought a CD for $19.95 and
a DVD for $26.85.
How much did she pay for the two items?

6. Tagak needed 2.43 m and 2.18 m of rope
for his dog team.
When he added the two lengths,
he got the sum 46.1 m.
Tagak realized he had made a mistake.
How did Tagak know?
What is the correct sum?

7. The decimal point is missing in each sum.
Use estimation to place each decimal point.
a) 3.56 + 2.79 = 635
b) 27.36 + 43.02 = 7038
c) 7.5 + 3.26 + 28.11 = 3887
d) 135.2 + 4.7 + 0.37 = 14027

8. The decimal point in each sum is in the wrong place.
Write the sum with the decimal point in the correct place.
a) 5.36 + 4.78 = 101.4
b) 38.92 + 27.35 = 6.627
c) 0.43 + 114.8 = 1152.3
d) 0.98 + 0.35 = 0.133

9. Write a story problem that uses the
addition of two decimals with hundredths.
Solve your problem.
Show your work.

Reflect

Explain why keeping track of place-value positions
is important when adding decimals.
Use an example to explain.

Make 2!

You will need coloured markers.
Your teacher will give you a set of decimal cards and hundredths grids.

The object of the game is to shade hundredths grids
to represent a decimal that is as close to 2 as possible.

➤ Shuffle the decimal cards.
  Place the cards face down in a pile.
  Turn over the top 4 cards.
➤ Players take turns choosing one of the 4 cards displayed.
  Each time, the card is replaced with the top card in the deck.
➤ On your turn, represent the decimal on one of the hundredths grids.
  Use a different colour for each decimal.
  You may not represent part of the decimal on one grid
  and the other part on the second grid.
  You may not represent a decimal that would more than fill a grid.
  If each of the decimals on the 4 cards is greater than either decimal left
  on your grids, you lose your turn.
➤ Continue playing until neither player can choose a card.
  Find the sum of the decimals you coloured on your grids.
  The player whose sum is closer to 2 is the winner.

Subtracting Decimals

· ·

This chart shows the average annual snowfall in several Canadian cities.

Choose two cities from the chart. Estimate how much more snow one city gets than the other. Then find the difference. Use any materials you think will help. Record your work.

Average Annual Snowfall

City	Snowfall (m)
Regina, SK	1.07
St. John's, NL	3.22
Toronto, ON	1.35
Vancouver, BC	0.55
Yellowknife, NT	1.44

Show *and* Share

Share your results with another pair of classmates. Discuss the strategies you used to find the difference in snowfalls.

Connect

· ·

St. John's, Newfoundland, gets an average of 3.22 m of snow a year.

Halifax, Nova Scotia, gets 2.61 m.

How much more snow does St. John's get than Halifax?
Subtract: 3.22 − 2.61

Here are 3 different strategies students used to find 3.22 − 2.61.

➤ Alex used Base Ten Blocks to compare the two numbers.

St. John's:

Halifax:

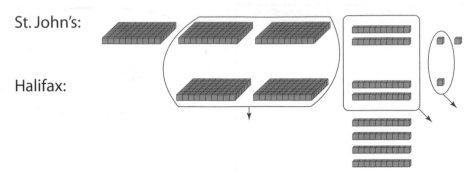

Alex removed the blocks that were the same in each number.
He had these blocks left.

St. John's:

Halifax:

Alex traded the ones flat for 10 tenths, then removed more blocks
that were the same in each number.

St. John's:

Halifax:

The blocks for 6 tenths 1 hundredth remain.
So, St. John's has 0.61 m more snow than Halifax.

➤ Lindsay used Base Ten Blocks on a place-value mat.
She modelled 3.22 on the mat.
Lindsay cannot take 6 tenths from 2 tenths,
so she traded 1 one for 10 tenths.

Lindsay used a
"take-away" model
to compare

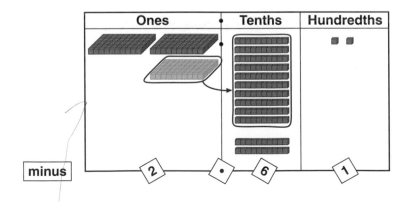

$$\begin{array}{r} \overset{2\ 12}{3.\cancel{2}2} \\ -\ 2.61 \\ \hline \end{array}$$

Lindsay then took away 2 ones 6 tenths 1 hundredth.

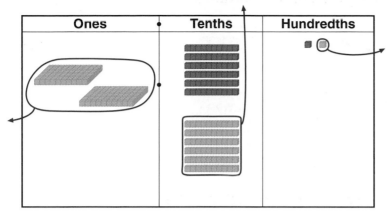

Ones	Tenths	Hundredths

0 ones   6 tenths   1 hundredth

When a decimal has no whole-number part, you write a zero in the ones place.

$$\begin{array}{r} \overset{2\ 12}{3.\cancel{2}2} \\ -\ 2.61 \\ \hline 0.61 \end{array}$$

Lindsay added to check her answer.

$$\begin{array}{r} \overset{1}{2.61} \\ +\ 0.61 \\ \hline 3.22 \end{array}$$

➤ Graeme used a number line to add on.

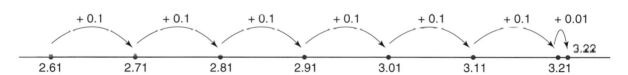

+ 0.1   + 0.1   + 0.1   + 0.1   + 0.1   + 0.1   + 0.01

2.61   2.71   2.81   2.91   3.01   3.11   3.21   3.22

Graeme added on: $0.1 + 0.1 + 0.1 + 0.1 + 0.1 + 0.1 + 0.01 = 0.61$

So, $3.22 - 2.61 = 0.61$

Graeme used front-end rounding to check his answer is reasonable.
He wrote 3.22 as 3.
He wrote 2.61 as 2.
$3 - 2 = 1$
The answer 0.61 is close to the estimate 1, so the answer is reasonable.

So, St. John's gets 0.61 m more snow than Halifax.

Practice

1. Use Base Ten Blocks to subtract. Estimate to check.
   a) $7.8 - 2.3$
   b) $6.7 - 3.8$
   c) $9.35 - 4.26$
   d) $10.62 - 4.07$

2. Subtract. Add to check.
   a) $6.04 - 3.78$
   b) $2.76 - 0.98$
   c) $9.03 - 7.28$
   d) $11.09 - 9.29$
   e) $12.26 - 3.91$
   f) $73.40 - 54.23$

3. Subtract.
   Think about equivalent decimals when you need to.
   a) $0.56 - 0.4$
   b) $16 - 4.26$
   c) $0.8 - 0.36$

4. Erin subtracted 12 from 37.8 and got a difference of 36.6.
   a) How did Erin know she had made a mistake?
   b) What is the correct answer?

5. Use the data in the table.

Average Annual Precipitation

City	Precipitation (cm)
Calgary, AB	39.88
Victoria, BC	85.80
Montreal, QC	93.97
Whitehorse, YT	26.90
Winnipeg, MB	50.44

   a) What is the difference in precipitation between Calgary and Whitehorse?
   b) How much more precipitation does Montreal get than Winnipeg?
   c) How much less precipitation does Whitehorse get than Winnipeg?
   d) What is the difference in precipitation between the cities with the greatest and the least precipitation?

6. Use the data in question 5.
   Find which two cities have a difference in precipitation of:
   a) 45.92 cm
   b) 8.17 cm
   c) 54.09 cm

7. The decimal point is missing in each difference.
Use estimation to place each decimal point.
a) 17.25 − 2.18 = 1507
b) 33.08 − 21.4 = 1168
c) 203.08 − 137.32 = 6576
d) 93.5 − 0.93 = 9257

8. The decimal point in each difference is in the wrong place.
Write the difference with the decimal point in the correct place.
a) 25.49 − 3.28 = 2.221
b) 1.35 − 0.78 = 57.0
c) 328.76 − 1.94 = 32.682
d) 257.9 − 98.83 = 1590.7

9. Why is it important to keep track of the place-value position of each digit when subtracting decimals?

10. In the men's long jump event, Marty jumped 8.26 m in the first trial and 8.55 m in the second trial. What is the difference of his jumps?

11. Candida got a $50 bill for her birthday.
She bought a camera for $29.95 and a wallet for $9.29.
How much money is left?

12. Write a story problem that uses the subtraction of two decimals with hundredths.
Trade problems with a classmate.
Solve your classmate's problem.

13. Brad estimated the difference between 11.42 and 1.09 as less than 10. Is Brad correct? Show 2 different ways to estimate that support your answer.

Math Link

Media

A headline in a newspaper writes a large number like this:

1.5 Million People Affected by Power Cut

We say 1.5 million as "one point five million."
1.5 million is one million five hundred thousand, or 1 500 000.

Reflect

How is subtracting decimals like subtracting whole numbers?
How is it different?
Use words, pictures, or numbers to explain.

Spinning Decimals

You will need Base Ten Blocks.
Your teacher will give you place-value mats and a spinner.
The object of the game is to make the greatest decimal
using the fewest Base Ten Blocks.

Players take turns.

➤ On your turn, you must take tens rods and unit cubes.
Spin the pointer 2 times.
After the first spin, you may choose to take that number of rods or
that number of cubes.
After the second spin, take that number of cubes or rods,
whichever you did not choose the first time.
➤ Make as many trades of Base Ten Blocks as you can.
Record the decimal for that turn.
➤ After 3 rounds of play, find the sum of your decimals.
The player with the highest score wins.

Adding and Subtracting Decimals

Some population numbers are written as decimals, in millions.
For example, in 2006, the population of Saskatchewan was
about 0.968 million, or 968 000.
In the same year, the population of Alberta was
about 3.290 million, or 3 290 000.

Explore

This table shows the approximate
populations of the western provinces and
territories in 2006.

Province or Territory	Population (millions)
Alberta	3.290
British Columbia	4.113
Manitoba	1.148
Nunavut	0.029
Saskatchewan	0.968
Northwest Territories	0.041
Yukon Territory	0.030

➤ Estimate first.
   Then find the total population of:
   • Alberta and the Yukon Territory
   • British Columbia and the Northwest Territories
   • Manitoba and Nunavut

➤ Estimate first.
   Then find the difference in populations of:
   • Saskatchewan and the Yukon Territory
   • British Columbia and Saskatchewan
   • the greatest and least populations

Show and Share

Share your results with another pair of classmates.
Discuss the strategies you used to estimate and to find the sums and differences.

Another number that is written as a decimal, in millions, is the money that a movie earns in Canada and the United States. The earnings are recorded in millions of US dollars.

A popular movie opened in theatres on Friday, August 13, 2004. That Friday, it earned US$4.328 million in Canadian and American theatres. It earned US$3.019 million the next day.

➤ To find the total earnings on Friday and Saturday, add: 4.328 + 3.019
Here are two ways to find the sum.

- Use Base Ten Blocks.
  Model 4.328 and 3.019 on a place-value mat.
  Add the thousandths.
  Trade 10 thousandths for 1 hundredth.
  Add the hundredths. Add the tenths. Add the ones.

$$\begin{array}{r} 1 \\ 4.328 \\ +\,3.019 \\ \hline 7.347 \end{array}$$

- Add from left to right.

$$\begin{array}{r} 4.328 \\ +\,3.019 \\ \hline 7.000 \\ 0.300 \\ 0.030 \\ +\,0.017 \\ \hline 7.347 \end{array}$$

Estimate to check the answer is reasonable.
Write 3.019 as 3.
Add: 4.328 + 3 = 7.328

7.347 is close to the estimate 7.328, so the answer is reasonable.

The combined earnings were US$7.347 million.

➤ To find the difference in the earnings on Friday and Saturday, subtract: 4.328 − 3.019
Here are two ways to find the difference.

- Use Base Ten Blocks.
  Model 4.328 on a place-value mat.
  You cannot take 9 thousandths from 8 thousandths.
  Trade 1 hundredth for 10 thousandths.

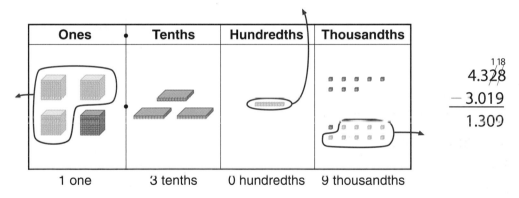

$$\begin{array}{r} \overset{1\,18}{4.3\cancel{2}\cancel{8}} \\ -\ 3.019 \\ \hline \end{array}$$

Take away 9 thousandths.
Take away 1 hundredth.
Take away 3 ones.

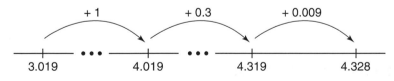

$$\begin{array}{r} \overset{1\,18}{4.3\cancel{2}\cancel{8}} \\ -\ 3.019 \\ \hline 1.309 \end{array}$$

| 1 one | 3 tenths | 0 hundredths | 9 thousandths |

- Use a number line and think addition.
  We added on: 1 + 0.3 + 0.009 = 1.309

```
        + 1            + 0.3           + 0.009
      ⌢              ⌢               ⌢
 ——+——•••——+——•••——+————————+——
 3.019      4.019      4.319         4.328
```

So, 4.328 − 3.019 = 1.309

Estimate to check the answer is reasonable.
Write 3.019 as 3.
Subtract: 4.328 − 3 = 1.328

1.309 is close to the estimate 1.328, so the answer is reasonable.

The movie earned US$1.309 million more on Friday than on Saturday.

Add to check that the answer is correct.
Add: 3.019 + 1.309
The sum should be 4.328.

$$
\begin{array}{r}
\overset{1}{}3.019 \\
+\,1.309 \\
\hline
4.328
\end{array}
$$

So, the answer is correct.

Practice

1. Add or subtract. Check your answers.
   a) $\begin{array}{r} 3.251 \\ +\,8.960 \\ \hline \end{array}$
   b) $\begin{array}{r} 17.324 \\ -\,9.166 \\ \hline \end{array}$
   c) $\begin{array}{r} 84.032 \\ -\,8.263 \\ \hline \end{array}$
   d) $\begin{array}{r} 4.629 \\ +\,0.576 \\ \hline \end{array}$

2. Estimate first. Then find each sum or difference.
   a) 2.876 − 0.975
   b) 71.382 + 9
   c) 0.58 + 0.736
   d) 0.14 + 4.038
   e) 7 − 0.187
   f) 0.999 − 0.99

3. Use each of the digits 0 to 7 once.
   Make 2 decimals with thousandths whose sum is close to 2
   and whose difference is close to 1.
   Explain your choices.
   Show your work.

4. The decimal point is missing in each sum and difference.
   Use estimation to place each decimal point.
   a) 2.567 + 5.431 = 7998
   b) 5.101 + 3.267 = 8368
   c) 7.636 − 0.963 = 6673
   d) 5.042 − 3.15 = 1892

5. The decimal point in each sum and difference is in the wrong place.
   Move each decimal point to the correct place.
   a) 9.123 + 2.45 = 115.73
   b) 6.7 + 2.451 = 91.51
   c) 84.623 − 25.418 = 5.9205
   d) 0.758 − 0.256 = 5.02

6. Mirko is making fruit punch.
   Will the contents of these 3 containers
   fit in a 3-L punch bowl?
   Explain.

7. Winsome is being trained as a
   guide dog for a blind person.
   At birth, she had a mass of 0.475 kg.
   At 6 weeks, her mass was 4.06 kg.
   At 12 weeks, her mass was 9.25 kg.
   a) By how much did her mass change
      from birth to 6 weeks?
   b) By how much did her mass change
      from 6 weeks to 12 weeks?

8. Write a story problem that can be solved
   by subtracting two decimals with thousandths.
   Solve your problem. Show your work.

9. Use each of the digits from 0 to 7 once
   to make this addition true.
   Find as many different answers as you can.

   $$\begin{array}{r} \square . \square\square\square \\ + \ \square . \square\square\square \\ \hline 5\ .\ 7\ 8\ 8 \end{array}$$

10. A student added 0.523 and 2.36 and got the sum 0.759.
    a) What mistake did the student make?
    b) What is the correct answer?

11. Four students have favourite totem poles.
    Scannah's pole is 1.36 m shorter than Uta's pole.
    Uta's pole is 2.57 m taller than Sta-th's pole.
    Yeil's pole is 31.53 m taller than Sta-th's pole.
    Yeil's pole is 35.25 m tall.
    How tall are Scannah's, Uta's, and Sta-th's poles?

12. The difference in the capacities of 2 containers is 0.653 L.
    What might the capacity of each container be?

13. Two numbers have thousandths other than zero.
    Could the difference of these numbers be 5.3? Explain.

Reflect

When Mahala subtracted 2.768 from 5.9, she wrote 5.9 as 5.900.
Why might she have done this?

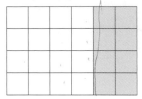

Unit 5 Show What You Know

LESSON

1

1. Write as many different fractions as you can to describe the shaded part of each picture.

   a)

   b)

   c)

2. Find an equivalent fraction for each fraction.

   a) $\frac{2}{5}$ **b)** $\frac{5}{8}$ **c)** $\frac{30}{40}$ **d)** $\frac{25}{50}$

2

3. Compare the fractions in each pair. Which strategies did you use?

   a) $\frac{3}{8}$ and $\frac{1}{2}$ **b)** $\frac{1}{8}$ and $\frac{2}{16}$ **c)** $\frac{3}{4}$ and $\frac{5}{16}$ **d)** $\frac{6}{8}$ and $\frac{6}{16}$

4. Draw a number line like the one below.

   0 ———————————————————————— 1

   Divide the number line to show halves, quarters, and sixths.
   Use the number line to order $\frac{3}{4}$, $\frac{1}{6}$, $\frac{1}{2}$, and $\frac{5}{6}$ from least to greatest.

4

5. Represent each fraction on a hundredths grid.
   Then write each number as a decimal.

   a) $\frac{7}{25}$ **b)** $\frac{3}{5}$ **c)** $\frac{1}{4}$ **d)** $\frac{9}{20}$

5

6. Use benchmarks on a number line.
   Order the decimals in each set from least to greatest.

   a) 0.90, 0.09, 0.81 **b)** 0.3, 0.33, 0.14 **c)** 0.56, 0.6, 0.5

6

7. Write a fraction and a decimal for each picture.

   a)

   b)

   represents 1 whole.

8. Write each fraction as a decimal.

   a) $\frac{55}{100}$ **b)** $\frac{208}{1000}$ **c)** $\frac{1}{4}$ **d)** $\frac{9}{1000}$

216

Unit 5

9. Write each decimal as a fraction.
   a) 0.257   b) 0.001   c) 0.9   d) 0.34

10. Write an equivalent decimal for each number.
    a) 0.7   b) 0.50   c) 1.84   d) 2.100

11. Describe the value of each digit in 3.675.

7

12. Use a number line to order the decimals from least to greatest.
    a) 0.24, 1.93, 1.9   b) 2.051, 2.3, 2.75

8

13. A canoe is 5.67 m long.
    How many centimetres is that?

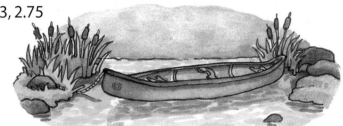

14. A nickel is about 21 mm wide.
    How many centimetres is that?

9

15. Five identical books cost $33.
    How much does 1 book cost?

10

16. Estimate each sum or difference.
    a) 2.48 + 2.99   b) 6.543 − 4.897
    c) 4.23 + 7.862   d) 23.78 − 0.36

11
12
13

17. Use the data in the table. For each type of pet,
    find the difference in the masses of the largest
    and smallest animals.

	Mass (kg)	
Animal	**Smallest**	**Largest**
Rabbit	0.397	11.991
Dog	0.113	155.582
Cat	1.361	44.452

18. Add or subtract.
    a) 3.84 + 7.63   b) 15.942 − 8.6
    c) 1.97 + 6.323   d) 18.25 + 9.375

UNIT

5   Learning Goals

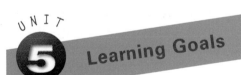

☑ create sets of equivalent fractions

☑ compare fractions with like and unlike denominators

☑ describe and represent decimals to thousandths

☑ relate decimals to fractions

☑ compare and order decimals to thousandths

☑ add and subtract decimals to thousandths

In the Garden

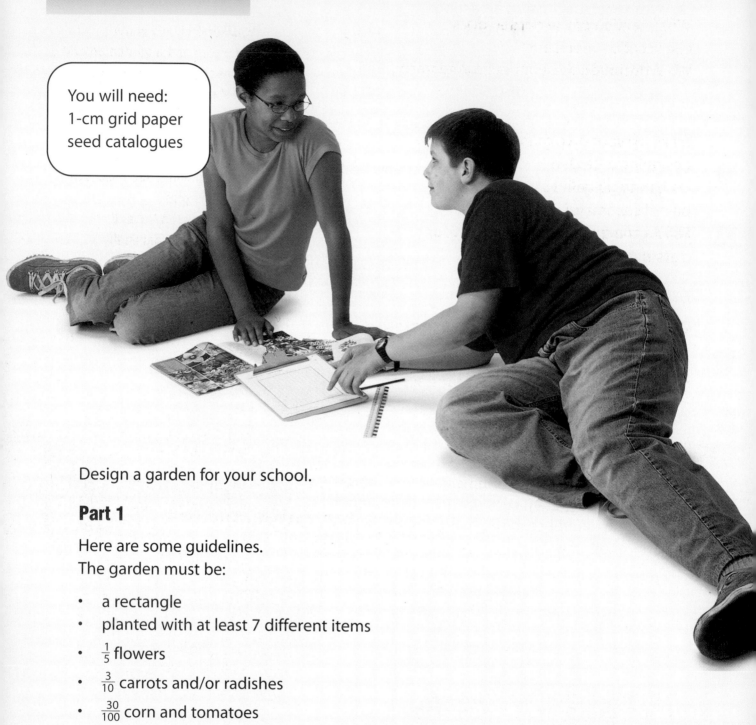

You will need:
1-cm grid paper
seed catalogues

Design a garden for your school.

Part 1

Here are some guidelines.
The garden must be:

- a rectangle
- planted with at least 7 different items
- $\frac{1}{5}$ flowers
- $\frac{3}{10}$ carrots and/or radishes
- $\frac{30}{100}$ corn and tomatoes

The tomatoes section is twice the size of the corn section.
Draw your garden on grid paper.
Label each section clearly.

What fraction of the garden does each section represent?
What decimal does each section represent?

Part 2

Make up your own guidelines for designing a garden.
Exchange guidelines with another pair of classmates.
Follow the guidelines to design your classmates' garden.

Part 3

Write 2 story problems about your garden:

- One problem involves adding decimals.
- The other problem involves subtracting decimals.

Exchange problems with another pair of classmates.
Solve your classmates' problems.
Check each other's work.

Check List

Your work should show
- ☑ a plan of the garden on grid paper, with each section clearly labelled
- ☑ the fraction or decimal each section represents
- ☑ how you calculated how to represent each section on the grid
- ☑ how you added and subtracted decimals

Reflect on Your Learning

How are fractions and decimals the same?
How are they different?

6
Building Bridges

Pratt Truss

Double Warren Truss

Howe Truss

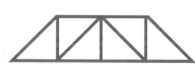

Howe Truss with counter braces

Learning Goals

- describe the sides of shapes
- describe the faces and edges of objects
- understand the terms: parallel, intersecting, perpendicular, vertical, and horizontal
- use attributes to identify and sort quadrilaterals

These are different types of truss bridges.

They were built during the great age of trains, about a hundred years ago.

A truss is a framework. It is made of wooden beams or metal bars.

The bridges are light, strong, and rigid.

Key Words

- attribute
- parallel
- intersect
- vertex
- horizontal
- vertical
- perpendicular
- right angle
- diagonal
- rhombus
- parallelogram
- trapezoid
- kite

- What is the most common geometric shape you see in the bridges?
- What other geometric shapes do you see? How are they the same? How are they different?
- Where are the lines of symmetry on the bridges?
- How can you check that the bridges are symmetrical?
- Which bridge do you think would support the greatest mass? Why?

LESSON 1

Describing Shapes

Look around the classroom.
Point out shapes with straight sides.
How else can you describe
the shapes you see?

Explore

Choose one of these shapes.
Keep your choice secret.

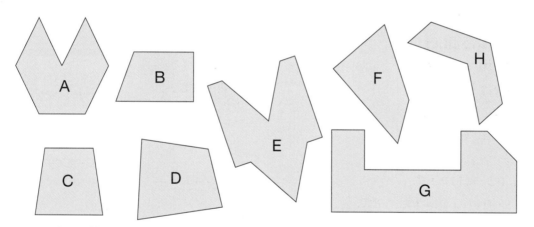

➤ Describe the shape to your partner in as many ways as you can.
Have your partner guess the shape.
➤ Trade roles.
➤ Repeat this activity 4 times.

Show *and* Share

Talk with another pair of classmates.
Share some of the ways you described the shapes.
How many sides does each shape have?
Find a way to sort the shapes.

We can describe a shape by telling about its **attributes**.
Here are some attributes of shapes.

➤ The lengths of the sides:
  • These shapes have some sides the same length.

  • These shapes have all sides the same length.

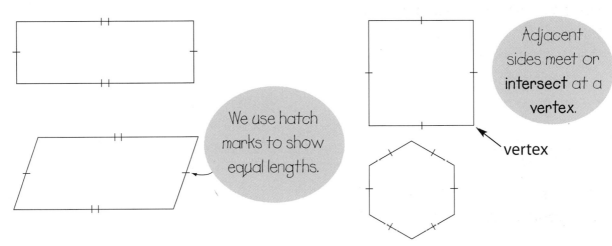

We use hatch marks to show equal lengths.

Adjacent sides meet or **intersect** at a **vertex**.

vertex

➤ The direction of the sides:
  • These shapes have at least one pair of **parallel** sides. These sides are always the same distance apart and never meet. When sides do not meet, we say the sides do not *intersect*.

  • These shapes have no parallel sides.

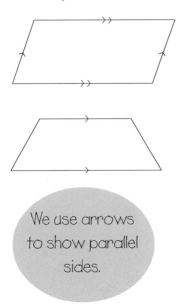

We use arrows to show parallel sides.

I can use a ruler to check for parallel sides. I make sure the sides are always the same distance apart.

➤ We can label each vertex with a different capital letter.
We then name a shape by its vertices. We write the vertices in order.

This is triangle ABC.

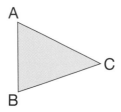

We use the letters to name the sides.
Triangle ABC has 3 sides:
AB, AC, and BC

This is quadrilateral MNPQ.

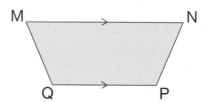

Quadrilateral MNPQ has 4 sides:
MN, NP, PQ, and QM
Sides MN and QP are parallel.
Sides MN and QP do not intersect.
Sides MN and NP intersect at vertex N.

Use these shapes for questions 1 and 2. Your teacher will give you copies of them.

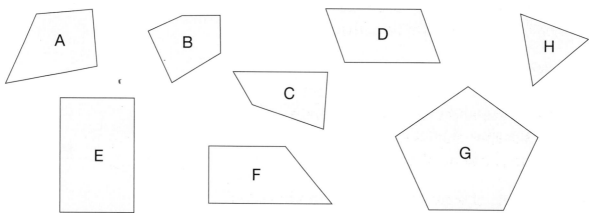

1. Which shapes have:
   a) all sides the same length?
   b) some sides the same length?
   c) parallel sides?

2. Choose 2 shapes above.
   Draw shapes like them on dot paper.
   How are the shapes the same? Different?
   Write about what you see.

3. Use a geoboard.
Make as many different shapes as you can with exactly 2 parallel sides.
Draw your shapes on dot paper.
Write about the attributes of each shape.

4. Use letters to name each shape.

a)

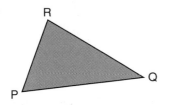

b)

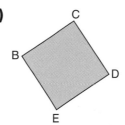

c)

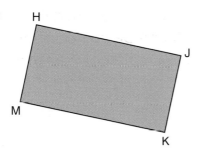

d)

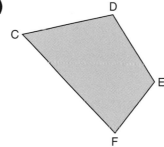

5. Use the shapes in question 4.
  a) For each shape, identify and name two sides that intersect.
  b) Which shapes have parallel sides?
    Identify and name the sides that are parallel.

6. In the classroom:
  a) Find 3 shapes that have parallel sides.
    How do you know the sides are parallel?
  b) Find 3 shapes that have intersecting sides.
    How do you know the sides intersect?

7. a) Which sets of letters below name this hexagon?
    Explain your thinking.
    CDEFGH   CDHGFE   ECDHGF   FEGHDC
  b) Describe the sides of the hexagon as
    many different ways as you can.

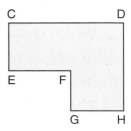

Reflect

How can you tell if a shape has parallel sides?
Use words or pictures to explain.

Investigating Perpendicular Sides

How are these shapes the same?
How are the shapes different?

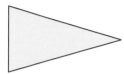

Explore

You will need a geoboard, geobands, and dot paper.

Make each shape below on a geoboard.
Then draw the shape on dot paper.
Each shape should have more than 3 sides.

- a shape that has a corner smaller
  than the corners in a square
- a shape that has a corner larger
  than the corners in a square
- a shape that has a corner that matches
  the corners in a square

Show *and* Share

Share your shapes with a classmate.
Which shapes have all the same corners?
Which shapes have more than one type of corner?
Did any shape have three types of corners?
If your answer is yes, describe the shape.

➤ Look at a picture on the wall.
If the picture is positioned correctly,
the top and bottom edges are **horizontal**.
The side edges are **vertical**.
We say that a horizontal edge and a vertical edge
are **perpendicular**.
That is, these edges intersect to form a **right angle**.
We draw a square where the edges meet to show
they are perpendicular.

Horizontal

Vertical

Perpendicular

➤ When two sides of any shape intersect
to make a right angle,
we say the sides are perpendicular.
These shapes have right angles.

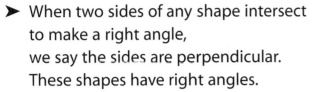

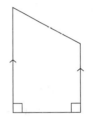

This is how
we show a
right angle.

This shape has 6 sides.
It is a hexagon.

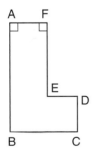

In hexagon ABCDEF,
AF is perpendicular to FE.
We write: AF ⊥ FE
Also, AF ⊥ AB

I can use the corner
of a square to
check if sides are
perpendicular.

1. Look at this photograph.
   Identify parts of the picture that:
   - intersect
   - are parallel
   - are perpendicular
   - appear to be horizontal
   - appear to be vertical

2. For each shape below, identify and name perpendicular sides.
   Which tool did you use?
   If a shape does not have any perpendicular sides, explain how you know.

   a)

   b)
   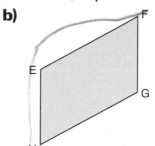

   c)
   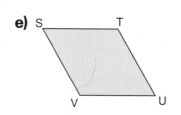

   d)
   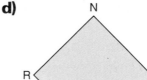

   e)
   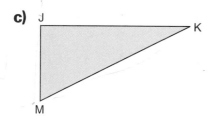

   f)
   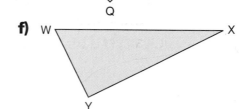

3. Look at the shapes in question 2.
   Assume the bottom of the page of this textbook is horizontal.
   For each shape above, where possible, identify and name:
   a) horizontal sides   **b)** vertical sides   **c)** intersecting sides

4. Use a geoboard and geobands. You will need square dot paper.
   Two edges of the geoboard are vertical, and the other 2 edges are horizontal.
   Make, then draw a shape that has:
   a) exactly 1 horizontal side and 2 vertical sides
   b) exactly 2 horizontal sides and 1 vertical side

5. Look at the shapes below.
Find a shape with:

   a) four right angles   **b)** two right angles   **c)** no right angles

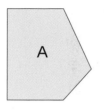
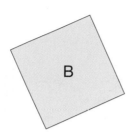

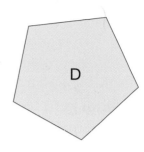

A   B   C   D

6. Use a geoboard and geobands.
Make as many different shapes as you can that have:
   a) exactly 1 pair of perpendicular sides
   b) exactly 2 pairs of perpendicular sides
   c) exactly 3 pairs of perpendicular sides
Draw each shape on dot paper. Label its vertices.
Identify and name any parallel sides.

7. How can you make or draw perpendicular lines without using dot paper?

8. What is the greatest number of right angles a hexagon can have?
Use a geoboard to help you find out.
Show your work.

9. On dot paper, draw as many different shapes as you can.
Include any or all of these attributes of sides each time:
parallel, perpendicular, vertical, horizontal

At Home

Reflect

How do you identify shapes
with perpendicular sides?
How can you tell if those sides
are vertical, or horizontal, or neither?
Use pictures and words to explain.

Look through newspapers and
magazines or on the Internet.
Find examples of shapes with sides that
are parallel, intersecting, perpendicular,
vertical, and horizontal.
Cut out or print the pictures.
Highlight the examples you found.

Investigating Quadrilaterals

Why is this shape a quadrilateral?
A **diagonal** joins two opposite vertices.
How many diagonals does this quadrilateral have?

You will need a ruler. Your teacher will give you a copy of the quadrilaterals below.
Share the work.

➤ How are the quadrilaterals alike? How are they different?
  Name each quadrilateral you can identify.
➤ Measure the lengths of the sides of each quadrilateral.
  What do you notice?
➤ Draw the diagonals in each quadrilateral. What do you notice?
➤ Choose 2 attributes. Sort the quadrilaterals.
  How can you record your sorting?

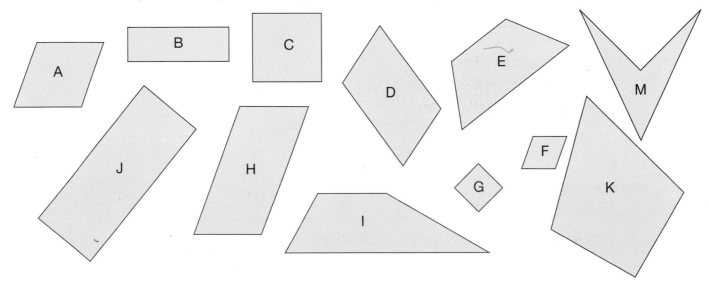

Show *and* Share

Compare your attributes and sorting with those of another pair of classmates.
Work together to sort the quadrilaterals a different way.

➤ Equal sides in quadrilaterals

• A square has 4 sides equal.

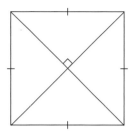

The diagonals of a square
are equal.
The diagonals are perpendicular.

• A **rhombus** has 4 sides equal.

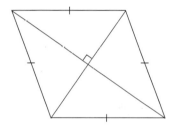

The diagonals of a rhombus
are perpendicular.

• A rectangle has 2 pairs of opposite
sides equal.

The diagonals of a rectangle
are equal.

• A **parallelogram** has 2 pairs of
opposite sides equal.

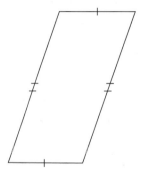

➤ Parallel sides in quadrilaterals

• All squares, rectangles, parallelograms, and rhombuses
have 2 pairs of parallel sides.

   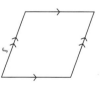

• A **trapezoid** has exactly 1 pair of parallel sides.

 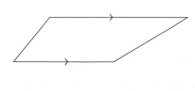

➤ Adjacent sides in quadrilaterals
A **kite** has 2 pairs of equal adjacent sides.

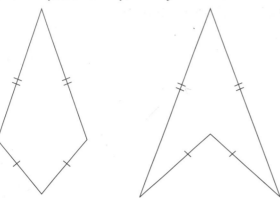

Practice . . . .

1. Use a geoboard.
    Make 5 different parallelograms.
    Draw the parallelograms on dot paper.
    Write how each parallelogram is different.

2. Use a geoboard.
    How many different quadrilaterals
    can you make:
    a) with 4 equal sides?
    b) with 2 pairs of parallel sides?
    c) with no equal sides and 2 parallel sides?
    Draw each quadrilateral on dot paper.

3. Use the shapes at the right.
    Find:
    a) a rhombus
    b) a trapezoid
    c) a shape that is a parallelogram
    and a rectangle
    d) a shape that is a square and
    a parallelogram

4. This riddle describes a quadrilateral.
    Solve this riddle:
    I have two pairs of parallel sides.
    All my sides are equal.
    What am I?
    How many different quadrilaterals can you name?

5. Sort the quadrilaterals below.
   a) Use the attributes: "Has diagonals of different lengths" and "Has 2 pairs of equal sides."

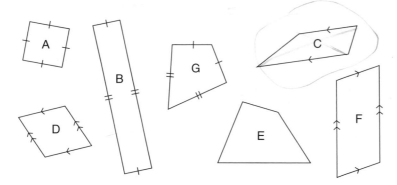

You could use a Venn diagram to sort.

   b) Choose two different attributes.
   Sort the quadrilaterals a different way.

6. Use dot paper. Draw a parallelogram.
   Write something about a parallelogram that is:
   a) never true   **b)** sometimes true   **c)** always true
   Explain your work.

7. Use the words "all," "some," or "no."
   Complete each sentence to make it true.
   a) ☐ rhombuses are parallelograms.
   b) ☐ squares are rhombuses.
   c) ☐ rhombuses are squares.
   d) ☐ parallelograms have diagonals of equal length.

8. Copy this shape on dot paper.
   a) Join the dots to divide the shape into
   5 congruent rectangles.
   b) Can you join the dots to make
   4 congruent rectangles?
   How do you know?

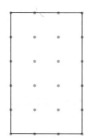

Remember that congruent shapes match exactly.

Reflect

Can you use the lengths of the sides of a quadrilateral to identify it? Use words and pictures to explain your answer.

Other Attributes of Quadrilaterals

Another attribute of a quadrilateral is the number of lines of symmetry it has.
How can you tell if a quadrilateral is symmetrical?

Your teacher will give you a copy of the quadrilaterals below.
Share the work.

➤ Which quadrilaterals have perpendicular sides? How can you tell?
Name each quadrilateral.

➤ Which quadrilaterals have line symmetry? How do you know?

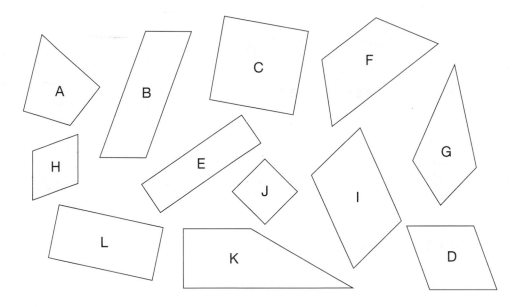

➤ Choose 2 attributes. Sort the quadrilaterals.
How did you know where to place each quadrilateral in your sorting?

Show *and* Share

Trade sortings with another pair of classmates.
Do not tell them your sorting rule.
Identify your classmates' sorting rule.

➤ All squares and rectangles have 4 right angles.
  Adjacent sides are perpendicular.

 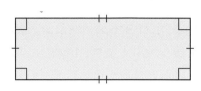

➤ A shape is symmetrical when it can be folded so that one part
  matches the other part exactly.
  The fold line is the line of symmetry.

  • Some quadrilaterals have no lines of symmetry.

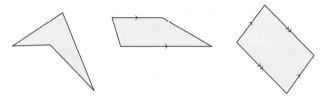

  • Some quadrilaterals have 1 line of symmetry.

  • Some quadrilaterals have 2 lines of symmetry.

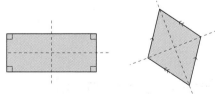

  • One quadrilateral has 4 lines of symmetry.

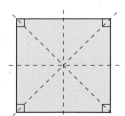

1. Choose 3 attributes of quadrilaterals.
   Use dot paper.
   Sketch and name as many quadrilaterals as
   you can that have each attribute.

2. How many different ways can you name each quadrilateral?
   Write the names.

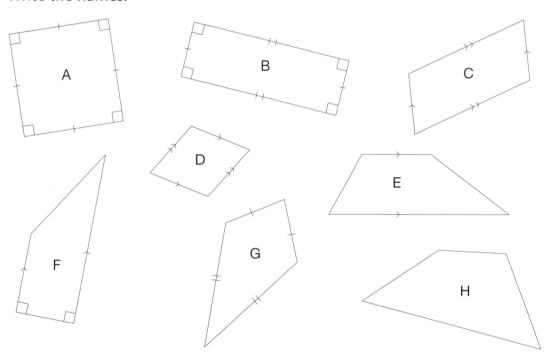

3. Use the quadrilaterals in question 2 and the Carroll diagram below.
   a) Sort the quadrilaterals.
      Use the attributes: "Has parallel sides"
      and "Has equal sides."
      Record your sorting.
   b) Choose 2 different attributes.
      Sort the quadrilaterals again.
      Record your sorting.

	Has parallel sides	Does not have parallel sides
Has equal sides		
Does not have equal sides		

4. You will need a geoboard and dot paper.
   Try to make a quadrilateral with each attribute.
   a) exactly 1 right angle   b) exactly 2 right angles   c) exactly 3 right angles
   Draw each quadrilateral on dot paper.
   Is there any quadrilateral you could not make? Explain.

5. How have these quadrilaterals been sorted?
Identify the attributes of each quadrilateral.
Write the sorting rule.

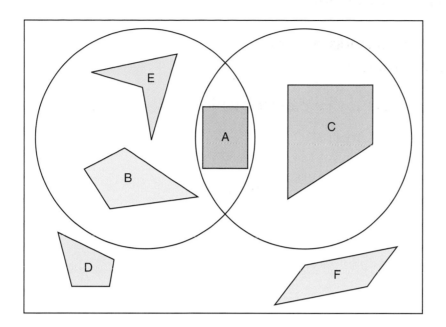

Use the shapes at the right for questions 6 to 8.

6. Sort the shapes into two groups.
One group has perpendicular sides.
The other group has no perpendicular sides.
Record your sorting.

7. Draw a Venn diagram.
Sort the shapes using these attributes:
"Has at least one right angle" and
"Has at least one pair of parallel sides"

8. Draw a Carroll diagram.
Think about all the attributes
of quadrilaterals.
Choose two attributes, then
sort the quadrilaterals.
Trade your completed Carroll diagram
with that of a classmate.
Identify your classmate's sorting rule.
Check that your answer matches
your classmate's rule.

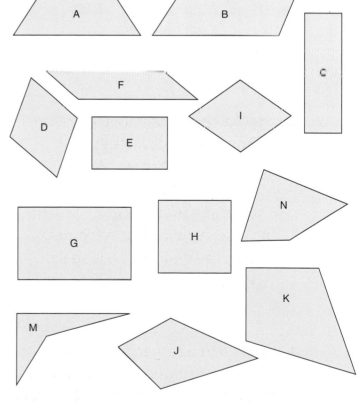

9. Work with a partner.
You will need a set of quadrilaterals.
Take turns to choose a secret attribute.
Find a set of quadrilaterals with that attribute.
Ask your partner to add a quadrilateral to the set.
Or, have your partner sketch a quadrilateral
that belongs.
If the quadrilateral does not belong,
tell your partner to try again.
Ask your partner to guess the attribute.

10. Draw a Venn diagram with two separate circles.
Which quadrilaterals could go in each circle?
Sketch the quadrilaterals.
Label each circle.
Explain your work.

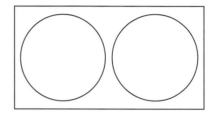

11. Use the clues to help you find the mystery attribute.
   • All these quadrilaterals have the attribute.

   • None of these quadrilaterals has the attribute.

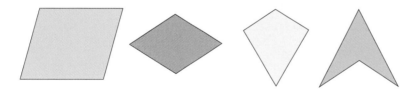

   • Which of these shapes have the attribute?

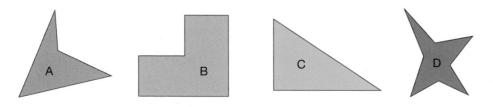

   a) What is the attribute?
   How do you know?
   b) Draw another shape with this attribute.

12. Name each shape.

a) Why is this quadrilateral
not a square?

b) Why is this quadrilateral
not a rectangle?

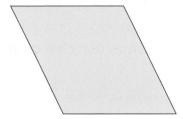

c) Why is this quadrilateral
not a rhombus?

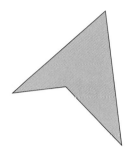

d) Why is this quadrilateral
not a kite?

Show your work.

Reflect

Which attributes are most useful to describe a quadrilateral? Why?
Could someone else think differently?
Check a classmate's response to this question.

Math Link

Your World

You see parallel lines in
railroad tracks, rails on a fence,
and double yellow lines on a
straight road.

Strategies Toolkit

A tangram is a square made from 7 shapes or **tans**.
The seven tans are: 2 small triangles,
1 medium triangle, 2 large triangles,
1 parallelogram, and 1 square.

Explore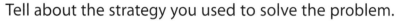

You will need a tangram and dot paper.
This large triangle is made from the
2 small triangles and the medium triangle.
Which shapes can *you* make with only 3 tans?
Which of these shapes are quadrilaterals?
Record your work.

Show *and* Share

Tell about the strategy you used to solve the problem.

Connect

Use the tans.
How many different ways can you make a trapezoid?

What do you know?
- You can use any of the tans.
- You must make a trapezoid.

Think of a strategy to help you
solve the problem.
- You can **solve a simpler problem**.
- Start with 2 tans, then try 3 tans, 4 tans, and so on.

Strategies

- **Make a table.**
- **Use a model.**
- **Draw a picture.**
- **Solve a simpler problem.**
- **Work backward.**
- **Guess and test.**
- **Make an organized list.**
- **Use a pattern.**

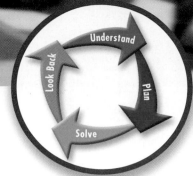

- • Choose 2 tans.
  Try to make a trapezoid.
  If you can, sketch it.
  If you cannot, trade 1 tan for a different tan and try again.
  Repeat for different pairs of tans.
- • Then choose 3 tans.
  Try to make a trapezoid.
- • Repeat for 4, 5, 6, then 7 tans.

How do you know that each shape you made is a trapezoid?

Practice

Choose one of the
Strategies

We know triangle, square, rectangle, parallelogram, rhombus, ...

trapezoid, kite, pentagon, hexagon, and octagon.

1. Think about the shapes you know.
   Which of these shapes can you make using all 7 tans?
   Show your work.

2. Try to make a square with 2 tans, 3 tans, 4 tans, 5 tans, 6 tans, and 7 tans.
   What did you find out?

3. Use any of the tans.
   a) How many different shapes can you make with 5 sides? 6 sides?
   b) Which of these shapes have parallel sides? Perpendicular sides?

Reflect

Which shapes were easiest to make with tans?
Which shapes were most difficult? Why?
Write about your ideas.

Exploring Faces and Edges of Objects

- Why are these objects called pyramids?

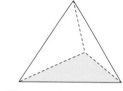

Square pyramid   Triangular pyramid

- Why are these objects called prisms?

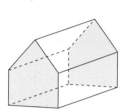 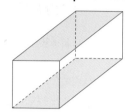

Pentagonal prism   Rectangular prism

Describe each object to your partner without saying its name.

Which objects above have:
- parallel faces?
- parallel edges?
- perpendicular faces?
- perpendicular edges?

Create a riddle that tells the attributes of an object but does not name it.

Show *and* Share

Trade riddles with another pair of classmates.
Identify your classmates' object.
Which words helped you to identify the object?

Connect •

Look at a wall in your classroom.

➤ Follow the wall down to the floor.
Look at the line that is formed where
the wall meets the floor.
The wall and floor *intersect* in this line.
The wall is *vertical*.
The floor is *horizontal*.
We say that the wall is *perpendicular* to the floor.

➤ Look at the vertical line where two
walls intersect and the horizontal line
where one of these walls meets the floor.
These lines are perpendicular.

Here is a triangular prism.

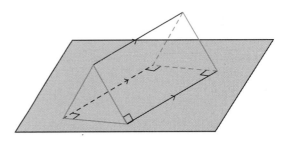

If the prism sits as shown on a table,
the red edges are horizontal.
They are also parallel.
Each blue edge is perpendicular to the red
edge where the edges intersect.

Here is the same prism with some faces shaded.
The red rectangular face is horizontal.
Each blue triangular face is vertical.
So, each triangular face is perpendicular to
the red rectangular face.
Since both triangular faces are vertical,
these faces are parallel.

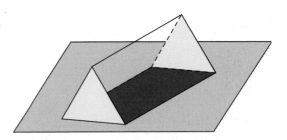

Practice

1. In your classroom, identify:
   a) two parallel walls
   b) two intersecting walls
   c) two perpendicular walls
   d) a horizontal edge
   e) a vertical edge
   f) two intersecting edges
   g) two parallel edges
   h) two perpendicular edges

2. Find each geometric object below in your classroom.

   On each object, identify, where possible:
   a) parallel edges
   b) parallel faces
   c) perpendicular faces
   d) perpendicular edges
   e) horizontal edges
   f) horizontal faces
   g) vertical faces
   h) vertical edges
   i) intersecting faces

3. Use the pictures and data from question 2.
   Create "What Am I?" riddles.
   Trade riddles with a classmate.
   Identify each object from your classmate's riddle.

4. Compare two prisms with different bases.
   Use the words you have learned in this lesson to answer the questions below.
   a) How are the prisms the same?
   b) How are they different?

Reflect

Choose two objects in the classroom, different from those in the questions above. Describe each object using these words: parallel, perpendicular, vertical, horizontal

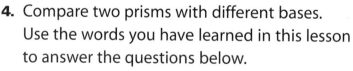

Face-Off!

The goal of this game is to show all the faces of a geometric object.

Game Rules

Your teacher will give you 36 cards.
Each card shows the face of a geometric object.
➤ The dealer deals 3 cards to each player.
  The deck of remaining cards is placed face down.
➤ The dealer places one of her cards face up.
  This is one face of an object.
➤ Each time a player places a card face up,
  the player takes a new card from the deck.
➤ The second player selects a card from his hand
  that shows another face of the object started by the dealer.
  If a player does not have a card that can be used,
  he takes a new card from the deck. The player loses his turn.

➤ The third player selects a card from her hand
  that is another face of the object.
➤ Play continues until all faces of the object are shown.
➤ The player who places the last card to complete all faces
  of the object, names the object, and gets a point.
➤ All the cards are shuffled and a new round begins.
➤ Play continues for 4 more rounds.
  The player with the most points wins.

In each round, players must complete a new object with their face cards.

Drawing Objects

Identify each object. Describe as many attributes as you can.

 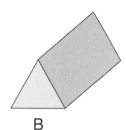 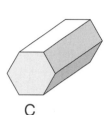 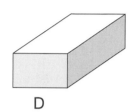

A   B   C   D

 Explore

You will need both triangular and square dot paper,
and models of the objects above.

➤ Match each object above with its front face below.
Explain how you know.

E   F   G   H

➤ Choose one front face and matching object.
Use dot paper.
Sketch the object.

➤ Trade sketches with your partner.
Identify your partner's object.

Show and Share

How did the dot paper help you draw the object?
What clues did you use to identify your partner's object?

Here are 2 ways to sketch an object.

➤ To draw this prism on triangular dot paper:

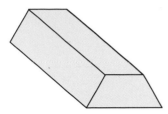

On triangular dot paper, each dot is the same distance from the 6 closest dots around it.

Step 1: Use a trapezoid as the front face. Join dots to draw a trapezoid.

Step 2: Draw a congruent trapezoid that is up and to the left of the first trapezoid.

These faces are parallel.

Step 3: Join corresponding vertices for the edges of the prism. These edges are parallel.

The blue edges that intersect are perpendicular.

➤ To draw a square pyramid on square dot paper:

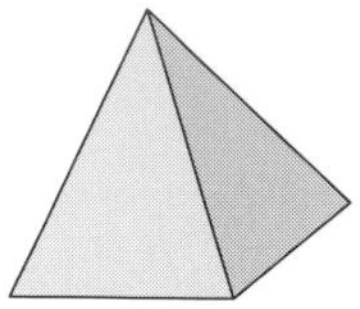

The base is horizontal.

Step 1: The base is a square, but we draw a parallelogram for the base.

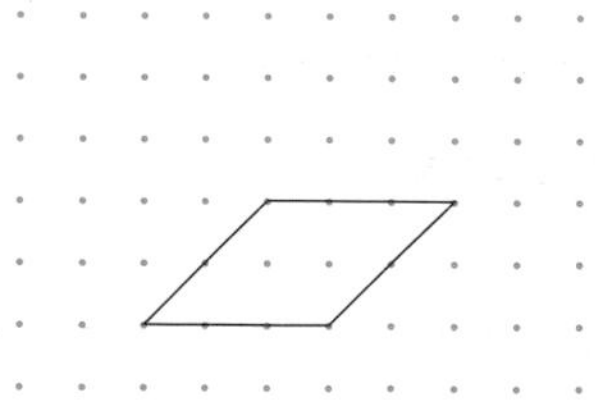

Step 2: Draw the diagonals of the base with broken lines. The diagonals intersect at the midpoint of the parallelogram.

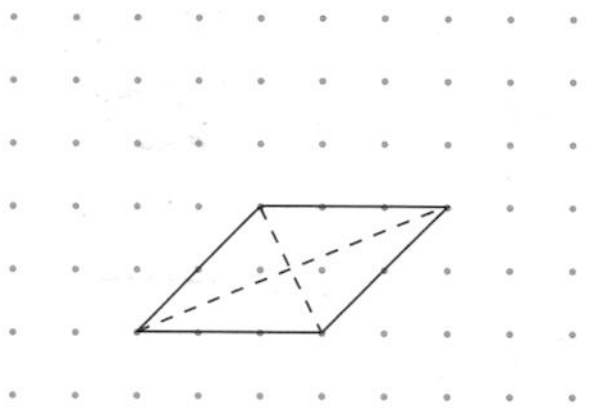

Step 3: Mark a point directly above the midpoint. This new point is the top vertex of the pyramid. Join this vertex to each vertex of the parallelogram.

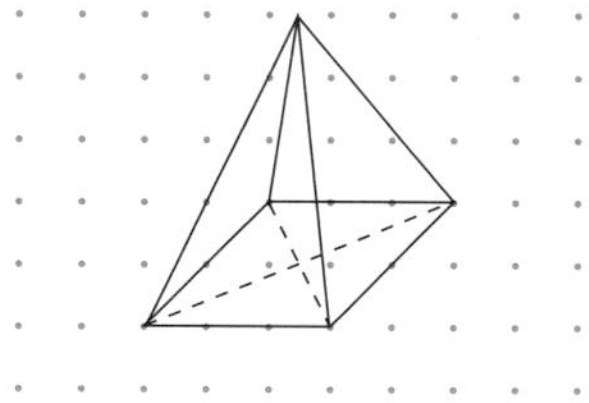

The sloping edges intersect at the top vertex.

Practice

1. Follow the steps in *Connect* to draw:
   a) the prism
   b) the square pyramid

2. Each picture below is the front face of a prism. Draw each prism.
   a) a cube
   b) a pentagonal prism

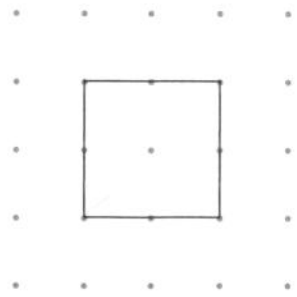

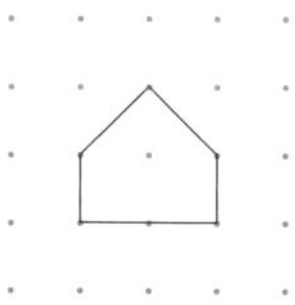

Use square dot paper or triangular dot paper.

3. Each picture below is the base of a pyramid. Draw each pyramid.
   a) a rectangular pyramid
   b) a hexagonal pyramid

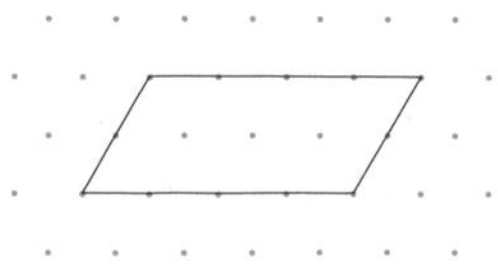

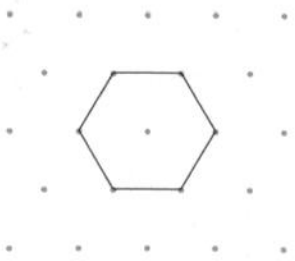

4. Name 3 objects outside the classroom that have:
   a) the shape of a prism
   b) the shape of a pyramid
   Describe each object in as much detail as possible.

5. Work with a partner.
   Use dot paper.
   Draw an object. Do not show your partner.
   Describe your object to your partner.
   Have her guess your object.
   Use any of these words to describe your object:
   perpendicular, parallel, horizontal, vertical, faces, and edges

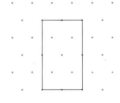

6. Draw as many prisms and pyramids as possible
   that have a triangle as a front face.
   Write about each object you draw.

7. A triangular prism with a horizontal base
   has this front face:

   Draw this prism.

8. Here is the front face of a
   rectangular prism.
   Draw a prism with this face.

6 cm

3 cm

At Home

Look through newspapers and
magazines or on the Internet.
Find examples of objects with edges
and faces that are parallel,
intersecting, perpendicular, vertical,
and horizontal.
Cut out or print the pictures.
Highlight the examples you found.

Reflect

How would you explain to
someone how to draw
a triangular pyramid?
Write the steps.
Include a drawing.

LESSON

1. a) Describe each shape at the right.
   b) Which shapes have at least
      2 equal sides?

2. Use the shapes in question 1.
   Which shapes have:
   a) perpendicular sides?
   b) parallel sides?
   c) no perpendicular sides?
   d) no parallel sides?

3. a) Use letters to name each shape
      at the right.
   b) For each shape, identify and name
      2 sides that intersect.
   c) Which shapes have parallel sides?
      Identify and name the sides that are parallel.

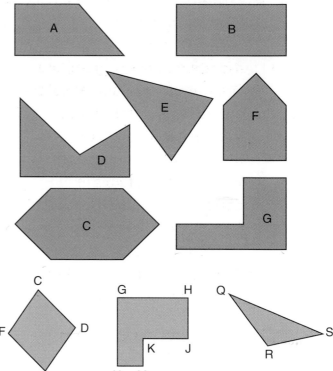

4. Look at the Venn diagram at the right.
   a) Name each quadrilateral.
      Write some attributes it has.
   b) How have the quadrilaterals been sorted?
      Write the sorting rule.

5. Look at the shapes in question 4.
   a) Use these attributes:
      "Has 2 sides equal" and
      "Has no parallel sides"
      Re-sort the shapes.
      Use a Venn diagram if it helps.
   b) Choose 2 different attributes.
      Sort the shapes.
      Trade sortings with a classmate.
      Find your classmate's sorting rule.

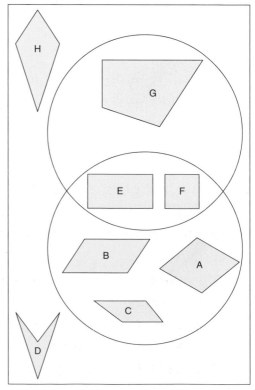

3
4

6. Use square or triangular dot paper.

   a) Draw each shape:
   rectangle, square, trapezoid,
   rhombus, parallelogram, kite

   b) Draw another quadrilateral that is
   different from the shapes in part a.

   c) Assume the bottom of each
   dot paper page is horizontal.
   Which quadrilaterals in
   parts a and b have:
   • horizontal sides?
   • vertical sides?

   d) Choose 2 attributes. Sort the quadrilaterals in parts a and b.
   What is the sorting rule?

6

7. For each object below:

   a) How many parallel faces?
   b) How many perpendicular faces?
   c) How many horizontal faces?
   d) How many vertical faces?

7

8. Look at the geometric objects
   in your classroom.
   Identify an object with the attributes
   shown below.
   Use square or triangular dot paper.
   Draw the object.

   a) an object with 2 pairs of parallel edges
   and no vertical edges

   b) an object with 2 horizontal faces and
   4 vertical faces

U N I T

6 Learning Goals

☑ describe the sides of shapes
☑ describe the faces and edges
   of objects
☑ understand the terms: parallel,
   intersecting, perpendicular,
   vertical, and horizontal
☑ use attributes to identify and
   sort quadrilaterals

Building Bridges

You will need:
- Bristol board
- a hole punch or a compass
- paper fasteners
- a centimetre ruler
- centimetre cubes or standard masses
- scissors

Part 1

Choose one type of bridge truss to build.
Your bridge must:
- span a 35-cm gap
- support a load
- stand up by itself

Your teacher will give you a copy of the truss pieces.
Use the truss pieces to cut strips of Bristol board.
How many of each size of strip do you need?
Cut a strip of Bristol board 14 cm wide
for the roadway.
How long does the road need to be?
Draw a line 2 cm in from each long edge.
Fold along the lines.

Build the bridge.
How will you brace the top?

Pratt Truss

Double Warren Truss

Part 2

Look at your bridge.
Identify as many of these attributes as you can:
- equal sides
- parallel sides
- perpendicular sides
- horizontal sides
- vertical sides
- lines of symmetry

Name the different quadrilaterals you see.

Part 3

Use two desks or some textbooks
to make a 35-cm gap.
Place your bridge across the gap.
Find the load your bridge can support.

Compare your bridge with those of other groups.
Which type of bridge can support the greatest mass?

Write about the bridges and the attributes that make them strong.

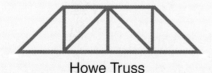

Howe Truss

Howe Truss with counter braces

Reflect on Your Learning

What have you learned about shapes and objects?
When you see a quadrilateral, which attributes do you
use to identify it?
Use words and pictures to explain.

UNIT

1

1. For each table, use a variable to write an expression for the number of dots in any figure. Check that the expression is correct.

a)

Figure Number	Number of Dots
1	3
2	4
3	5
4	6

b)

Figure Number	Number of Dots
1	0
2	1
3	2
4	3

c)

Figure Number	Number of Dots
1	10
2	11
3	12
4	13

2

2. Describe the meaning of each digit in the number 139 057.

3

3. How could you use repeated halving to find 100 ÷ 4?

4

4. The tallest known giraffe was about 6.10 m tall.
   The tallest known human was about 2720 mm tall.
   Which was taller? How much taller?
   Give your answer in millimetres.

5. Provide a referent for each unit of measure.
   Explain your choice.
   a) one metre   b) one centimetre   c) one millimetre

6. A rectangle has perimeter 22 cm.
   a) Sketch and label all possible rectangles with side lengths
      that are whole numbers of centimetres.
   b) Describe the rectangle with the greatest area.
   c) Describe the rectangle with the least area.

7. A racer drank a total of 1 L of water during
   a bike race.
   She drank 300 mL half way through the race.
   How much water did the racer drink during
   the rest of the race?

8. Use counters or draw a picture to find which pairs of fractions are equivalent.
   a) $\frac{3}{5}$ and $\frac{9}{25}$ **b)** $\frac{4}{16}$ and $\frac{2}{8}$ **c)** $\frac{2}{3}$ and $\frac{10}{15}$ **d)** $\frac{16}{18}$ and $\frac{4}{9}$

9. Which fraction in each pair is greater?
   Use equivalent fractions to find out.
   a) $\frac{5}{8}$ and $\frac{3}{4}$ **b)** $\frac{7}{9}$ and $\frac{2}{3}$ **c)** $\frac{3}{4}$ and $\frac{2}{3}$ **d)** $\frac{4}{5}$ and $\frac{13}{15}$

10. Write an equivalent decimal for each decimal.
   a) 0.54   **b)** 0.5   **c)** 0.050   **d)** 0.7

11. For which decimals in question 10 can you write 2 equivalent decimals?
   Explain why this is possible.

12. Find each sum or difference.
   Which strategy did you use each time?
   a) $4.53 - 1.98$ **b)** $3.251 + 2.982$ **c)** $5.937 - 1.09$ **d)** $6.73 + 7.321$

13. Sami had $10.47. He spent $4.69.
   How much money does Sami have left?

14. Use dot paper.
   Draw 4 different shapes with some parallel sides.
   Identify each shape you draw.
   Explain how you know you have named the shape correctly.

15. Label the vertices of each shape you drew in question 14.
   Assume the top and bottom of the dot paper are horizontal.
   For each shape, name:
   a) intersecting sides   **b)** parallel sides
   c) perpendicular sides   **d)** vertical sides
   e) horizontal sides   **f)** equal sides

16. Justify your answer to each question below.
   a) Is a rhombus a parallelogram?
   b) Is a parallelogram a rectangle?
   c) Is a rectangle a square?
   d) Is a square a rhombus?

Statistics and

Weather Watch

Learning Goals

- understand the difference between first-hand data and second-hand data
- construct and interpret double bar graphs
- use the language of probability
- compare the likelihoods of outcomes

Probability

Key Words

first-hand data

second-hand data

double bar graph

horizontal axis

vertical axis

legend

impossible

possible

certain

likely

unlikely

probable

improbable

probability

outcome

experiment

- How can we find out how much precipitation fell in one day?
- How can we find out the highest and lowest temperatures in one day?
- What types of weather are more likely in your area this week? How did you decide?
- Can we ever be certain about tomorrow's weather? Why or why not?

First-Hand Data and Second-Hand Data

To find out what people like, do, think, or need, we ask questions.
For example, how many bicycle stands will your class need?

Explore

➤ Your teacher will draw this table on the board.
How do you usually get to school?
Take turns to draw a tally mark in the correct row.
Count the tallies to complete the third column of the table.

• What do you know from the data in the table?

Method of Travel	Tally	Number of Students
Bicycle		
Bus		
Car		
Walk		
Other		

➤ Elementary school students across Canada answered the same question. Here are the results for 100 students.

• Why might someone need to know these data?
• Compare your data with the given data.
How are the data the same?
How are they different?

Method of Travel	Number of Students
Bicycle	3
Bus	36
Car	26
Walk	31
Other	4

Show and Share

Work with another classmate.
Write a question you could answer using your data. Answer the question.
Write a question you could answer using the given data. Answer the question.

| Understand the difference between first-hand and second-hand data.

Data you collect yourself are called **first-hand data**.
Data collected by someone else are called **second-hand data**.

➤ Mrs. Rasoda's class studied weather.
The students measured the rainfall for 5 days.
For Mrs. Rasoda's class, these results are first-hand data.
For you, these results are second-hand data.

Day	Rainfall
Monday	5 mm
Tuesday	9 mm
Wednesday	0 mm
Thursday	12 mm
Friday	0 mm

During the 5 days that measurements were taken, we know that:

• More rain fell on Thursday than on any other day.
• There were 2 days when no rain fell.

➤ The students also looked at second-hand
data from a government Web site.

City	Annual Average Precipitation
Winnipeg	504 mm
Regina	364 mm
Edmonton	461 mm
Calgary	399 mm
Vancouver	1167 mm

From these data, the students know that:

• Vancouver usually has more precipitation than any
other 2 cities together.
• Regina has the least precipitation of the 5 cities.

1. Mathieu goes fishing at a lake near his home.
   He counts how many fish he catches in one hour.
   Are these first-hand or second-hand data? Explain.

2. Sylvie is interested in endangered animals.
   She wants to find out how many sea lions live off the west coast of B.C.
   Should Sylvie use first-hand or second-hand data? Why?

3. Tell whether you would use first-hand or second-hand data
   to answer each question. Explain your choices.
   a) Do your friends watch more English or French videos?
   b) Which foods contain the most vitamin C?
   c) How many people live in Canada?
   d) What are the favourite TV shows of students in your school?

4. Work with a partner to collect first-hand data.
   a) Think of one thing you would like to know about your
      classmates. What question will you ask?
   b) Conduct a survey. Tally your results.
   c) Display your findings in a table.
   d) What did you find out about your classmates?
   e) Tell why first-hand data were needed to
      answer your question.

5. Think of a question you could answer with
   second-hand data.
   Look for a table or graph that gives the
   information you need.
   Use newspapers, magazines, or the Internet.
   Why are second-hand data the better choice
   for this question?

Math Link

Science

A marine biologist collects
first-hand data when she
observes whales in the
ocean. The biologist uses
second-hand data when
she receives information
on the Internet from other
scientists around the
world.

Reflect

What is the difference between first-hand data
and second-hand data?
Include one example of each type of data
in your answer.

Interpreting Double Bar Graphs

Explore

Lyne surveyed her classmates to find out what they usually wear on their feet at home. She drew two bar graphs.

Graph 1

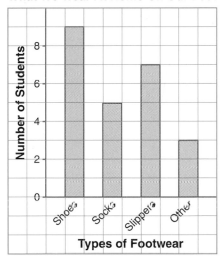

Graph 2

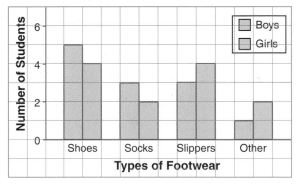

➤ How are the two graphs the same? How are they different?

➤ What can you tell from one graph that you cannot tell from the other graph?

Show *and* Share

Work with another pair of classmates. Write a question you could answer using the first graph. Write a question you could answer using the second graph. Answer both questions.

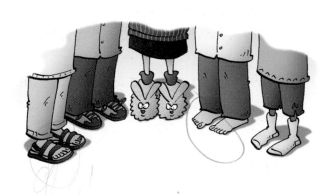

What do you usually eat for breakfast?
Students across Canada answered that question.

➤ Here are 2 bar graphs that show the typical answers of 100 boys and 100 girls.

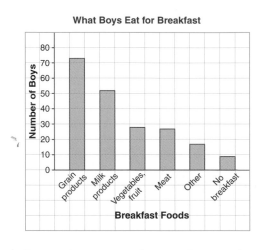

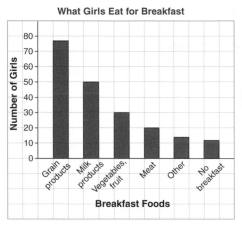

Some students eat more than one type of food.

From these graphs, we know that:

• More students eat grain products than any other food.
• Most students eat breakfast, but some do not.

➤ A **double bar graph** displays two sets of data at once.
You can use the graph to make comparisons between the data sets.

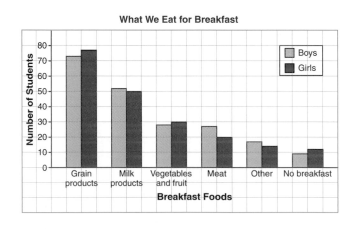

Horizontal is across. Vertical is up.

The *title* tells what the graph is about.
The **horizontal axis** shows the breakfast foods.
The **vertical axis** shows how many students eat each food.
The *scale* is 1 square represents 10 students.
The double bar graph has a **legend** that tells what the 2 colours represent.

From the double bar graph, we know that:

- More boys than girls have meat for breakfast.
- More girls than boys have no breakfast.

Any bar graph may be drawn with its bars horizontal instead of vertical.

Practice

1. Look at these double bar graphs.
   a) What attributes does every graph have?
   b) How are the graphs different?

A. Medals Won in the 2006 Arctic Winter Games

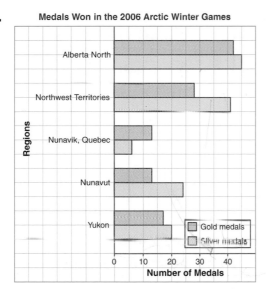

B. Thickness of Sea Ice

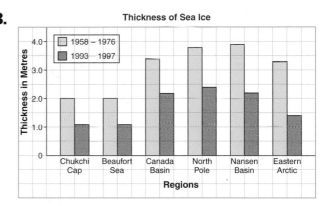

C. Category 4 and 5 Hurricanes in 30 Years

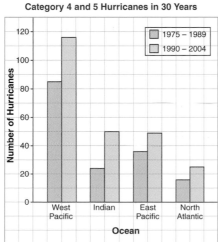

D. Some Languages Spoken by Aboriginal People, 2001

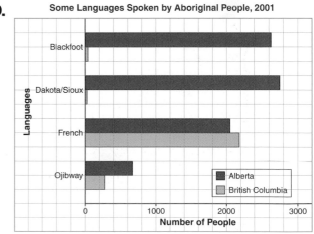

2. Choose two graphs from question 1. For each graph:
   a) Write a question you could answer using the graph.
   b) Answer your question.
   c) Trade questions with a classmate.
      Answer your classmate's question.

3. Kelly is in a combined Grades 4 and 5 class.
   She surveyed her classmates about their favourite recess activity.
   Kelly then drew this double bar graph.

Grades 4 and 5 Favourite Recess Activities

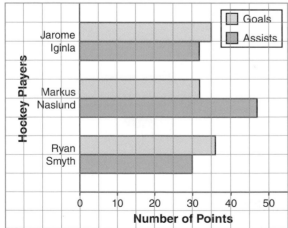

   a) What is the most popular activity for Grade 4 students?
      For Grade 5 students?
   b) How many students are in each grade?
   c) What else can you tell from the graph?

4. Suppose you are the manager of a new NHL hockey team.
   Which of these three hockey players would you pick:
   Jarome Iginla or Markus Naslund or Ryan Smyth?
   Use data from the double bar graph to explain your choice.

Hockey Players' Statistics

5. a) What does this double bar graph show?

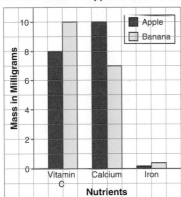

Some Nutrients in Apples and Bananas

Use the double bar graph to answer these questions.

b) Which fruit provides more vitamin C?

c) Which fruit provides more calcium?

d) An orange contains about 70 mg of vitamin C.
How do apples and bananas compare to oranges for vitamin C?

e) Write a question about this graph. Answer your question.

6. Look at this double bar graph.
What could it represent?
Use a copy of the graph.
Write a title and legend for the graph.
Label each axis.
What is the scale?

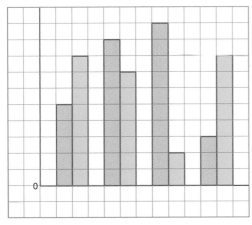

Reflect

How are a bar graph and a double bar graph alike?
How are they different?
When would you use each graph?

3

Constructing Double Bar Graphs

The students in two Grade 5 classes were asked this question: "What is your favourite physical activity?"

The students' responses are shown in the graph.
What do you know from the graph?

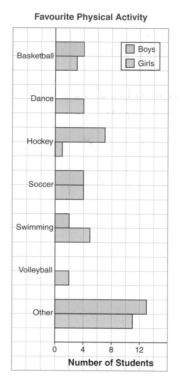

Favourite Physical Activity

Number of Students

Explore

Suppose you want to find which season the students in your class like best.
Decide on a survey question.
Collect data from equal numbers of boys and girls.
Record the data in a table.
Draw a double bar graph.

Show *and* Share

Share your graph with another pair of students.
How are your graphs the same? Different?
What conclusions can you make based on your graph?
Suppose you had surveyed twice as many boys as girls.
How might this have changed your conclusions?

The Grade 5 class sells snacks at morning and afternoon recesses.
This table shows one day's sales.

David used a double bar graph to display these data.

Snack Sales

Snack	Morning	Afternoon
Fruit	$24	$20
Cereal Bars	$30	$12
Popcorn	$6	$12
Pretzels	$6	$6

➤ First, he drew and labelled 2 axes.
   Then, he chose a scale.
   One square represents $4.

➤ He drew two bars for each
   snack in the table.
   In each pair, he coloured
   the *Morning* bar red and
   the *Afternoon* bar green.

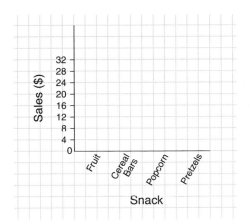

➤ He drew a legend to show what each
   colour of bar represents.
   Finally, David gave the graph a title.

The double bar graph shows how the data sets compare.

Look at the heights of pairs of bars:
• Fruit sales were a little higher
  in the morning than in the afternoon.
• Cereal bar sales were much higher
  in the morning than in the afternoon.
• Twice as much popcorn was sold
  in the afternoon than in the morning.
• Pretzels sales were the same at both recesses.

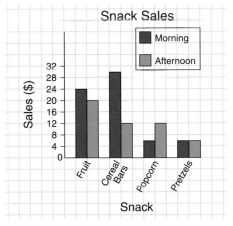

1. a) Draw a double bar graph to display the data in the table.
   b) What conclusions can you draw from the graph?

Students' Favourite Board Games

Game	Number of Girls	Number of Boys
Monopoly	8	9
Scrabble	15	6
Life	12	8
Clue	4	16

2. Work with a partner.
   a) Each of you rolls a number cube 25 times. Record the results of each roll in a table.
   b) Draw a double bar graph to show your data and your partner's data.
   c) Make comparisons between the data sets.

3. a) Draw a double bar graph to display the data in the table.
   b) Write a question about the graph. Answer the question.
   c) What else do you know from the graph?

Precipitation

City	January	July
Charlottetown	106 mm	86 mm
Fredericton	110 mm	87 mm
Halifax	134 mm	107 mm
St. John's	150 mm	89 mm

4. Jonathan Cheechoo is a star hockey player and a member of the Cree First Nation. In 2005/2006, he scored more goals than any other player in the NHL. Here are Jonathan's data for 4 months of that year.

Month	Goals	Assists
January	8	8
February	7	4
March	10	6
April	11	7

a) Graph the data.
b) In which month were Jonathan's goals and assists equal? How does the graph show this?
c) In which month did Jonathan score the fewest goals? How does the graph show this?
d) Is Jonathan more likely to score a goal, or help another player score? Give reasons for your answer.

5. a) Draw a double bar graph to display these data.

b) What do the table and graph show?

c) Does every female grizzly bear have a mass of 200 kg? Explain your answer.

d) Which has the greater mass: a male black bear or a female polar bear? How can you tell from the table? From the graph?

e) Which bear has a mass that is one-half that of a male grizzly bear?

f) Which bear has a mass that is three times that of a female grizzly bear?

g) Write another question you can answer using the graph. Answer your question.

Greatest Mass of Different Bears

Type of Bear	Mass of Female	Mass of Male
Black bear	135 kg	275 kg
Grizzly bear	200 kg	400 kg
Polar bear	300 kg	600 kg

6. Do people with long arms also have long feet? Work with 3 classmates to complete part a. Complete parts b and c on your own.

a) Measure each student's arm length and foot length, to the nearest centimetre.

b) Display the data on a double bar graph.

c) Answer the question posed above. Use the graph to explain your answer. Show your work.

At Home

Reflect

When is it better to draw a double bar graph than two separate bar graphs?

Find examples of double bar graphs in newspapers, magazines, and on the Internet.
What is being compared in each graph? Why do you think a double bar graph was drawn?

Using *Census at School* to Find Second-Hand Data

How do you and your classmates compare to other students across Canada?
You can find out on a Web site called *Census at School*.
It provides data about students from age 8 to 18.

You can use questions from *Census at School* to collect first-hand data about your own classmates.
Then, you can check the Web site for second-hand data about students from other parts of the country.
You can even find out how students in other parts of the world answered the same questions.

Your teacher can register your class so you can complete a questionnaire online. The data from your class are then included with those already on the database.

Here are some of the questions you can answer.

- Do you have allergies?
- Which pets do you have?
- What is your favourite physical activity?
- How do you usually travel to school?

Suppose you select this question:

Are you right-handed, left-handed, or ambidextrous?

A table similar to that below appears.

From the table, we know that:

About 82 girls out of 100 girls in elementary school are right-handed.

About 12 boys out of 100 boys in elementary school are left-handed.

Right-handed, left-handed or ambidextrous?

	Elementary		Secondary		All students
	Girls	Boys	Girls	Boys	
	%				
Right-handed	82.12	75.47	83.25	77.31	79.10
Left-handed	7.55	11.81	8.17	10.83	9.64
Ambidextrous	10.33	12.72	8.58	11.86	11.26

This symbol means that the numbers are given out of 100.

Source: Census at School – Canada, 2005/2006.

• What else can you find out from this table?

• Draw a double bar graph to display the data for elementary school students.
  Remember to write each number to the closest whole number.

We write each number of students to the closest whole number because we cannot have a fraction of a person.

Visit the *Census at School* Web site.

• Select a topic that interests you.
  Print the data if you can.

• Write 3 questions you can answer using the data you find.
  Answer your questions.

• If the data are suitable, draw a double bar graph to display them.
  Write all that you know from the graph that you did not know from the table.

The Language of Probability

Can you find a flower that talks?

HEY,
HOW'S
IT
GROWING?

Is the month after June always July?

Some events are **impossible**.

Events that could happen are **possible**.

Some events are **certain**.

Explore

Make a table with these headings.
Write 5 events under each heading.

Impossible	Possible but Unlikely	Possible and Likely	Certain

Show *and* Share

Share your events with another pair of students.
Do you agree about the likelihood of each event? Explain.

Connect

If an event is *likely* to happen, it is **probable**.
If an event is *unlikely* to happen,
it is **improbable**.

Luis has these coins in his pocket.

9 pennies   2 nickels   2 dimes

One coin falls out.
How likely is it that this coin is:

a ?   a ?   a ? ?   a ? ?

> The **probability** of an event is a measure of how likely the event is to happen.

- It is impossible for the coin to be a 🪙 because Luis doesn't have any quarters.

- It is likely that the coin is a 🪙 because most of Luis' coins are pennies.

The coin is *most likely* to be a 🪙.

- It is unlikely that the coin is a 🪙 or a 🪙 because Luis has only 2 of each coin.

The coin is *equally likely* to be a 🪙 or a 🪙.

You can use a line to show how likely it is an event will happen.

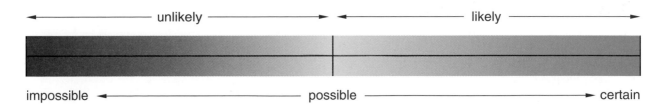

1. Use the words "impossible," "possible," "certain," "unlikely," or "likely" to describe each event.

   a) It will snow tomorrow.
   b) You will have orange juice with your lunch today.
   c) You will see a whale next week.
   d) You will go camping in the spring.
   e) Tomorrow is Friday.
   f) The sun will rise tomorrow.

2. Describe each event.
   Use these words: impossible, unlikely, likely, certain
   a) Someone in your class will win a raffle.
   b) Someone in your class is 10 years old.
   c) It will rain tomorrow.
   d) You will attend the Carnaval de Québec next February.
   e) You will have math homework next Wednesday.

3. You will need a copy of this Venn diagram.
   a) Sort these events.
      A. A rock dropped into water will sink.
      B. You will be at school and at home at the same time.
      C. A bird will fly over your school today.
      D. An ice cube will be cold.
      E. A real goldfish will sing.
   b) Where did you put events that are impossible? Explain why.
   c) Write down 3 different events.
      Sort these events in the Venn diagram.

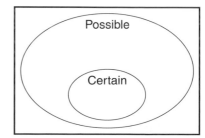

4. Roll a number cube until you get a 3.
   a) Keep a tally of how many rolls it takes.
   b) Which word describes how likely it is
   that a 3 will come up on the next roll:
   certain, possible, impossible?
   Explain.

5. Suppose you close your eyes, then pick one
   marble from this bag.
   Say which colour:
   a) You are likely to pick.
   b) You are unlikely to pick.
   c) You will never pick.

6. Draw a bag of marbles for which:
   a) Picking a pink marble is a likely event.
   b) Picking a green marble is an unlikely event.
   c) Picking an orange marble is possible.
   d) Picking a black marble is impossible.
   Explain how you chose the marbles you drew.

7. Suppose you put these counters in a bag.

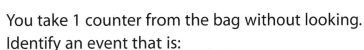

You take 1 counter from the bag without looking.
Identify an event that is:
a) possible   **b)** impossible   **c)** certain
Explain how you identified each event.

At Home

Reflect

Which event is likely to happen
at school today?
Which event is unlikely
to happen at school today?
Explain your choices.

What are two likely events
and two unlikely events that
could happen at home this
week?

Using Spinners to Compare Likelihoods

How will you know what to wear when you leave the house tomorrow?

You cannot be certain of the weather. In each season, some weather conditions are more likely than others.

Explore

Your teacher will give you a spinner.
Colour the spinner to match the colour name in each sector.
You will need an open paper clip as a pointer, and a sharp pencil point to hold the pointer at the centre of the spinner.

When you spin the pointer, it will land on one of these sectors: blue, orange, pink, or green

➤ Which result is most likely?
➤ Which result is least likely?
➤ Are any results equally likely?

Spin the pointer 20 times.
Record your results in a tally chart.
How do your results compare with your predictions?
If your results do *not* match your predictions, why do you think this happened?

Show *and* Share

Compare your results with those of another pair of students.
Talk about your predictions and how you made them.

➤ This spinner has 7 equal sectors.
So, there are 7 possible outcomes
when the pointer lands.

- One outcome that is *possible*
  is landing on 3.
  Other possible outcomes are
  landing on: 1, 2, 4, 5, 6, 7
- One outcome that is *impossible*
  is landing on 8.
  Other impossible outcomes are
  landing on: 9, 10, 11, 12, …

➤ This spinner has 4 equal sectors.

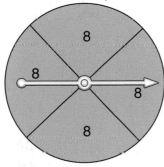

The outcome that is *certain* is landing on 8.
There is no other possible outcome.

➤ This spinner has 8 equal sectors.

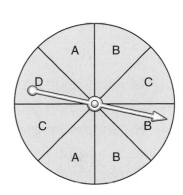

- There are 2 sectors labelled A
  and 2 sectors labelled C.
  So, landing on A and landing on C
  are *equally likely*.
- There is 1 sector labelled D.
  So, landing on D is *less likely*
  than landing on A.
  Landing on D is also less likely
  than landing on B or on C.
- There are 3 sectors labelled B.
  So, landing on B is *more likely*
  than landing on C.
  Landing on B is also more likely
  than landing on A or on D.

1. This spinner is from a board game.
   The pointer is spun.
   a) Which colour is the pointer most likely to stop on?
      How do you know?
   b) It is equally likely that the pointer will stop on
      one of two colours.
      What are the two colours? How do you know?
   c) Write a statement about the pointer using
      the word "impossible."

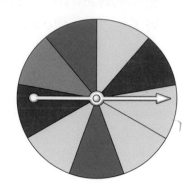

2. The pointer on each spinner is spun.
   How likely is the pointer to land on each colour:
   red, blue, green, orange, yellow?
   Use the words "less likely", "equally likely", or "more likely".

   a) 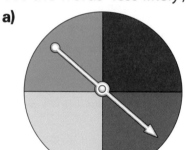 b) 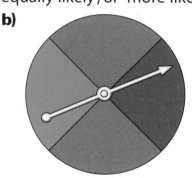 c)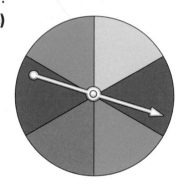

3. Your teacher will give you copies of blank spinners.
   Colour a spinner to match each statement below.
   a) landing on red is possible
   b) landing on blue is impossible
   c) landing on green is certain
   d) landing on green and landing on blue are equally likely
   e) landing on yellow is less likely than landing on pink
   f) landing on brown is more likely than landing on purple

4. Look at the spinners you coloured in question 3.
   Write another statement about one of the spinners that uses each word
   or phrase below.
   a) possible   b) impossible
   c) less likely   d) equally likely
   e) more likely

5. The pointer on this spinner is spun.

    a) What are the possible outcomes?

    b) Compare the likelihoods of the outcomes.
Use the words "more likely," "equally likely,"
or "less likely."

6. Alex and Rebecca spin the pointer
on this spinner.
Alex gets a point if the pointer lands
on an even number.
Rebecca gets a point if it lands
on an odd number.
Each person spins the pointer 20 times.
The person with more points wins.
Who is more likely to win? How do you know?

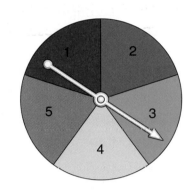

7. Anna and Nicolas disagree on the likelihoods
of where the pointer will land.
Anna thinks that the pointer landing on 2
is more likely because it has two spaces
on the spinner.
Nicolas thinks that the pointer landing on 1
is more likely than the pointer landing
on any other number.
Who is correct? Why?

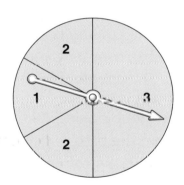

Reflect

Suppose you have a spinner with
equal sectors and different colours.
What do you know about the likelihood
of landing on each colour?
Use words, pictures, or numbers to explain.

Conducting Experiments

Explore •

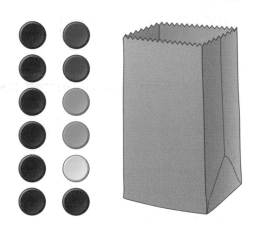

You will need a paper bag and counters.
Put 1 yellow, 2 blue, 2 green,
and 7 red counters in a bag.

➤ Suppose you took out 1 counter,
without looking.
Is each outcome below impossible, unlikely,
likely, or certain? Explain.
Which outcomes are equally likely? Explain.
A. The counter is blue.
B. The counter is green.
C. The counter is yellow.
D. The counter is red.
E. The counter is orange.

➤ Without looking, take 1 counter
from the bag.
Record the colour in a tally chart like this:
Replace the counter and shake the bag.
Do this 50 times.
Explain your results.

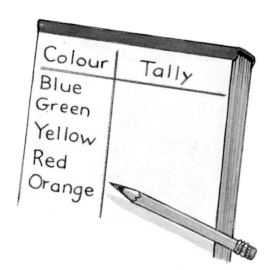

Show *and* Share

Share your results with another pair of classmates.
How do your results compare with theirs?
Are the results the same?
Should the results be the same? Explain.

Connect

Taking a counter from a bag is an **experiment.**

Suzanne and Marius conduct this experiment:
Suzanne puts these tiles in a paper bag:
6 red, 2 black, 1 yellow, and 1 blue
Without looking, Marius takes
a tile from the bag.
Suzanne records the colour of
the tile in a tally chart.
Marius returns the tile to the bag.
This experiment was conducted 100 times.

Marius is more likely to take a red tile than a blue tile.

Colour of Tile	Tally	Number of Tiles
Red ■	⦀⦀ ⦀⦀ ⦀⦀ ⦀⦀ ⦀⦀ ⦀⦀ ⦀⦀ ⦀⦀ ⦀⦀ ⦀⦀ ⦀⦀ ⦀⦀ II	62
Black ■	⦀⦀ ⦀⦀ ⦀⦀ III	18
Yellow	⦀⦀ IIII	9
Blue ■	⦀⦀ ⦀⦀ I	11

← Here are the results of the experiment.

- Six of the 10 tiles are red.
  So, it is more likely that a ■ is taken.
  The results show this.
  62 ■ were taken. Only 18 ■ were taken.
- Only 1 tile is yellow.
  So, it is less likely that a ⬜ is taken.
  The results show this.
  Only 9 ⬜ were taken compared with 62 ■ and 18 ■.
- There is 1 yellow tile and 1 blue tile.
  So, taking a ⬜ and taking a ■ are equally likely.
  The results show this.
  The numbers of ⬜ and ■ are very close: 9 and 11, respectively.
- All the tiles are coloured.
  So, it is certain that a coloured tile is taken.
  The results show this. All 100 tiles taken were coloured.
- There are no ■ in the bag.
  So, it is impossible to take a ■.
  The results show this.
  No green tiles were taken.

1. **a)** Suppose you toss a coin.
   Which outcome is more likely: heads or tails?
   b) Toss a coin 40 times.
   Record your results in a tally chart.

	Tally	Total
Heads		
Tails		

   c) How do your results compare to your answer to part a? Explain.

2. Work with a partner.
   Roll a number cube 30 times.
   Record the result of each roll in a tally chart.
   Use your results and one of these words:
   likely, unlikely, impossible, certain
   Describe the likelihood of each event.
   a) rolling a 6
   b) rolling a 7
   c) rolling a number from 1 to 6
   d) rolling a number greater than 2

Number	Tally	Total
1		
2		
3		
4		
5		
6		

3. Work with a partner.
   Place 5 red tiles and 1 yellow tile in a paper bag.
   Take turns taking a tile from the bag and replacing it.
   Record your results.
   Do this 30 times.
   a) Which colour tile is more likely to be taken?
   Do your results match your answer? Explain.
   b) Which colour tile is less likely to be taken?
   Do your results match your answer? Explain.
   c) Which colour tile will never be taken?
   Explain how your results confirm your answer.

For each of questions 4 to 6, answer this question:
Who is more likely to win the game?
Use likelihoods to explain how you know.

4. The pointer is spun.
   Player A gets a point if the pointer
   lands on an even number.
   Player B gets a point if the pointer
   lands on an odd number.

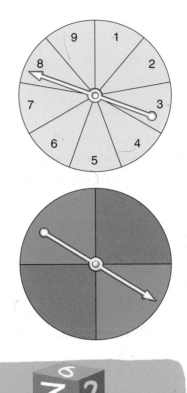

5. The pointer is spun.
   Player A gets a point if the pointer
   lands on ⬤.
   Player B gets a point if the pointer
   lands on ⬤.

6. A number cube labelled 1 to 6 is rolled.
   Player A gets a point if 1 or 2 shows.
   Player B gets a point if 3, 4, 5, or 6 shows.

7. Which spinner most likely has
   these results after 100 spins?
   60 blue and 40 red
   Explain your thinking.

Spinner A   **Spinner B**

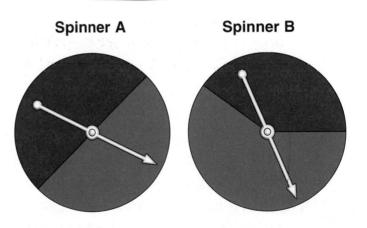

Reflect

Suppose you and a friend plan to toss a coin.
Your friend says that she nearly always tosses heads.
What would you say?

LESSON 7

Designing Experiments

Explore

You will need an envelope, 10 red paper clips, and 10 green paper clips.

Take turns to design an experiment to get one of the results below.
You have to decide how many paper clips of each colour
to put in the envelope.

Result A: removing a ⫘ is less likely than removing a ⫘

Result B: removing a ⫘ is more likely than removing a ⫘

Result C: removing a ⫘ and removing a ⫘ are equally likely

Conduct all three experiments.
For each experiment, remove a paper clip from the envelope
and replace it 20 times.
Record your results.

Did each experiment turn out the
way you expected? Explain.

Show *and* Share

Compare your experiments with
those of another group of students.
How are the experiments
for Result A the same?
How are they different?
Repeat this comparison for
Result B, then Result C.
Suppose you conducted the other
group's experiments.
Do you think your results would
have been the same? Explain.

Sue and Tim were designing experiments with 2 colours of tiles in a paper bag.
Sue designed an experiment where taking a blue tile
was more likely than taking a red tile.
Sue put 2 red tiles and 8 blue tiles in the bag.

Tim took a tile, recorded its colour,
then returned the tile to the bag.
Here are the results.

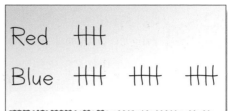

Tim took a blue tile more often than he took a red tile.
The experiment turned out the way Sue expected.

Practice

1. Your teacher will give you 3 copies of a large spinner.
   Design, then colour each spinner so that:
   a) Landing on red is less likely than landing on green.
   b) Landing on red and landing on green are equally likely.
   c) Landing on red is more likely than landing on green.
   Explain why you coloured each spinner the way you did.

2. You will need an open paper clip as a pointer and
   a sharp pencil point to hold it in place.
   For each spinner in question 1, conduct an experiment to check
   that the spinner you coloured works the way you expected.
   How many times do you think you should spin each pointer?
   Explain your answer.

3. You will need coloured counters and a paper bag.
   Suppose you take one counter from the bag without looking.
   Design one experiment so that:
   • You are unlikely to take a green counter.
   • You are likely to take a blue counter.
   • Taking a red counter is impossible.
   a) How many counters of each colour did you put in the bag?
   b) Explain why you chose the counters you did.

4. Conduct the experiment you designed for question 3.
Did the experiment give you the results you expected? Explain.

5. Suppose you have number cards from 1 to 20 and a paper bag.
An experiment is taking a number from the bag without looking.
Design each experiment:
   a) Taking an even number and taking an odd number
   are equally likely.
   b) Taking an odd number is more likely than taking
   an even number.
   c) Taking a number from 1 to 10 is more likely than
   taking a number from 11 to 20.
   d) Taking number 13 is impossible.
   Conduct each experiment to check that it works the way you expect.
   Write about how you designed each experiment and
   how well it worked.

6. Fatima is playing this game for the first time.
She throws a dart at the target.
   a) Is it likely Fatima will hit the bull's-eye?
   Explain your answer.
   b) Explain why hitting white and
   hitting red are *not* equally likely.
   c) Design a target so that hitting red and
   hitting white are equally likely.

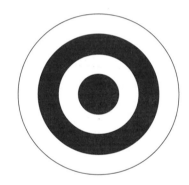

7. Design a spinner so that when the pointer is spun:
   • Landing on red is most likely.
   • Landing on blue is impossible.
   • Landing on green and landing on yellow are equally likely.
   • Landing on purple is least likely.
   Explain your work.

Reflect

Did your probability experiments always turn out the way
you expected? Explain.
Include examples in your explanation.

Sum Fun

You will need 2 number cubes each labelled 1 to 6.

➤ Take turns to roll the number cubes.

➤ Find the sum of the 2 numbers rolled.
   If the sum is even, you score a point.
   If the sum is odd, your partner scores a point.

➤ Record the results in a table.

➤ The first player to score 20 points wins.

➤ Who do you think will have more points after 36 turns?
   Explain.

Jean	Jack
Odd Sum	Even Sum
‖‖ ‖	‖‖ ‖‖

➤ List the outcomes of the game.

➤ Which is more likely: an even sum or an odd sum?
   Or, are these sums equally likely?
   How do you know?

Strategies Toolkit

Explore

Arlo did an experiment.
He used a spinner with green,
yellow, red, and blue parts.
Here are his results.

What might Arlo's spinner look like?

Colour	Tally
Green	⧼⧽ ⧼⧽
Yellow	⧼⧽ ⧼⧽ ⧼⧽ ⧼⧽ ⧼⧽ ⧼⧽
Red	⧼⧽ ⧼⧽
Blue	⧼⧽ ⧼⧽

Show and Share

Describe the strategy you used to solve this problem.

Connect

Jolanta did a spinner
experiment.
Here are her results.
What might her spinner
look like?

Colour	Tally
Green	⧼⧽ ⧼⧽ ⧼⧽ |||
Yellow	⧼⧽ ⧼⧽ ||

Strategies

- Make a table.
- Use a model.
- Draw a picture.
- Solve a simpler problem.
- Work backward.
- Guess and test.
- Make an organized list.
- Use a pattern.

What do you know?
- The spinner has 2 colours: green and yellow.
- The pointer landed on green 18 times and yellow 12 times.

Think of a strategy to help you solve the problem.
- You could **work backward**.
- Use the results to draw the spinner.

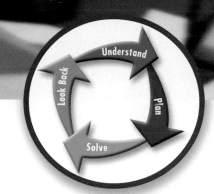

How are the numbers in the tally chart related?

How many congruent parts of the spinner are yellow? How many are green?

Draw the spinner.

How many different spinners can you draw?

Practice

Choose one of the **Strategies**

1. Sketch the spinner that likely gave each set of data.

   a)

Black	‖‖ ‖‖ ‖
Red	‖‖ ‖‖‖
Orange	‖‖ ‖‖ ‖‖
Green	‖‖ ‖‖ ‖

   b)

1	‖‖ ‖‖ ‖
2	‖‖ ‖‖‖
3	‖‖ ‖‖ ‖

2. The numbers 1, 2, 3, and 4 were written on the faces of an object.
   The object was rolled 40 times.
   The results are in the tally chart.
   Name the object you think was used.
   Explain your choice.

1	‖‖ ‖‖ ‖
2	‖‖ ‖‖‖
3	‖‖ ‖‖‖
4	‖‖ ‖‖ ‖

Reflect

How does working backward help to solve a problem?
Use words and numbers to explain.

LESSON

1

1. Tell whether you would use first-hand or second-hand data to answer the following questions:
   a) Do your friends prefer to read fiction or non-fiction books?
   b) Do more Canadians live in cities or outside cities?
   c) How many people in British Columbia speak Cantonese at home?
   d) How many people in Manitoba speak French?
   e) Which movies are most popular with the students in your class?

2
3

2. This table shows some students' favourite hiking snacks.
   a) How many students were surveyed?
   b) Draw a double bar graph to display these data.
   c) Make comparisons between the data sets. Write as many as you can.
   d) What can you tell more easily from the graph than the table?

Favourite Hiking Snacks

Snack	Number of Grade 5 Students	Number of Grade 6 Students
Granola bar	14	11
Nuts	5	9
Pretzels	7	3
Dried fruit	4	7

4

3. Use the words "likely," "unlikely," "impossible," "possible," or "certain" to describe each event.
   a) It will rain tomorrow.
   b) You will be in school this afternoon.
   c) You will go canoeing in January.
   d) You will travel to the moon in the future.

4. Each letter of the word PEPPER is written on a card.
   The cards are shuffled.
   One card is picked without looking.
   a) Which letter is most likely to be picked?
   b) Which letter is least likely to be picked?
   c) Which letter is impossible to pick?
   d) Are any two letters equally likely to be picked?
      How do you know?

5

5. The pointer on this spinner is spun.
Compare the likelihoods of landing on the letters.
Use any of the words:
less likely, equally likely, more likely

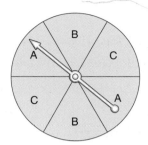

6

6. Suppose you took one marble from this bag
without looking.
Is each outcome below impossible, unlikely, likely, or certain?
a) The marble is green.   **b)** The marble is blue.
c) The marble is red.   **d)** The marble is yellow.

7. Work with a partner.
Place tiles in a paper bag to match the marble colours
in question 6.
Take turns removing a tile from the bag and replacing it.
Record your results. Do this 30 times.
Do your results confirm your answers to question 6?
Explain how you know.

7

8. Suppose you have a paper bag and coloured tiles.
You take one tile from the bag without looking, then replace it.
Design one experiment so that:
• You are more likely to take a red tile than
a yellow tile.
• Taking a blue tile is impossible.
• Taking a red tile and taking a green tile are
equally likely.
a) Tell how many tiles of each colour you would
place in the bag.
b) Explain why you chose the tiles you did.

9. Conduct the experiment you designed for
question 8.
Did the experiment give you the results you
expected? Explain.

UNIT

7 Learning Goals

☑ understand the difference
between first-hand data and
second-hand data
☑ construct and interpret
double bar graphs
☑ use the language of
probability
☑ compare the likelihoods
of outcomes

Weather Watch

Look at this table of weather data.
Are these first-hand or second-hand data?

Precipitation	Iqaluit, Nunavut	Vancouver, B.C.
Average January rainfall	0.1 mm	139.1 mm
Average January snowfall	228.0 mm	166.0 mm
Average July rainfall	59.2 mm	39.6 mm
Average July snowfall	1.0 mm	0

Part A

Use the data to draw a double bar graph on 1-cm grid paper.
Your graph should compare Iqaluit and Vancouver.
It should show the January rainfall, January snowfall,
July rainfall, and July snowfall in each place.

Write each measurement to
the closest millimetre before you
graph the data.

Check List

Your work should show

☑ double bar graphs with a title, a legend, and labelled axes

☑ answers to the questions in Part B

☑ pictures that show likely and unlikely weather in two other Canadian cities

Part B

Use your graph to help answer these questions.

- Is a rainy January day likely, unlikely, or impossible in Iqaluit? In Vancouver?

- Where are you more likely to have a rainy day in July?

- Where are you more likely to have a snowy day in July?

- Is a snowy July day in Vancouver impossible? Explain your answer.

- What else do you know from looking at your graph?

Part C

Find weather data for two other Canadian cities.
Repeat Parts A and B for the two cities.
Fold 2 pieces of paper into 4 sections.
For each city, draw a picture to show January and July weather that is likely and unlikely in each place.

Reflect on Your Learning

How does what you learned in this unit relate to your life outside school? Give examples.

Transformations

At the Amusement Park

Learning Goals

- translate, reflect, and rotate a shape
- draw and describe images after transformations
- identify a transformation

Key Words

· · · · · · · · · · · · · · · · · · · ·

translation

translation image

translation arrow

reflection

reflection image

line of reflection

rotation

rotation image

quarter turn

half turn

three-quarter turn

clockwise

counterclockwise

point of rotation

transformations

Look at the map of the amusement park.

· What rides do you see?
· How do people move on each ride?
· What is your favourite ride at an amusement park?
  How do you move on that ride?

Translations

A firefighter slides down a pole.

A flag slides up a pole.

A child slides down a playground slide.

Which other ways do people or objects slide?

Explore

You will need Pattern Blocks, dot paper, and a ruler.

➤ Choose a Pattern Block.
Place it on the dot paper.
Trace the block.
Slide the block in a straight line, in any direction.
Do not turn the block.
Use a ruler if it helps.
Trace the block in its new position.
How do the two positions of the block compare?

➤ Take turns to move a block and describe how its two positions compare.

Show *and* Share

Compare drawings with another pair of classmates.
How do the original shape and the shape in its new position compare?

Connect •

When a shape moves along a straight line, without turning,
it is *translated* from one position to another.
The movement is a **translation** or a *slide*.

When we draw the shape in its new position,
we draw a **translation image** of the shape.

The translation is described by the numbers
of squares moved right or left and up or down.
The translation below is:
5 squares right and 4 squares down.

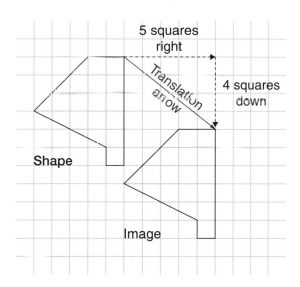

We say how many squares right or left before we say how many up or down.

If we cannot translate the shape, we trace the shape,
then translate the tracing.

The **translation arrow** shows how the shape moved.
The arrow joins matching points on the shape and its image.

A shape and its translation image have the same orientation;
that is, they face the same way.

1. Copy each shape on grid paper. Use tracing paper.
   Translate the shape using the given translation.
   Draw the image and a translation arrow.
   Describe the position and orientation of the image.

   a) 7 squares left and
   3 squares up

   b) 5 squares right
   and 4 squares down

   c) 3 squares left and
   6 squares down

    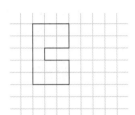 

2. Does each picture show a translation?
   How do you know?
   If a picture does show a translation, describe it.

   a)

   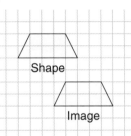

   b)

   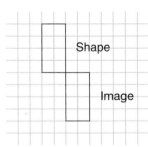

   c)

   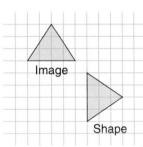

   d)

   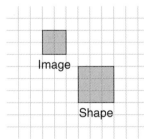

3. Write the translation that moved each shape to its image.

   a)

   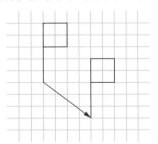

   b)

   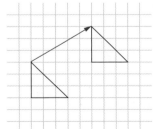

   c)

   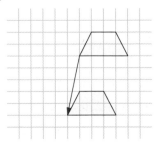

4. a) Draw this shape on grid paper.
   Predict where the image will be after
   this translation:
   3 squares left and 5 squares up
   Draw the image to check your prediction.

b) Draw the shape again.
   Predict where the image will be after
   this translation:
   5 squares left and 3 squares up
   Draw the image to check your prediction.

5. Draw a shape on dot paper.
   Translate the shape in any direction.
   Draw its image.
   Record the translation.
   Describe the position and orientation of the image.

6. Draw two identical shapes in two different places
   on grid paper.
   Make sure the shapes have the same orientation.
   Label one shape "Image" and the other "Shape".
   Which translation will move the shape to its image?

7. Copy these shapes on grid paper.

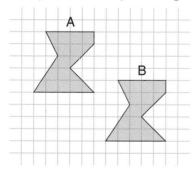

a) Describe which translation moves Shape A to Shape B.
b) Describe which translation moves Shape B to Shape A.

Reflect

Use grid paper.
Draw a shape and its translation image.
Explain how you know your picture shows a translation.

Strategies Toolkit

Explore

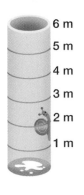

The hare and the tortoise had a race.
The race was 5 times around the running track.
The hare ran 4 times around in 1 h,
then stopped for a rest.
The tortoise did not stop.
She took 1 h to go once around the track.
The hare woke up after 4 h.
Who won the race?

Show *and* Share

Explain how you solved the problem.

Strategies

- **Make a table.**
- **Use a model.**
- **Draw a picture.**
- **Solve a simpler problem.**
- **Work backward.**
- **Guess and test.**
- **Make an organized list.**
- **Use a pattern.**

Connect

A snail is at the bottom of a well.
It climbs 2 m every day, but it slides
back 1 m at night.
The well is 6 m deep.
How many days does it take the snail
to get out of the well?

Understand

What do you know?
- Each day, the snail climbs
  2 m up the well.
- Each night, the snail slides back 1 m.
- The snail has to climb 6 m to get out.

Plan

Think of a strategy to help you solve the problem.
- You can **draw a picture.**
- Show where the snail is each day.

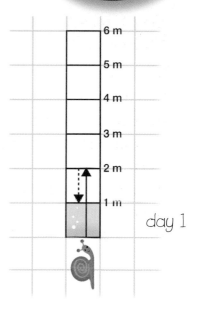

Use grid paper to record how far the snail moves.
Use a different colour for each day.
Count the days when the snail reaches the top of the well.
When does the snail get out of the well?

Write a similar problem.
Have a classmate solve your problem.

6 m
5 m
4 m
3 m
2 m
1 m

day 1

Practice

Choose one of the Strategies

1. Shannon is shorter than Bruce.
   Olivia is shorter than Alex but taller than Bruce.
   Who is the tallest? Shortest?

2. Hannah and Liam are using a compass.
   They move 30 m north, then 30 m west, and then 30 m south.
   Which direction do Hannah and Liam go to get back to where they started?
   How far must they go?

N
W ← → E
S

Reflect

How does drawing a picture help you to solve a problem?

Reflections

A **reflection** can be used to make an interesting picture.
Is this person floating above the ground?
Where else do you see reflections?

Explore

You will need Pattern Blocks, dot paper,
a ruler, and a Mira.

➤ Draw a line through the centre
of the dot paper.
Place a Mira on this line.

➤ Place a block on one side of the line.
Your partner places her block on
the image she sees in the Mira.

➤ Take turns to place one block,
then another block on its image.
Each time, describe the position
and orientation of the image.

➤ Take turns to draw around a block and its image.
  Draw around blocks that touch the Mira line.
  Draw around blocks that cross the Mira line.
  In each case, how does the shape compare with its image?

Show *and* Share

Compare your pictures with those of another pair of classmates.
How is each shape and its image placed with respect to the Mira line?

Connect ·

When a shape is *reflected* in a
mirror, we see a **reflection image**.

The line segment that joins a point
to its image is perpendicular to the
line of reflection.

A point and its image are the same
distance from the line of reflection.

A shape and its reflection image have
opposite orientations; that is, they
face opposite ways.

A reflection is sometimes called a *flip*.
When a shape is reflected, it is flipped over.

Math Link

Your World

Many patterns and designs show a shape and its reflection images.
Identify a shape and its reflection images in this design.
Where are the lines of reflection?

Use a Mira when it helps.

1. Copy each shape and line of reflection on grid paper.
   Draw each reflection image.
   Describe the position and orientation of the image.

   a)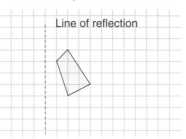

   b)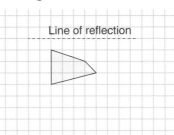

   c)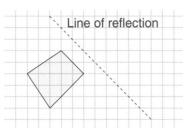

   d)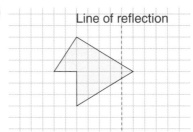

2. Which pictures show a reflection? How do you know?
   Describe where the line of reflection is.

   a)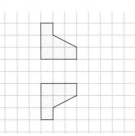

   b)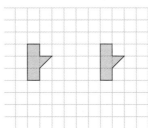

   c)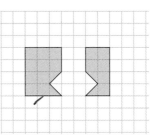

3. In question 2, do any pictures show a translation?
   If so, describe the translation.

4. Each picture shows a shape and its reflection image.

   a)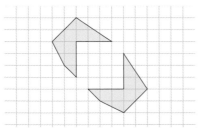

   b)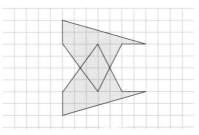

   Copy each picture on grid paper.
   Draw the line of reflection. Explain how you did this.
   How do you know the line of reflection is drawn correctly?

5. Copy each shape and line of reflection on dot paper.
Predict where each reflection image will be.
Draw each image to check your prediction.

a)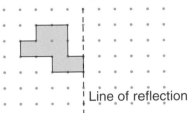

Line of reflection

b)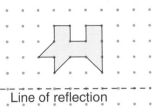

Line of reflection

6. Print the letters of the alphabet as capital letters.
   a) Draw a horizontal line above each letter.
   Place a Mira on the line.
   Which letters look the same in the Mira?
   b) Draw a vertical line beside each letter.
   Place a Mira on the line.
   Which letters look the same in the Mira?
   c) Create three words whose images
   read the same as the words when
   a Mira is placed above the letters.

7. Draw a shape on dot paper.
   Draw and label a line of reflection.
   Draw the image of the shape in the line of reflection.
   a) Use a ruler.
   Join two matching points on the shape and its image.
   b) Use a ruler.
   Measure the distance between each point and the line of reflection.
   What do you notice?
   c) What do you notice about the angle between the line you drew
   in part a and the line of reflection?
   Show your work. Explain your thinking.

Reflect

How are a translation and a reflection alike?
Draw a shape and its image that could show both
a reflection and a translation.

Rotations

A bicycle wheel turns about the centre
of the wheel.

What other examples are there of things that turn?
Explain how they turn.

Explore

You will need several pieces of paper, tracing paper, a ruler,
a compass, and scissors.

➤ Use a ruler.
Draw a shape with straight sides
in the centre of a piece of paper.

➤ Use tracing paper.
Draw an identical shape on
another piece of paper.
Cut out this shape.
Place it on top of the first
shape you drew.

➤ Put your compass point at
one vertex.
Turn the shape to a new position.
Draw the shape in its new position.
Label this shape Image A.

➤ Return your shape to its
original position.
Turn the shape in the opposite direction.
Draw the shape in its new position.
Label this shape Image B.

➤ In each case, how do the positions of the original shape
and its image compare?

Show and Share

Compare your picture and ideas with another pair of classmates.
Did you have the same ideas about how a shape compares
with its image after a rotation? Explain.

 **Connect** ·

When a shape turns about a point,
it is *rotated* from one position to another.

The movement is a **rotation**, or *turn*.
When we draw the shape in its new position,
we draw a **rotation image** of the shape.

After 1 complete turn, a shape is back
to where it started.

When the minute hand on a clock moves from 12 to 3, it moves a **quarter turn**.	When the minute hand moves from 12 to 6, it moves a **half turn**.	When the minute hand moves from 12 to 9, it moves a **three-quarter turn**.
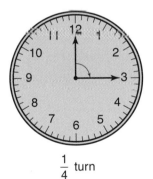	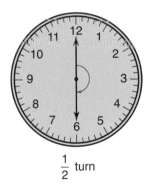	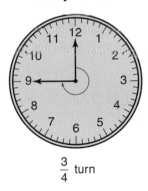
$\frac{1}{4}$ turn	$\frac{1}{2}$ turn	$\frac{3}{4}$ turn

A shape can rotate **clockwise**
about a vertex V:

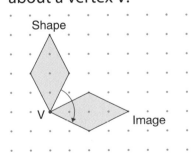

A shape can rotate **counterclockwise**
about a vertex V:

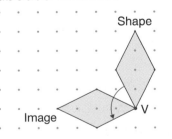

Any turn less than 1 complete turn is a fraction of a turn clockwise or counterclockwise.

This shape has rotated a $\frac{1}{4}$ turn clockwise, about vertex A.
This point is called the **point of rotation**.

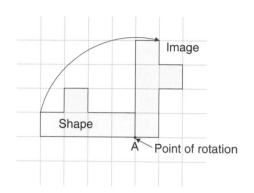

This shape has rotated a $\frac{1}{4}$ turn counterclockwise, about vertex B.

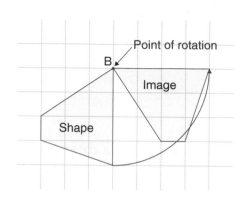

A rotation is described by:

• the direction of the turn (clockwise or counterclockwise),

• the fraction of the turn, and

• the point of rotation

A shape and its rotation image have different orientations. The shape and its image face different ways for any rotation that is less than 1 complete turn.

A reflection, a rotation, and a translation are **transformations**.

Practice

1. Copy each shape below on grid paper. For each shape:
   • Rotate the shape about vertex V, using the rotation given.
   • Draw the rotation image.
   • Describe the position and orientation of the image.

   a) a $\frac{1}{4}$ turn counterclockwise

   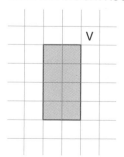

   b) a $\frac{1}{2}$ turn clockwise

   c) a $\frac{3}{4}$ turn clockwise

   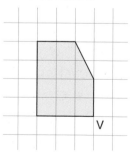

2. Each picture below shows a shape and its rotation image. Describe the rotation. Include the direction of the turn.

a)

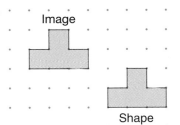

b)

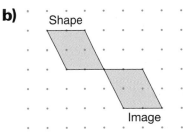

3. Which pictures show a rotation?
How do you know? Describe the rotation.

a)

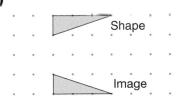

b)

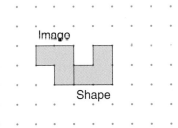

c)

Shape

Image

d)

Image

Shape

4. Did any of the pictures in question 3 show a translation? A reflection? If so, identify the picture and describe the transformation.

5. Copy this shape.
Trace the shape on tracing paper.
Use the tracing to rotate the shape.
Predict the position of the image after each rotation below.
Draw each image to check your prediction.

a) a $\frac{1}{4}$ turn clockwise about vertex A

b) a $\frac{3}{4}$ turn counterclockwise about vertex A

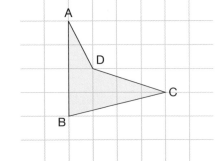

6. Copy this shape.
Use tracing paper to rotate the shape:
a) a $\frac{1}{2}$ turn clockwise about vertex E
b) a $\frac{1}{2}$ turn counterclockwise about vertex E
What do you notice about the rotation images?

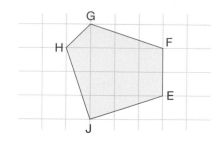

7. Copy this shape on grid paper.
   a) Rotate the shape about a vertex.
       Describe the direction of the turn, the fraction of the turn, and the point of rotation.
       Draw the image.
   b) Repeat part a for a different direction.
   c) Repeat part a for a different fraction.
   d) Repeat part a for a different point of rotation.
   Show your work.

8. Describe the transformation that moves the shape to each image.
Can you describe any movements in more than one way? Explain.
   a) Image A
   b) Image B
   c) Image C
   d) Image D

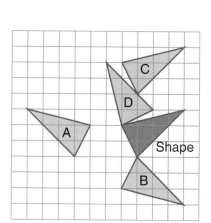

Reflect

When you see a shape and its image, how do you know if they show a reflection, a rotation, or a translation?
Use diagrams to explain.

At Home

Look for an example of each transformation.
Describe each transformation and explain how you identified it.

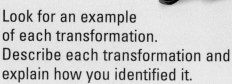

Exploring Different Points of Rotation

A shape can rotate about a point of rotation that is not on the shape.

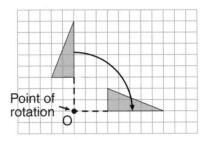

Point of rotation
O

Explore

You will need grid paper, Pattern Blocks, and a ruler.

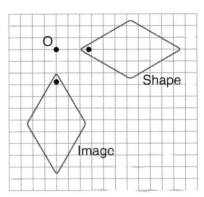

➤ A blue Pattern Block was placed on grid paper and traced.
The block was rotated about point O and traced again.
Describe different ways the block could have moved.
Tell about the fraction of the turn, the direction, and the point of rotation.
How do the shape and its image compare?

➤ Trace the blue Pattern Block on grid paper as shown.
Extend one side and mark this endpoint O.
Use point O as the point of rotation.
Choose clockwise or counterclockwise.
Rotate the block a $\frac{1}{2}$ turn about point O.
Trace its new position.

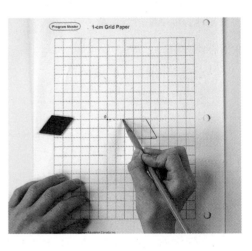

Show and Share

Exchange your tracings with a pair of students who rotated their block in the direction opposite to yours.
What do you notice? Explain.

LESSON FOCUS | Rotate a shape about a point of rotation not on the shape.

311

➤ We can use tracing paper to find the image when we rotate a shape.

- Place the tracing paper so the bottom right corner is on point P.
- Trace the shape.
- Hold the tracing paper in place with your pencil at point P.
  Rotate the tracing paper a $\frac{1}{4}$ turn clockwise.
- Note the position of the image of the shape.
- Lift the tracing paper and draw the image in place.
  Label the image.

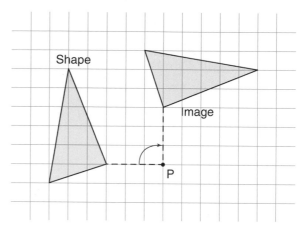

➤ We can predict the position of the image formed when we rotate a shape. Visualize the shape as a flag whose pole joins any vertex to the point of rotation. The pole rotates, but its length does not change.

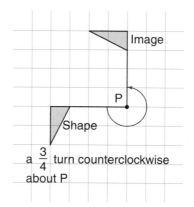

a $\frac{3}{4}$ turn counterclockwise about P

Use tracing paper when needed.

1. Copy each rectangle and point P on grid paper.
   Draw each image after a $\frac{1}{4}$ turn clockwise about point P.

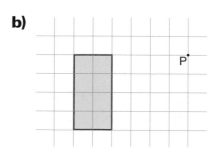

a)

b)

2. Copy each trapezoid and point P on grid paper.
Draw each image after a $\frac{1}{2}$ turn clockwise about P.

a)

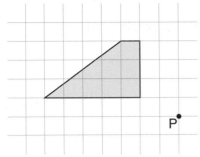

b)

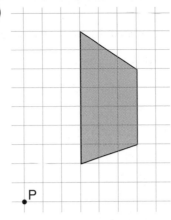

3. Describe each rotation.
Include:
• the fraction of the turn
• the point of rotation
• the direction

a)

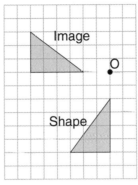

b)

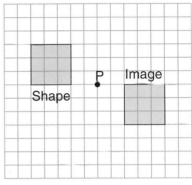

4. Copy this trapezoid and point O
on grid paper.

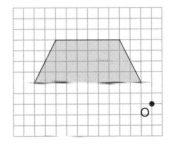

   a) Draw the image after a $\frac{1}{4}$ turn
   clockwise about point O.
   b) Draw the image after a $\frac{1}{2}$ turn
   counterclockwise about point O.
   c) How can you tell if you have drawn the
   correct images?

5. Draw a quadrilateral on grid paper.
Choose a point outside the quadrilateral.
Rotate the quadrilateral about the point you chose.
Draw its rotation image.
Describe the rotation.

Reflect

When you see a shape and its rotation image, how can you
tell if the point of rotation is on or off the shape?

Transformations on a Computer

Use dynamic geometry software.
Open a new sketch.
Check that the distance units are centimetres.
Display a grid.

If you need help at any time, use the Help menu.

Translating a Shape

Construct a rectangle. Select the rectangle.
Translate the rectangle 4 squares left and 2 squares down.
Print the rectangle and its translation image.

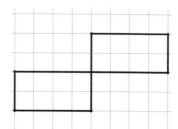

Reflecting a Shape

Construct a triangle.
Select one side of the triangle as the line of reflection.
Select the triangle. Reflect it in the line of reflection.
Print the triangle and its reflection image.

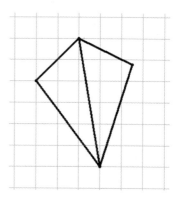

Rotating a Shape

Construct a parallelogram.
Select a vertex of the parallelogram as the point of rotation.
Select the parallelogram. Rotate it a $\frac{1}{4}$ turn counterclockwise.
Print the parallelogram and its rotation image.

Identifying Rotations

Work with a partner. Take turns.

➤ Construct a shape on the grid.
Choose a rotation and construct the rotation image.
Print the picture.
Have your partner identify the rotation.
Remind her to include:
  • the point of rotation
  • the fraction of the turn
  • the direction of the turn

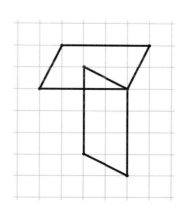

➤ Repeat the steps above for different points of rotation, different fractions of a turn, and different directions.

Predicting the Image

Work with a partner.
Take turns.

➤ Construct a shape on the grid.
   Print the shape.
   Choose a translation.
   Tell your partner what it is.
   Have your partner predict where
   the translation image will be.
   Translate the shape
   and draw its image.
   Print the shape and its image to verify
   your partner's prediction.

➤ Repeat the steps above for a reflection.

➤ Repeat the steps above for a rotation.

Identifying a Transformation

Work with a partner.
Take turns.

➤ Choose a transformation.
   Construct a shape and its image.
   Have your partner look at the screen and
   identify the transformation.

➤ Repeat the steps above for different
   transformations and different shapes.

Reflect

How does each shape and its image compare?
Do the comparisons match those you made from pictures
you drew in earlier lessons? Explain your ideas.

1. Copy the shape on grid paper.

   a) Translate the shape in any direction you like.
      Draw its translation image.

   b) Draw a line of reflection.
      Draw the reflection image.

   c) Choose a point of rotation and a fraction of a turn.
      Rotate the shape and draw its rotation image.

   d) Describe the position and orientation of each image
      in parts a, b, and c.
      How does each description help you identify
      the transformation?

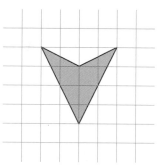

2. Draw a shape on grid paper.

   a) Translate the shape any way you like.
      Draw its translation image.
      Record the translation.
      Include each direction and
      the number of squares moved.

   b) Reflect the shape.
      Draw its reflection image.
      Label the line of reflection.
      Find how far the shape and its image
      are from this line.

   c) Rotate the shape.
      Draw its rotation image.
      Describe the rotation.
      Include the direction of the turn,
      the fraction of the turn,
      and the point of rotation.

3. Describe a transformation that would move
   shape A to each image.
   a) Image B   b) Image C
   c) Image D   d) Image E

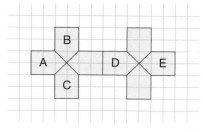

1

4. Describe the translation that moves:
   a) Shape B to Image A
   b) Shape D to Image C

1
3
4

5. In question 4, which other transformation would move each shape to its image?

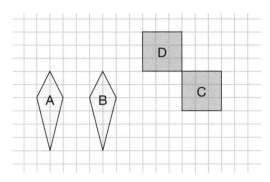

6. Copy this shape on grid paper.
   Predict the position of the image after each transformation below.
   Draw each image to check your prediction.
   a) a reflection in the line of reflection
   b) a translation 3 squares right and 4 squares up
   c) a $\frac{1}{4}$ turn counterclockwise about O

Line of reflection

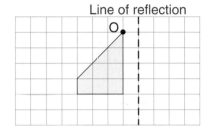

5

7. Copy this triangle and point O on grid paper.
   Draw the image after a $\frac{1}{4}$ turn clockwise about O.

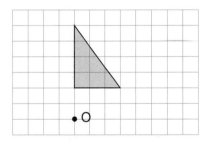

1
3
4
5

8. Describe the transformation that moves the shape to its image.

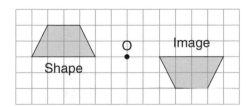

UNIT

8 Learning Goals

✓ translate, reflect, and rotate a shape

✓ draw and describe images after transformations

✓ identify a transformation

Design a ride for an amusement park.
The ride must move people
in at least 2 *different* ways.

Turns counterclockwise.

Unit 8

Moves up and down.

Check List

Your work should show
- ☑ how you designed a ride
- ☑ a clear presentation of your ride
- ☑ an explanation of how the ride moves
- ☑ how you used geometric language to describe your work

Think about how you will present your ride to the class.

Will you
– make a drawing?
– make a model?
– write about it?
– talk about it?

How does your ride move people in at least 2 different ways?

Reflect on Your Learning

What did you learn about how shapes can move?
Use words and pictures to explain.

Investigation

Dinomaze

Part 1

Dinosaurs were first discovered in England in 1824.
Since then, many dinosaur fossils have been found in Western Canada.
Some dinosaurs, such as the Edmontosaurus and the Columbosauripus have been
named after a Canadian city or province.

- Use books, magazines, or the Internet to learn which
  dinosaurs have been found in each province
  or territory of Canada.
  Record your findings in a table, chart, or on a map.

Great care is taken when fossils are excavated to avoid
breaking the remains. The location of a fossil find is important,
so a region is often searched systematically, using a grid.

Part 2

Play *Dinomaze* with a partner.
This game uses dinosaurs as obstacles,
and number cubes to determine a translation.
You will need a copy of the game board,
a red number cube and a green number cube,
and 2 different coloured counters.

Rules:
- Each player rolls a number cube.
  The player who rolls the greater number starts.

- Take turns to roll both cubes.
  The green cube tells how many squares to move right or left.
  The red cube tells how many squares to move up or down.

- You must always move horizontally first, and then vertically.

- A dinosaur square is an obstacle.
  You cannot cross a dinosaur square, or land on it.

- If you cannot move in one direction, you must move in the opposite
  direction if it is possible. If you cannot move, you miss that turn.

- Both players cannot be on the same square at the same time.
  The only exception to this is the START square.

- The winner is the first player to land on the END square.

Play the game several times.
- Which strategies did you use to help you win?
- Which series of translations would take you
  to the END in 6 turns or fewer?
- Which series of translations would take you
  to the END in the fewest turns?

Take It Further

Use grid paper.
Design your own *Dinomaze* game.
You may choose a different
shaped game board,
or use spinners instead
of number cubes.

UNIT

1

1. Use a variable. Write an expression for each number pattern.
   Write the next 5 terms in each pattern.
   Explain how you know the expressions and terms are correct.
   a) 9, 10, 11, 12, 13, …   **b)** 28, 27, 26, 25, 24, …

2

2. These data show how the population of Nunavut
   changed in 5 years.
   Use these data to predict the population of Nunavut in 2007.
   Explain your strategy for predicting.
   If possible, use the Internet to find the population
   of Nunavut in 2007.
   How close was your prediction?

Year	Population
2002	28 700
2003	29 200
2004	29 600
2005	30 000
2006	30 800

3

3. How can you use multiplying by 10 to find 9×8?

4. Find each product or quotient.
   Which strategy did you use each time?
   a) 4×600 **b)** 30×20 **c)** 10×300 **d)** $132 \div 3$
   e) 27×68 **f)** $357 \div 8$ **g)** 74×55 **h)** $919 \div 7$

4

5. Give 3 examples of items you would measure in millimetres.

6. A rectangle has area 40 cm^2.
   a) Sketch and label all possible rectangles with side lengths
   that are whole numbers of centimetres.
   b) Describe the rectangle with the greatest perimeter.
   c) Describe the rectangle with the least perimeter.

7. Provide a referent for each unit of measure. Explain your choice.
   a) one cubic centimetre   **b)** one cubic metre   **c)** one litre   **d)** one millilitre

8. Make the object at the right with centimetre cubes.
   Find its volume.

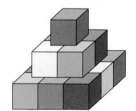

9. Use 36 centimetre cubes.
   How many different rectangular prisms can you make?
   How do you know you have made all possible prisms?

10. Use a number line to order these fractions from least to greatest.

$\frac{11}{12}$ $\frac{1}{6}$ $\frac{3}{4}$ $\frac{7}{12}$ $\frac{2}{3}$

11. Which other strategies could you have used to order
the fractions in question 10?
Use one of the strategies you name to check the order in question 10.

12. Write each decimal as a fraction.
   a) 0.3   **b)** 0.42   **c)** 0.535   **d)** 0.06

13. Write each fraction as a decimal.
   a) $\frac{21}{100}$ **b)** $\frac{21}{1000}$ **c)** $\frac{9}{10}$ **d)** $\frac{90}{1000}$

14. Order these decimals from greatest to least.
1.325, 1.32, 1.235, 1.5, 1.253, 1.352
Which strategy did you use?

15. a) Name as many shapes as you can that have some perpendicular sides.
   b) Use dot paper. Draw each shape you name.

16. Use dot paper. Draw 8 different quadrilaterals.
   a) How are the quadrilaterals alike?
     How are they different?
   b) Choose a sorting rule. Sort the quadrilaterals.
     Record your sorting.
   c) Trade sortings with a classmate.
     List the attributes of each quadrilateral.
     Identify your classmate's sorting rule.

17. Use triangular or square dot paper.
Look at a rectangular prism.
Draw the prism on dot paper.
Label each vertex of the prism.
Identify edges that:
   a) are parallel   **b)** intersect   **c)** are perpendicular
   d) are vertical   **e)** are horizontal

18. Look at the prism you drew in question 17. Identify faces that:
   a) are parallel   **b)** intersect   **c)** are perpendicular
   d) are vertical   **e)** are horizontal

7

19. Tell whether you would use first-hand data or second-hand data to answer each question. Explain each choice.
   a) Which pop group or singer is the most popular with Grade 5 students in Canada?
   b) How tall is each member of your family?
   c) How many pets does each student in your class have?
   d) Which territory has the greatest area?

20. One hundred boys and 100 girls were asked: "What is your favourite subject?" The data are shown at the right.
   a) Draw a double bar graph.
   b) Write 3 questions you could answer using the graph.
   c) Trade questions with a classmate. Answer your classmate's questions.

Subject	Number of Boys	Number of Girls
Art	8	24
Computers	8	5
English	2	6
French	2	4
Math	16	12
Music	4	7
PE	44	26
Science	6	5
Social studies	4	5
Other	6	6

21. The pointer on this spinner is spun.
   a) Which outcomes are equally likely?
   b) Name two outcomes where one outcome is more likely than the other.
      Name as many pairs of outcomes as you can.
   c) Name two outcomes where one outcome is less likely than the other.
      Name as many pairs of outcomes as you can.

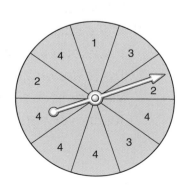

324

22. Use the spinner in question 21.
Name an outcome that is:
a) possible **b)** certain **c)** impossible

8

23. Use dot paper.
Draw a quadrilateral.
a) Draw the translation image of the quadrilateral
after the translation:
7 squares left and 3 squares up
b) Draw a slanted line of reflection.
Draw the reflection image of the quadrilateral.
c) Choose a vertex as the point of rotation.
Draw the rotation image of the quadrilateral
after a $\frac{1}{4}$-turn counterclockwise.
d) Describe the position and orientation of each
image in parts a to c.

24. You will need 3 pieces of grid paper.
a) Copy the shape at the right.
Choose a translation.
Draw the translation image.
b) Copy the shape at the right.
Choose a line of reflection.
Draw the reflection image.
c) Copy the shape at the right.
Choose a point of rotation,
a fraction of a turn,
and the direction for the rotation.
Draw the rotation image.
d) Make sure that only the original shape and its images
appear on your drawings.
Trade drawings with a classmate.
Identify each transformation.
Justify your answers.

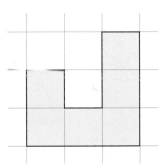

Illustrated Glossary

a.m.: A time between midnight and just before noon.

Area: The amount of surface a shape or region covers. We measure area in square units, such as square centimetres or square metres.

Axis (plural: axes): A number line along the edge of a graph. We label each axis of a graph to tell what data it displays. The horizontal axis goes across the page. The vertical axis goes up the page.

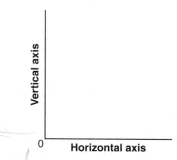

Bar graph: Displays data by using bars of equal width on a grid. The bars may be vertical or horizontal.

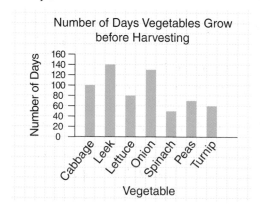

Base: The face that names an object. For example, in this triangular prism, the bases are triangles.

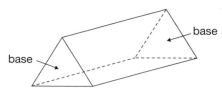

Benchmark: Used for estimating by writing a number to its closest benchmark; for example,

1. For whole numbers: 47 532 is closer to the benchmark 47 500 than to the benchmark 47 600.

2. For fractions: $\frac{1}{3}$ is closer to $\frac{1}{2}$ than to 0 or to 1.

3. For decimals: 0.017 is closer to 0.020 than to 0.010.

Capacity: A measure of how much a container holds. We measure capacity in litres (L) or millilitres (mL).

Carroll diagram: A diagram used to sort numbers or attributes.

Centimetre: A unit used to measure length.
We write one centimetre as 1 cm.
1 cm = 0.01 m
1 cm = 10 mm
100 cm = 1 m

Certain event: An event that always happens.

Clockwise: The hands on a clock turn in a clockwise direction.

Clockwise

Compatible numbers: Pairs of numbers that are easy to work with; for example,

1. The numbers 340 + 160 are compatible for adding because 40 + 60 = 100.
2. Multiples of 10 or 100 are compatible for estimating products because they are easy to multiply.

Compensation: A strategy for estimating; rounding one number up and rounding the other number down when the numbers are added.

Congruent shapes: Two shapes that match exactly.

Consecutive numbers: Numbers that follow in order;
for example, 4, 5, 6, 7, …

Core: See **Repeating pattern**.

Counterclockwise: A turn in the opposite direction to the direction the hands on a clock turn.

Counterclockwise

Cube: An object with 6 faces that are congruent squares. Two faces meet at an edge. Three or more edges meet at a vertex.

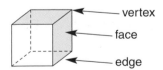

Cubic centimetre (cm³): A unit to measure volume.
A centimetre cube has a volume of one cubic centimetre.
We write one cubic centimetre as 1 cm³.

Cubic metre: A unit to measure volume.
One cubic metre is the volume of a cube with edge length 1 m.
We write one cubic metre as 1 m³.

Data: Information collected from a survey or experiment.

Decagon: A polygon with 10 sides.

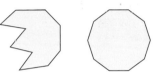

Decimal: A way to write a fraction. The fraction $\frac{2}{10}$ can be written as the decimal 0.2.

Decimal point: Separates the whole number part and the fraction part in a decimal. We read the decimal point as "and." We say 3.2 as "three **and** two-tenths."

Degree: A unit to measure temperature. We write one degree Celsius as 1°C.

Denominator: The part of a fraction that tells how many equal parts are in one whole. The denominator is the bottom number in a fraction.

Diagonal: A line segment that joins opposite vertices of a shape.

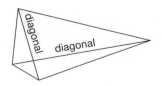

Difference: The result of a subtraction. The difference of 5 and 2 is 3:
$$5 - 2 = 3$$

Dimensions: 1. The measurements of a shape or an object. A rectangle has 2 dimensions, length and width. A cube has 3 dimensions, length, width, and height.
2. For an array, the dimensions tell the number of rows and the number of columns.

Displacement: The volume of water moved or displaced by an object put in the water. The displacement of this cube is 50 mL or 50 cm³.

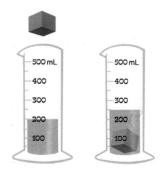

Dividend: The number to be divided. In the division sentence 77 ÷ 11 = 7, the dividend is 77.

Divisor: The number by which another number is divided. In the division sentence 77 ÷ 11 = 7, the divisor is 11.

Double bar graph: Displays two sets of data at once.

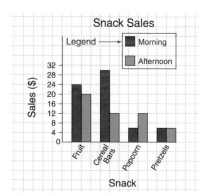

Edge: Two faces of a solid meet at an edge. See also **Cube**, **Prism**, and **Pyramid**.

Equally likely events: Two or more events, each of which is as likely to happen as the other. For example, if you toss a coin, it is equally likely that the coin will land heads up as tails up.

Equally probable: See **Equally likely events**.

Equation: 1. Uses the = symbol to show two things that represent the same amount. 5 + 2 = 7 is an equation.
2. Uses the = symbol with a variable, an operation such as +, −, ×, or ÷, and numbers to show two things that represent the same amount; for example, 20 = p + 6. See **Solution of an equation**.

Equivalent decimals: Decimals that name the same amount. 0.4, 0.40, and 0.400 are equivalent decimals.

Equivalent fractions: Name the same amount; for example, $\frac{1}{3}, \frac{2}{6}, \frac{3}{9}, \frac{10}{30}$ are equivalent fractions.

Estimate: Close to an amount or value, but not exact.

Event: The outcomes or a set of outcomes from a probability experiment. For example, when a die labelled 1 to 6 is rolled, some events are: rolling a number greater than 3, rolling an even number, rolling a 6.

Expanded form: Shows a number as a sum of the values of its digits; for example,

1. For whole numbers:

123 456 = 100 000 + 20 000 + 3000 + 400 + 50 + 6

2. For decimals:

5.713 = 5 + 0.7 + 0.01 + 0.003

Experiment: In probability, a test or trial used to investigate an idea.

Expression: Uses a variable and numbers to represent a pattern; for example, $d + 2$ represents the number of dots on Figure d in the pattern shown in the table below.

Figure Number	Number of Dots
1	3
2	4
3	5
4	6
5	7

Face: Part of an object. See also **Cube**, **Prism**, and **Pyramid**.

Factors: Numbers that are multiplied to get a product. In the multiplication sentence $3 \times 7 = 21$, the factors of 21 are 3 and 7.

Fair game: A game where all players have the same chance of winning.

First-hand data: Data you collect yourself.

Front-end rounding: Using only the first digit of each number to get an estimate; for example,

1. For adding: $23\,056 + 42\,982$ is about $20\,000 + 40\,000 = 60\,000$
2. For multiplying: 72×23 is about $70 \times 20 = 1400$

Gram: A unit to measure mass. We write one gram as 1 g. $1000\text{ g} = 1\text{ kg}$

Hexagon: A polygon with 6 sides.

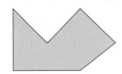

Horizontal: A line that is parallel to the horizon.

Horizontal axis: See **Axis**.

Hundredth: A fraction that is one part of a whole when it is divided into 100 equal parts. We write one-hundredth as $\frac{1}{100}$ or 0.01.

Image: The shape that is the result of a transformation. This is a rectangle and its image after a translation of 6 squares right and 1 square up.

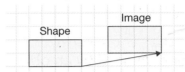

Impossible event: An event that cannot happen.

Improbable event: An event that is unlikely to happen but not impossible.

Improper fraction: A fraction that shows an amount greater than one whole. The numerator is greater than the denominator. $\frac{3}{2}$ is an improper fraction.

Increasing pattern: A pattern where each frame or term is greater than the previous frame or term.

1, 3, 8, 10, 15, 17, 23, …

Intersect: 1. For shapes, when two sides meet, they intersect in a point called the vertex.

2. For objects, when three or more edges meet, they intersect in a point called the vertex. When two faces meet, they intersect in an edge. See **Cube**.

Irregular polygon: A polygon that does not have all sides equal or all angles equal. Here are two irregular hexagons.

Key: See **Pictograph**.

Kilogram: A unit to measure mass. We write one kilogram as 1 kg.
1 kg = 1000 g

Kilometre: A unit to measure long distances. We write one kilometre as 1 km. 1 km = 1000 m

Kite: A quadrilateral with two pairs of adjacent sides equal.

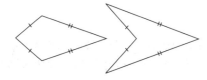

Legend: Tells the scale on a double bar graph and what each bar represents. See **Double bar graph**.

Likely event: An event that will probably happen.

Line of reflection: A line in which a shape is reflected. See **Reflection**.

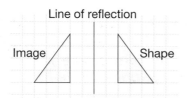

Line of symmetry: Divides a shape into two congruent parts. If we fold the shape along its line of symmetry, the parts match.

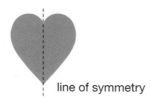

line of symmetry

Linear dimension: Length, width, depth, height, thickness.

Litre: A unit to measure the capacity of a container. We write one litre as 1 L.
1 L = 1000 mL

Mass: Measures how much matter is in an object. We measure mass in grams or kilograms.

Metre: A unit to measure length. We write one metre as 1 m.
1 m = 100 cm
1 m = 1000 mm

Milligram: A unit to measure mass. We write one milligram as 1 mg.
1000 mg = 1 g

Millilitre: A unit to measure the capacity of a container. We write one millilitre as 1 mL.
1000 mL = 1 L
1 mL = 1 cm³

Millimetre: A unit to measure length. We write one millimetre as 1 mm. One millimetre is one-tenth of a centimetre: 1 mm = 0.1 cm
10 mm = 1 cm
One millimetre is one-thousandth of a metre: 1 mm = 0.001 m
1000 mm = 1 m

Multiple: Start at a number, then count on by that number to get the multiples of that number. To get the multiples of 3, start at 3 and count on by 3:
3, 6, 9, 12, 15, …

Multiplication fact: A sentence that relates factors to a product.
3 × 7 = 21 is a multiplication fact.

Net: An arrangement that shows all the faces of an object, joined in one piece. It can be folded to form the object.

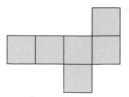

Number line: Has numbers in order from least to greatest. The spaces between pairs of consecutive numbers are equal.

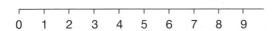

Numerator: The part of a fraction that tells how many equal parts to count. The numerator is the top number in a fraction. In the fraction $\frac{2}{3}$, the numerator is 2. We count 2 thirds of the whole.

Object: Has length, width, and height. Objects have faces, edges, vertices, and bases. We name some objects by the number and shape of their bases.

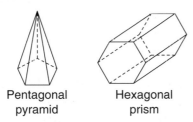

Pentagonal pyramid · Hexagonal prism

Octagon: A polygon with 8 sides.

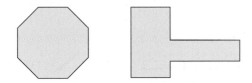

Operation: Something done to a number or quantity. Addition, subtraction, multiplication, and division are operations.

Outcome: One result of an event or experiment. Tossing a coin has two possible outcomes, heads or tails.

p.m.: A time between noon and just before midnight.

Parallel: 1. Two lines that are always the same distance apart are parallel.

2. Two faces of an object that are always the same distance apart are parallel; for example, the shaded faces on the rectangular prism below are parallel.

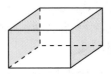

Parallelogram: A quadrilateral with 2 pairs of opposite sides parallel.

Partial products: Used as a strategy for multiplying 2-digit numbers; for example,

$$42 \times 57 = (40 + 2) \times (50 \times 7)$$
$$= (40 \times 50) + (40 \times 7) + (2 \times 50) + (2 \times 7)$$
$$= 2000 + 280 + 100 + 14$$
$$= 2394$$

There are 4 partial products.

Pattern rule: Describes how to make a pattern. For the pattern 1, 2, 4, 8, 16, …, the pattern rule is: Start at 1. Multiply by 2 each time.

Perimeter: The distance around a shape. It is the sum of the side lengths.
The perimeter of this rectangle is:
2 cm + 4 cm + 2 cm + 4 cm = 12 cm

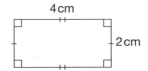

Perpendicular: 1. Two lines that intersect at a right angle are perpendicular.

2. Two faces that intersect on a rectangular prism or a cube are perpendicular.

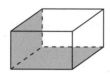

Pictograph: Uses pictures and symbols to display data. Each picture or symbol can represent more than one object. A key tells what each picture represents.

Equipment Rentals for Week of July 2

Type of Equipment	
Rollerblades	🚶🚶🚶🚶🚶🚶🚶🚶🚶🚶🚶🚶
Bicycles	🚶🚶🚶🚶🚶🚶🚶🚶🚶🚶🚶🚶
Skateboards	🚶🚶🚶🚶🚶🚶🚶

🚶 = 20 People

Place-value chart: It shows how the value of each digit in a number depends on its place in the number; see page 44 for whole numbers and page 184 for decimals.

Placeholder: A zero used to hold the place value of the digits in a number. For example, the number 603 has 0 tens. The digit 0 is a placeholder.

Point of rotation: The point about which a shape is rotated. See **Rotation**.

Polygon: A shape with three or more sides. We name a polygon by the number of its sides. For example, a five-sided polygon is a pentagon.

Possible event: An event that may happen.

Prediction: You make a prediction when you decide how likely or unlikely it is that an event will happen.

Prism: An object with 2 bases.

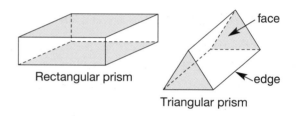

Rectangular prism

Triangular prism

Probability: Tells how likely it is that an event will occur.

Probable event: An event that is likely but not certain to happen.

Product: The result of a multiplication. The product of 5 and 2 is 10: $5 \times 2 = 10$

Proper fraction: Describes an amount less than one. A proper fraction has a numerator that is less than its denominator. $\frac{5}{7}$ is a proper fraction.

Pyramid: An object with 1 base.

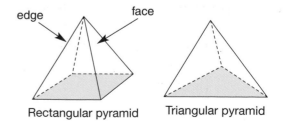

Rectangular pyramid

Triangular pyramid

Quotient: The number obtained by dividing one number into another. In the division sentence 77 ÷ 11 = 7, the quotient is 7.

Quadrilateral: A shape with 4 sides.

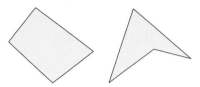

Rectangle: A quadrilateral, where 2 pairs of opposite sides are equal and each angle is a right angle.

Rectangular prism: See **Prism**.

Rectangular pyramid: See **Pyramid**.

Referent: Used to estimate a measure; for example, a referent for:
a length of 1 mm is the thickness of a dime.
a length of 1 m is the width of a doorway.
a volume of 1 cm³ is the tip of a finger
a volume of 1 m³ is the space taken up by a playpen.
a capacity of 1 L is a milk pitcher.
a capacity of 1 mL is an eyedropper.

Reflection: Reflects a shape in a line of reflection to create a reflection image. See **Line of reflection**.

Reflection image: The shape that results from a reflection. See **Reflection**.

Regular shape: See **Regular polygon**.

Regular polygon: A regular polygon has all sides equal and all angles equal. Here is a regular hexagon.

Related facts: Sets of addition and subtraction facts or multiplication and division facts that have the same numbers. Here are two sets of related facts:

2 + 3 = 5	5 × 6 = 30
3 + 2 = 5	6 × 5 = 30
5 − 3 = 2	30 ÷ 6 = 5
5 − 2 = 3	30 ÷ 5 = 6

Remainder: What is left over when one number does not divide exactly into another number. For example, in the quotient 13 ÷ 5 = 2 R3, the remainder is 3.

Repeating pattern: A pattern with a core that repeats. The core is the smallest part of the pattern that repeats. In the pattern: 1, 8, 2, 1, 8, 2, 1, 8, 2, …, the core is 1, 8, 2.

Rhombus: A quadrilateral with all sides equal and 2 pairs of opposite sides parallel.

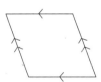

Right angle: Two lines that are perpendicular make a right angle.

Rep-tile: A polygon that can be copied and arranged to form a larger polygon that has the same shape.

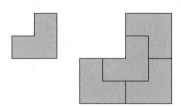

Rotation: Turns a shape about a point of rotation in a given direction. This is a triangle and its image after a rotation of a $\frac{1}{4}$ turn counterclockwise about one vertex:

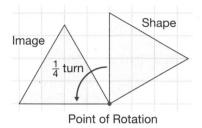

Rotation image: The shape that results from a rotation. See **Rotation**.

Scale: The numbers on the axis of a graph show the scale.

Second: A small unit of time. There are 60 seconds in 1 minute. 60 s = 1 min

Second-hand data: Data collected by someone else.

Solution of an equation: The value of a variable that makes the equation true; for example, $p = 14$ is the solution of the equation $20 = p + 6$.

Speed: A measure of how fast an object is moving.

Square: A quadrilateral with equal sides and 4 right angles.

Square centimetre: A unit of area that is a square with 1-cm sides. We write one square centimetre as 1 cm².

Square metre: A unit of area that is a square with 1-m sides. We write one square metre as 1 m².

Standard form: The number 579 328 is in standard form; it has a space between the thousands digit and the hundreds digit.
See **Place-value chart**.

Standard units: Metres, square metres, cubic metres, kilograms, and seconds are some standard units.

Sum: The result of addition. The sum of 5 and 2 is 7:
5 + 2 = 7

Survey: Used to collect data. You can survey your classmates by asking them which is their favourite ice-cream flavour.

Symmetrical: A shape is symmetrical if it has one or more lines of symmetry.

Tenth: A fraction that is one part of a whole when it is divided into 10 equal parts. We write one-tenth as $\frac{1}{10}$ or as 0.1.

Term: One number in a number pattern. For example, the number 4 is the third term in the pattern 1, 2, 4, 8, 16, …

Thousandth: A fraction that is one part of a whole when it is divided into 1000 equal parts. We write one-thousandth as $\frac{1}{1000}$, or 0.001.

Tonne: A unit used to measure a very large mass. We write one tonne as 1 t. 1 t = 1000 kg

Transformation: A translation (slide), a reflection (flip), and a rotation (turn) are transformations.

Translation: Slides a shape from one location to another. A translation arrow joins matching points on the shape and its image. This shape has been translated 6 squares left and 2 squares up.

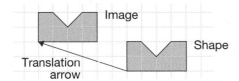

Translation arrow: See **Translation**.

Translation image: The shape that results from a translation. See **Translation**.

Trapezoid: A quadrilateral with exactly 1 pair of sides parallel.

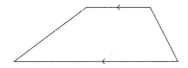

Triangular prism: See **Prism**.

Triangular pyramid: See **Pyramid**.

Unlikely event: An event that will probably not happen.

Variable: A letter, in italics, that is used to represent a number in an equation, or a set of numbers in a pattern. See **Equation** and **Expression**.

Vertex (plural: vertices): 1. The point where two sides of a shape meet. **2.** The point where three or more edges of an object meet.

Vertical: A line that is perpendicular to the horizon.

Vertical axis: See **Axis**.

Volume: The amount of space occupied by an object or the amount of space inside an object. Volume can be measured in cubic centimetres or in cubic metres.

Index

Acknowledgments

Pearson Education would like to thank the Bank of Canada and the Royal Canadian Mint for the illustrative use of Canadian bills and coins in this textbook. In addition, the publisher wishes to thank the following sources for photographs, illustrations, and other materials used in this book. Care has been taken to determine and locate ownership of copyright material in this text. We will gladly receive information enabling us to rectify any errors or omissions in credits.

Photography

Cover: Cornelia Doerr/AGE fotostock/firstlight.ca; pp. 2–3 Ian Crysler; p. 4 Canadian Press/Alex Galbraith; p. 7 Ian Crysler; p. 11 Florin Tirlea/Shutterstock; p. 12 Ray Boudreau; p. 13 Ian Crysler; p. 17 Ian Crysler; p. 21 Ian Crysler; p. 29 Ian Crysler; p. 32 Ray Boudreau; pp. 34–35 tbkmedia.de/Alamy; p. 34 (inset top) Megapress/Alamy; p. 34 (inset centre) Colin Rowe/Klixpix/First Light; p. 34 (inset bottom) Megapress/Alamy; p. 36 Bryan & Cherry Alexander Photography/Alamy; p. 39 Ian Crysler; p. 41 Ian Crysler; p. 42 Ian Crysler; p. 44 Johnathan Ferrey/Getty Images Sports; p. 45 Ian Crysler; p. 47 Ian Crysler; p. 48 CP PHOTO/Jeff McIntosh; p. 49 CP PHOTO/COC/Andre Forget; p. 50 Ian Crysler; p. 52 Miles Ertman/Masterfile; p. 54 Ian Crysler; p. 56 Alan Sirulnikoff/First Light; p. 57 Elena Elisseeva/Shutterstock; p. 59 Canadian Press/AP Photo/Francois Mori; p. 60 Ian Crysler; p. 61 Ian Crysler; p. 62 moodboard/Corbis; p. 68 (left) CP PHOTO/Richard Lam; p. 68 (right) CP PHOTO/Edmonton Sun—Darryl Dyck; p. 70 © Royalty-Free/CORBIS/MAGMA; p. 71 John A. Rizzo/Photodisc/Getty Images; p. 72 Ian Crysler; p. 76 Ian Crysler; p. 80 Ian Crysler; p. 83 Corel Collection Nesting Birds; p. 85 Ian Crysler; p. 87 Jim Corwin/Alamy; p. 89 Ian Crysler; p. 91 Ian Crysler; p. 92 Ian Crysler; p. 95 Ian Crysler; p. 96 Ian Crysler; p. 97 Keith Douglas/First Light; p. 98 Ian Crysler; p. 101 Ian Crysler; p. 104 (top) Digital Vision/firstlight.ca; p. 104 (bottom) Canadian Press/AP Photo/Ann M. Job; p. 107 Myrleen Ferguson Cate/PhotoEdit; p. 108 Ian Crysler; p. 109 Ian Crysler; p. 111 Digital Vision/Getty Images; p. 112 Corel Collection Recreational Activities; p. 116 (top) Larsh Bristol Photography; p. 116 (centre) Corel Collection Barns and Farms; p. 116 (bottom) Ian Crysler; p. 117 (top) S Meltzer/Photolink/Getty Images; p. 117 (bottom) Ian Crysler; p. 122 Ian Crysler; p. 125 Ian Crysler; p. 131 Ian Crysler; p. 132 Ian Crysler; p. 135 Ian Crysler; p. 138 Ian Crysler;

p. 142 Ian Crysler; p. 145 Ian Crysler; p. 148 Ian Crysler; p. 149 Ian Crysler; p. 151 Ian Crysler; p. 152 Ian Crysler; p. 155 Ray Boudreau; p. 156 Ray Boudreau; pp. 162–163 Ian Crysler; p. 164 Deborah Davis/PhotoEdit, Inc.; p. 166 Ian Crysler; p. 170 Ian Crysler; p. 174 Ian Crysler; p. 183 Ian Crysler; p. 187 Copyright, All Enthusiast, Inc.; p. 191 Ray Boudreau; p. 192 Marevision/MaXx Images; p. 193 (top) Arco Images/Alamy; p. 193 (bottom) Paul Souders/Corbis; p. 194 Ian Crysler; p. 195 Ian Crysler; p. 199 (top) Kindra Clineff/Index Stock Imagery; p. 199 (bottom) Ian Crysler; p. 204 Ian Crysler; p. 205 (top) Canadian Press/Robert Dall; p. 205 (bottom left) CP PHOTO/St. John's Telegram—Gary Hebbard; p. 205 (bottom right) CP PHOTO/Halifax Daily News—Darrell Oake; p. 207 Ian Crysler; p. 210 Ian Crysler; p. 215 (top) Courtesy of Manurewa High School New Zealand in partnership with RNZFB Guide Dog Services; p. 215 (bottom) Ken Straiton/First Light; p. 218 Ian Crysler; 220–221 Corel Collection Bridges; p. 226 Ian Crysler; p. 228 Harry Hu/Shutterstock; p. 229 Ian Crysler; p. 239 Henry Horenstein/Index Stock Imagery, Inc.; p. 242 Ian Crysler; p. 244 Ian Crysler; p. 245 Ray Boudreau; p. 247 Ian Crysler; p. 249 Ray Boudreau; p. 251 (left and centre) Ian Crysler; p. 251 (right) Stephen Saks/Index Stock/MaXx Images; p. 252 Ian Crysler; pp. 256–257 Oliver Mackay/First Light; p. 257 (inset top) CP PHOTO/Larry MacDougal; p. 257 (inset centre) CP PHOTO/Robert Dall; p. 257 (inset bottom) CP PHOTO/Edmonton Sun—Darryl Dyck; p. 259 CP PHOTO/Chuck Stoody; p. 266 Ian Crysler; p. 268 AP Photo/Tony Avelar/CP Photo; p. 269 Ian Crysler; p. 270 Richard Hutchings/PhotoEdit; p. 271 Ian Crysler; p. 274 Corbis Royalty-Free; p. 275 Ray Boudreau; p. 281 Ian Crysler; p. 284 Ian Crysler; p. 287 Ian Crysler; p. 292 (top) CP PHOTO/Jeff McIntosh; p. 292 (bottom) Ian Crysler; p. 293 (top) Ron Watts/First Light; p. 293 (bottom) Ron Watts/First Light; p. 296 Ian Crysler; p. 297 Ian Crysler; p. 302 Ian Crysler; p. 306 Ian Crysler; p. 307 Photodisc/Getty Images; p. 310 Ray Boudreau; p. 311 Ian Crysler; p. 318 Ray Boudreau; p. 320 Buddy Mays/CORBIS; p. 321 Ian Crysler

Illustrations

Steve Attoe, Kasia Charko, Leanne Franson, Linda Hendry, Brian Hughes, Paul McCusker, Grant Miehm, Suzanne Mogensen, Allan Moon, NSV Productions, Dusan Petricic, Michel Rabagliati, Bill Slavin, Neil Stewart/NSV Productions, Craig Terlson